ROUTLEDGE LIBRARY EDITIONS: CURRICULUM

Volume 36

THE PREPARATION FOR LIFE CURRICULUM

THE PREPARATION FOR LIFE CURRICULUM

BRIAN WILCOX, JACQUELINE DUNN,
SUE LAVERCOMBE AND LESLEY BURN

Routledge
Taylor & Francis Group

LONDON AND NEW YORK

First published in 1984 by Croom Helm

This edition first published in 2019
by Routledge
2 Park Square, Milton Park, Abingdon, Oxon OX14 4RN

and by Routledge
711 Third Avenue, New York, NY 10017

Routledge is an imprint of the Taylor & Francis Group, an informa business

British Library Cataloguing in Publication Data
A catalogue record for this book is available from the British Library

ISBN: 978-1-138-31956-1 (Set)
ISBN: 978-0-429-45387-8 (Set) (ebk)
ISBN: 978-1-138-31951-6 (Volume 36) (hbk)
ISBN: 978-1-138-32206-6 (Volume 36) (pbk)
ISBN: 978-0-429-45390-8 (Volume 36) (ebk)

Publisher's Note
The publisher has gone to great lengths to ensure the quality of this reprint but points out that some imperfections in the original copies may be apparent.

Disclaimer
The publisher has made every effort to trace copyright holders and would welcome correspondence from those they have been unable to trace.

THE PREPARATION FOR LIFE CURRICULUM

BRIAN WILCOX
JACQUELINE DUNN
SUE LAVERCOMBE
LESLEY BURN

CROOM HELM
London ● Sydney ● Dover, New Hampshire

© 1984 Brian Wilcox
Croom Helm Ltd, Provident House, Burrell Row,
Beckenham, Kent BR3 1AT
Croom Helm Australia Pty Ltd, First Floor,
139 King St., Sydney, NSW 2001, Australia
Croom Helm, 51 Washington Street, Dover,
New Hampshire 03820, USA

British Library Cataloguing in Publication Data

The Preparation for life curriculum.
    1. Education, Secondary—England—
Curricula
I. Wilcox, B.
373.19'0942   LB1629.5.G7

ISBN 0-7099-3604-4

Library of Congress Cataloging in Publication Data
Main entry under title:

The Preparation for life curriculum.

    Bibliography: p.
    Includes index.
    1. Comprehensive high schools—Great Britain—
Curricula—Case studies. 2. Curriculum planning—
Great Britain—Case studies. 3. Career education—
Great Britain—Case studies. 4. Vocational guidance—
Great Britain—Case studies. 5. Life skills—Great
Britain—Case Studies. I. Wilcox, B. (Brian)
LB1629.5.G7P74 1984 373.19 84-12749
ISBN 0-7099-3604-4

Printed and bound in Great Britain

CONTENTS

Preface

Acknowledgements

One of the recurring themes of the Great Debate and its aftermath has been the insistence that a fundamental aim of schools, and secondary schools in particular, is the preparation of their pupils for all aspects of adult life. A major preoccupation has been with ways of adapting the last two years of compulsory education so as to facilitate the transition to working life of those pupils who leave school at the earliest opportunity - especially those with poor academic attainments and little commitment to the values and demands of schools. This has led to an increased recognition of the need for more systematic careers education and guidance, enhanced programmes of work experience, and generally the establishment of better links between schools and the world of work.

As the youth unemployment situation has worsened however, careers teachers, perhaps more than their colleagues in other departments, have experienced the trauma of having some of the basic assumptions of their subject rendered problematic as a result of major structural changes occurring in the economy. One response to this situation has been to give greater emphasis to preparing pupils for unemployment and enforced leisure and to the acquisition of 'coping' and 'survival' skills.

In the face of such challenges many schools are restructuring their fourth and fifth year curricula both in organisational and content terms. Some of the changes which can be discerned include: expanding the core curriculum with a consequent reduction in the amount of time devoted to 'options'; devising new approaches to pupil assessment with the needs of potential employers particularly in mind; and integrating careers education, health education and certain aspects of social studies programmes in new integrated courses under such titles as social education, preparation for adult life and social and life skills.

This book provides an evaluative account of the experience of four comprehensive schools involved in a project concerned, inter alia, with modifying their curricula along the kind of lines indicated above. The project was one of a network of several dozen autonomous ones, established throughout Western Europe as a result of an EEC initiative, concerned with the transition of young people into working life.

The book is based on the results of a programme which closely followed the evolution of the project in the schools over a three year period. During that time project lessons were regularly observed, interviews were conducted with both the teachers and pupils involved, questionnaire surveys were carried out, relevant statistical data were collected and analysed, and school documents scrutinised. The data from all of these sources constitute a substantial curriculum development archive.

The book as a whole can be regarded as a detailed case study. It differs from other studies of schools which adopt a case study approach by being based on several schools, rather than one, and by making the curriculum a central rather than a peripheral concern. It is likely to be of special interest to teachers in secondary schools concerned with careers education, health education, social studies and social and life skills, and to those like headteachers and directors of studies who have particular responsibility for the curriculum as a whole. It will also be helpful to those in LEAs responsible for advising school staffs about innovations in this curriculum area and about curriculum development generally.

The account presented here has particular salience in the light of two recent national curriculum initiatives, i.e. the DES Lower Attainers Project and the MSC Technical Vocational Education Initiative.

Brian Wilcox
City of Sheffield Education Department

ACKNOWLEDGEMENTS

We would like to thank the headteachers and staff of the four schools involved in the project for their willingness to have their activities form the basis of a sustained enquiry. We gained greatly from the opportunity of observing and working closely with teachers and are indebted to them for their unfailing help and enthusiasm.

We would particularly like to acknowledge the invaluable support and encouragement we received from the project director, Mike Smith.

During the years of the project we gained greatly from our regular meetings with the national evaluator, Professor Alan Little, and his co-worker, Dr. Carol Varlaam, and also with those associated with the other UK projects. It has been a great privilege to take part in the unique evaluation network which the project programmes across the European Community generated.

Nearer home the continuing support of the Chief Education Officer, Michael Harrison, and the former Chief Adviser, Eric Hulland, has been greatly appreciated, particularly by the one of us with full-time responsibilities in the advisory service.

We acknowledge with gratitude the contribution made in Chapter 9 by Joan Garforth (adviser, research and evaluation, for the City of Sheffield Education Department) and also that made to Chapter 11 by Heather Carr, a former statistics student at Sheffield City Polytechnic.

Our thanks also go to the project secretaries (Jean Binney and Christine Yousefi) who, over the duration of the project, were responsible for typing the 35 or so individual research reports on which this book draws.

Finally, we would like to pay tribute to the efforts of Christine Watt, who had the formidable task of preparing the 'camera ready copy' of the book itself. Her considerable skill, good humour and readiness always to seek the best solutions to difficult problems of layout cannot be praised too highly.

Chapter 1

A PROJECT TO CHANGE THE CURRICULUM OF SECONDARY SCHOOLS

INTRODUCTION

The period since the mid 1970s has been characterised by an unprecedented intensity of debate about the nature of the school curriculum. This has been prompted by a series of DES and HMI reports on the curriculum - the number of which almost certainly far exceeds those of any previous period in the history of the public education system. The titles of the main reports since 1977 are listed in chronological order in Table 1.

The questions in these documents about the nature of the school curriculum were posed in a period when education had moved from a situation of expansion to one of contraction and retrenchment. It was also the time when the layman's usual justification of schooling, i.e. to obtain a ticket to the job market, became increasingly less convincing as school leaver unemployment rapidly escalated. The relentless advance of the new technologies was forcing teachers and others to confront its implications for the creation, storage and dissemination of knowledge and hence for schools and education generally. In addition the consequences of two decades or so of rapid and dramatic social and moral change meant that it was no longer possible to assume a consensus of values existing between schools and society at large. As a result the curriculum came to be scrutinised,

1

Table 1: Official Reports on the Curriculum and Related Matters 1977-1981

DES (1977)	Educating our Children: four subjects for debate. A background paper for the regional conferences. (London: HMSO)
House of Commons (1977)	Education in Schools: a consultative document. (London: HMSO)
DES (1977)	Curriculum 11-16. Working papers by HM Inspectorate: a contribution to current debate. (London: HMSO)
DES (1978)	Primary Education in England: A survey by HM Inspectorate. (London: HMSO)
DES (1979)	Local Authority Arrangements for the School Curriculum: Report on the Circular 14/77 review. (London: HMSO)
DES (1979)	Aspects of Secondary Education in England: A survey by HM Inspectors of schools. (London: HMSO)
DES (1980)	A Framework for the School Curriculum. (London: HMSO)
DES (1980)	A View of the Curriculum. HMI series: Matters for Discussion 11. (London: HMSO)
DES (1981)	Curriculum 11-16. A review of progress: A joint study by HMI and five LEAs. (London: HMSO)
DES (1981)	The School Curriculum. (London: HMSO)
House of Commons (1981)	The Secondary School Curriculum and Examinations with special reference to the 14 to 16 year old age group, Vol. 1: Second report from the Education, Science and Arts Committee. (London: HMSO)

---

debated, and subjected to attempts to change it as never before.

The curriculum, together with 'accountability' and 'assessment and evaluation', constituted an educational trinity which increasingly dominated the debate of the late 70s and early 80s.

A frequently reiterated theme in the debate was the nature of the fourth and fifth year curriculum of secondary schools and the importance of facilitating the transition to working life of those pupils who left school at the earliest opportunity – especially those with poor academic attainments and little commitment to the values and demands of schools. As youth unemployment worsened however greater emphasis was laid on preparing pupils for unemployment and enforced leisure and to the acquisition of 'coping' and 'survival skills'. This book describes the experiences of 4 comprehensive schools in facing such challenges over the period 1978 to 1981. These schools like many others throughout the country attempted to refashion their fourth and fifth year curriculum both in organisational and content terms by such means as: expanding the core curriculum with a consequent reduction in the amount of time devoted to 'options'; devising new approaches to pupil assessment with the needs of potential employers particularly in mind; and the development of new integrated courses under such titles as social education, preparation for adult life, and social and life skills.

The schools concerned were participants in a locally directed Transition from School to Working Life project which was in turn one of a network of several dozen similar autonomous projects established throughout Western Europe as a result of an initiative of the European Community.

The book is based on the results of a programme of research which closely followed the evolution of the project in the schools over a three year period. During that time project lessons were regularly observed, interviews were conducted with both the teachers and pupils involved, questionnaire surveys were carried out, relevant statistical data were collected and analysed, and school documents scrutinised. The research data from all of these sources constitute a substantial curriculum development archive similar in some respects to Stenhouse's conception of a Contemporary Educational Records Archive (Stenhouse, 1978). Our book provides a detailed case study not only of an important aspect of the secondary school curriculum but also of the process of curriculum development at the level of the individual school and LEA.

It is perhaps significant that just as this project, and those associated with it in the European network, came to an end the Secretary of State for Education, Sir Keith Joseph, initiated a centrally funded programme to assist LEAs in developing a curriculum relevant to the needs of the lower 40% of the ability range in the 4th and 5th years. Close on the announcement of this, the Manpower Services Commission stepped into the arena of the school curriculum with its Technical and Vocational Educational Initiative (TVEI) which provided some 14 LEAs with funds to develop the 14-18 curriculum with a more technical and vocational bias (MSC, 1983).

THE EUROPEAN BACKGROUND TO THE PROJECT

In February 1976 a resolution was passed by the Council and Ministers of Education of the European Community expressing a commitment to a programme which would promote, inter alia, measures aimed at facilitating the transition of young people into working life. As a result of a further ministerial resolution in the December of that year a Community-wide action programme was implemented to assist in the evaluation and development of national policies with the following priority themes:

- the educational and training requirements of school leavers who have difficulty in finding and retaining appropriate employment;
- the problems of poor motivation among young people towards education and work, and the measures which might be adopted to stimulate interest and participation;
- the needs of special target groups such as girls, young migrants, and the physically or mentally handicapped;
- the development of guidance and counselling with particular regard to collaboration between those responsible for education, guidance, training and placement;
- the improvement of vocational preparation and the promotion of co-operation between the education and employment sectors;

- the promotion of measures to improve the initial and in-service training of teachers so that they may more effectively prepare young people for working life.

The central activity of the programme was the establishment of 47 pilot projects and sub projects throughout Europe (IFAPLAN, 1980). In England projects were established in Bradford, ILEA and Sheffield. In addition there were three projects in the Republic of Ireland and one each in Scotland and Wales.

Early in 1977 the DES initiated discussions with the City of Sheffield Education Department about the possibility of participation in the pilot programme. Following on from this a small working party of officers prepared a project proposal during the Summer of 1977 which was subsequently accepted in November of the same year for joint funding by the DES and the EEC. The decision was taken to second the Department's senior adviser for secondary education as director for the project's duration. This was to be for three years from 1st September 1978 although the project was later extended for a further year, i.e. to run to 31st August 1982. The director was able to assume his duties on a part-time basis from January 1978 and so carry out intensive consultations with schools, other organisations and individuals before the formal start of the project in the September. In the period March to July 1978 project advisory and steering committees were set up, regular meetings of project schools initiated, and financial details worked out. In the same period most of the appointments to the project central team and schools were made.

THE SHEFFIELD PROJECT: STRUCTURE AND ORGANISATION

Aims and Objectives

The Sheffield project was to be concerned with the development of a cooperative approach between schools, guidance and counselling agencies, further education colleges, employers and social services to improve the preparation for adult/working life of low achievers during the last two years of compulsory education and subsequently if unemployed. The main objectives were:

- to examine, and modify where necessary, school curricula offered to the target group pupils in order to increase their motivation for work, improve their attitude to school and to better prepare them for employment;
- to develop teaching methods and materials and to disseminate these to institutions involved and later to other institutions;
- to provide an enhanced programme of careers education and guidance;
- to explore means by which schools, further education colleges and industrial training boards may work together to provide a more 'appropriate' education for the target group;
- to develop a relevant in-service training programme for teachers;
- to improve communication within and between schools and relevant agencies (including the industrial and commercial world);
- to foster school/parent communication and parental involvement in order to help to ameliorate problems of persistent truancy and absenteeism;
- to develop firm links between schools and industrial and commercial concerns in order to influence thinking and attitudes on both sides and in particular to influence curriculum provision in schools and recruitment and training procedures in industry and commerce. (Sheffield MDC, 1978)

The Schools Involved

Four schools were involved in the project. These are referred to throughout simply as A, B, C and D. The first three were involved in the full range of project development whilst the fourth (D) had the status of an associate school. School A and the associate school D were situated in the north of the city some three and a half miles and three miles respectively from the centre. School B lay about three miles south-east of the centre and school C was approximately five miles away in the north-west. B and D were campus schools having a youth wing and an adult education centre on the same site as the school. All the schools were based on a single site and were, prior to comprehensive reorganisation in 1969, secondary modern schools.

The four schools had relatively homogeneous catchments biased towards the lower socio-economic groups. Data on parental occupations based on estimates provided by the headteachers in 1975/76 are given in Table 2.

Table 2: Estimated Percentage of Children in September 1975 Intake coming from Homes with Parental Occupations of Different Categories

	School A	School B	School C	School D
Professional	1	0	2	1
Clerical	2	2	4	8
Skilled worker	29	11	32	20
Semi-skilled worker	49	36	37	29
Unskilled worker	19	51	25	43

The schools were amongst the seven secondary schools in the city in which teachers received an extra salary supplement (social priority supplement) in recognition of the extra difficulties involved in teaching children from disadvantaged environments.

The schools differed in size, with C being the smallest (546 pupils on roll), A and B having almost equal numbers of pupils (1,042 and 1,031 respectively), and D being intermediate in size with 693 pupils. Two of the schools had intakes at 12+, one at 11+ and the other a dual intake at 11+ and 12+. All four schools catered for pupils up to the age of 18 and had small sixth forms (see Table 3).

Pupil teacher ratios in three of the schools were comparable to one another and close to the city average for secondary schools of 16.5:1 whereas C had a more favourable ratio of 14.0:1.

The academic achievement of the schools as measured by public examination results was roughly comparable with the numbers of 'O' level and 'O' level equivalent passes per pupil aged 15 as at 1st September 1977 (corrected for double entry) ranging from 0.57 to 0.88.

Project to change secondary curriculum

Table 3:   Age of Pupil Entry, Pupils on Roll, and
Pupil Teacher Ratio

	School A	School B	School C	School D
Age of pupil entry	11+ & 12+	12+	11+	12+
No. of pupils on roll as at April 1978	1042	1031	546	693
No. of pupils in 6th form	21	39	19	27
% pupils in 6th form	2%	4%	4%	4%
Pupil teacher ratio as at April 1978	16.5:1	15.9:1	14.0:1	16.6:1

Absenteeism was a problem, particularly with
the older pupils. A city wide survey of fifth year
pupils carried out in the Autumn term of 1977
showed the four schools to be amongst those with
the lowest rate of attendance. The attendance
rates for A and B were both 68%, C and D were
somewhat higher with rates of 73% and 82%.

Target Groups

The group of pupils at whom the project was
initially aimed, i.e. the target group, was defined
in the original submission document (Sheffield MDC,
1977) as those falling within the lowest 40%
attainment category during their last two years at
school. Such pupils would include those with low
IQ, poor educational attainment, poor attitudes to
school and lacking in motivation. A number of
pupils in these categories would also be persistent
absentees from school.

In the negotiations which preceded the
commencement of the project in September 1978 it

8

became clear that one of the schools approached was unhappy with the notion of identifying a target group for special treatment. However, because the school had established a substantial reputation in careers education and liaison with industry, it was thought that it should be involved in the project, particularly in order to make its expertise and experience in this area available to other schools. It therefore agreed to participate on an 'associate' basis. Three other schools were involved with full project status and the composition of the target group differed somewhat in each. In the first year of the project, schools A and C identified a target group for mainly administrative reasons although the modifications made to the curriculum applied to the total year group. However, at school B a target group was selected from the fourth year which followed a distinct project curriculum not available to other pupils.

In school A the lower 40% of the fourth and fifth year group was selected by year tutors using scores obtained by pupils at the end of their third year on NFER tests of vocabulary and reading. In school B a target group representing approximately 30% of the year group was formed from the pupils in the remedial band together with a number from the rest of the year group identified by teachers as low achievers and/or poor attenders. School C designated the total year group as the target group while emphasising the needs of those pupils with poor educational attainment, low motivation and poor attitudes to school. For administrative purposes a group was designated as falling specifically within the project target group criteria. By the end of the second year of the project the head of school B was feeling that the target group distinction was an unsatisfactory one. It was thought that it gave a low status to all things done under the project's auspices - the project being effectively seen as provision for an enlarged remedial group. By the third year school B had recast its project programme to provide a series of options which were technically available to all pupils in the year group. The overall effect of this was to blur the boundary between pupils in the remedial band and those in the rest of the year.

Project Organisation

The project team consisted of the director, a secretary, a careers officer, an education social worker and two research assistants. The team was accommodated within the Education Department and was thus able to draw on its office and administrative services. The team was responsible for:

- general administration of the project;
- development and organisation of meetings and contacts;
- servicing of meetings and conferences;
- organisation of in-service training;
- monitoring of activities in Sheffield and elsewhere;
- input from external sources;
- dissemination of information including reports;
- curriculum development support;
- secretarial back-up services;
- mediation and trouble shooting;
- research and evaluation. (Sheffield MDC, 1978)

Additional appointments were also made to the participating schools for the duration of the project. Thus all four schools had their secretarial/clerical establishment increased by one part-time member and three main project schools each had an extra full-time teacher appointed. It was also possible for the schools (except the associate school) to designate a senior member of staff as the project coordinator - in two cases the person concerned was promoted to a higher scale in recognition of the extra duties involved.[1]

A project advisory committee including representation from the education service, the education committee, industry and commerce, headteachers and parent governors of the participating schools was established and met on a termly basis. A less broadly based steering committee having a more executive role than the advisory group was also set up although as the project progressed this role was increasingly taken on by the meetings convened periodically by the director with the senior staff of the participating schools.

A number of working parties were established composed of the director, teachers and representatives from other agencies, to deal with such issues as careers education, records and reporting, trades union studies, in-service education and residential education. The project generated a programme of in-service education by means of: residential and non-residential conferences; special courses for project schools organised by external agencies; sponsored attendance by individuals and small groups at relevant local, regional and national courses and school based courses. Visits made by the director, project staff, and teachers to other projects both in the United Kingdom and Europe generally, together with reciprocal visits made to Sheffield provided another dimension of in-service education and professional development.

The project aimed to foster a close liaison between schools and industry. This was achieved principally by: further development of pupil work experience; the secondment of teachers to industry by means of the CBI Introduction to Industry scheme; and involvement in the BIM Twinning scheme. Of these, the only completely new initiative for each of the project schools was the latter. This involved 'twinning' the headteacher with a senior manager of a local firm in the hope that this relationship would foster a wider contact between school and firm and their respective staffs. In addition links with the trades union side of industry were established by means of conferences and through the development of teaching materials for trades union studies. The latter was specifically facilitated by the secondment of a lecturer from the trades union studies unit in one of the local further education colleges.

Throughout the duration of the project a series of publications was produced in order to keep all of those involved informed of progress and development. The main source of general information was the 'Bulletin' which was produced on average twice per year. A wide variety of other documents was circulated regularly, e.g. the project annual reports, conference reports, reports of study visits, and research reports. In addition, and increasingly as the project neared its end, relevant teaching materials, many of which were the outcomes of project activities, were published and made available locally and beyond.

In order to promote systematic exchange and cooperation between pilot projects, a Central Animation and Evaluation Team (CAET) was established as a special department of a social research institute IFAPLAN based in Cologne. CAET also coordinated the network of evaluators appointed to assess the development of projects in individual countries. In addition each project was expected to develop its own local or internal evaluation. There were thus three levels of evaluation.

Community level   Total programme of projects evaluated by CAET.

National level   Projects in each participating country were evaluated externally.

Local level   In each country individual projects were evaluated internally.

In the Sheffield project an on-going evaluation of activities was seen as the professional responsibility of all of those involved. This was expressed formally through the annual reports submitted to CAET and the national evaluator by the director, the specialist project staff (careers officer and social worker) and teaching staff in school. In addition the project budget allowed the appointment of two full-time research assistants. They formed a small research and evaluation team which was directed by the principal author in his capacity as the LEA's senior adviser for research and evaluation. A brief account of the approach adopted in the evaluation of the project is given in the appendix at the end of the book.

NOTES

[1] In the third case the teacher concerned was already on the top scale (scale 4).

Chapter 2

CHANGES IN THE CURRICULUM STRUCTURE OF THE SCHOOLS

During the course of the project the curriculum of the schools underwent a number of changes. Schools did not begin the project neatly with a new curriculum. Rather, changes were made over time - the curriculum evolved. In the first year of the project limited changes were made in the S4 curriculum. In the second year these changes were carried over into S5 [1] and further changes made to the curriculum of the new S4. Modifications continued so that by the third year a new curriculum structure had been established in S4 and S5 in at least three of the schools. In the case of the other school the curriculum structure had not stabilised by the third year and further change occurred in the following year. In a sense, of course, no curriculum is ever stable - it is a question of the rate of evolution varying from one school to another.

A comparison of the curriculum of different schools is a complex task. In principle it can be attempted at several different levels. The most general level provides a description of the amount of time allocated to the different subjects or activities which pupils encounter. Description at a more detailed level is, of course, possible, e.g. in terms of the knowledge and skills which the subjects attempt to foster, i.e. the content structure. Finally an account can be given of the way in which the content structure is actually taught to pupils in the classroom. This chapter offers a description of the S4 and S5 curriculum of the project schools at the first of these three levels. Later chapters penetrate below this to the second and third level by drawing on the results of teacher questionnaires and classroom observation.

In looking at the curriculum of the four schools it is necessary, as indicated above, to do so across a period of time. Although longitudinal studies of individuals, particularly children, are an established method of educational research, longitudinal accounts of schools appear to be rare. A recently reported exception is the study of changes in a sample of secondary schools over a ten year period carried out by King (1981). King, however, concentrated on organisational and behavioural changes rather than curricular ones.

In our study it was possible to examine the changes in the curriculum organisation of the four schools over a four year period. This was made possible by access to three sources of information. First, curriculum analyses of the schools were available for the years concerned. These had in fact been collected from all secondary schools since 1976 as a routine exercise independent of the project using a notational system developed by the LEA (Wilcox and Eustace, 1980). Secondly, the annual project reports produced by the schools provided a more detailed account of the curricular and other changes which had taken place. Thirdly, the visits made by the research team to schools throughout the duration of the project had produced further relevant information from teacher interviews and lesson observation.

School A

In 1977/78, i.e. before the commencement of the project, both the fourth and fifth years were organised on the basis of mixed ability registration groups. English, mathematics, religious education, careers education and physical education/games formed a common core occupying 16 of the 40 periods per week (ppw). For the remaining 24 periods pupils took subjects which were chosen from each of six option blocks. Table 4 summarises the main changes which took place in the S4 and S5 curriculum over the four years 1977/78 to 1980/81. Comparing the situation in 1980/81 (third year of the project) to that in 1977/78 (the pre-project year) it can be seen that the number of periods devoted to the fourth and fifth year core was increased by four ppw from 16 to 20. This was achieved by reducing the number of options from six to five. The core curriculum was modified by increasing the number of periods of

English from five to six, introducing four periods of sociology to replace careers education and providing RPE in place of one period of mathematics for a proportion of the target group. A brief description of the latter two modifications is necessary at this stage. Sociology was a new course which aimed to integrate careers education, health education and certain aspects of social studies. RPE is an abbreviation for Record of Personal Experience, Qualities and Qualifications (Stansbury, 1976) - a system which enables pupils to write short descriptive accounts of personally significant activities in which they have been involved. A fuller description of both of these innovations is given in later chapters. In addition new courses in mathematics and science were devised with the needs of the target group in mind.

As can be seen from Table 4 this new curriculum was established in a step by step fashion. In the first year of the project (1978/79) changes were largely confined to increasing the amount of careers education (and consequently its content) in S4 and S5, and introducing RPE and the new mathematics and science courses in S4. In the following year (1979/80) the integrated sociology course replaced the separate careers education provision in S4. By the third year sociology was established in both S4 and S5.

School B

Unlike the other schools involved in the project, school B maintained a separate remedial band of two or three forms in each year group up to the fifth. Apart from the remedial band the remainder of each year group was organised on the basis of mixed ability registration forms.

In the fourth and fifth years the bulk of pupils followed a core curriculum of English, mathematics, careers education and physical education for 15 ppw. For the remaining 25 ppw, pupils chose one subject from each of five option blocks. As can be seen from Table 5 this structure remained essentially unchanged over the period covered, i.e. from 1977/78 to 1980/81. In the main the project affected the curriculum offered to the less able pupils generally and to those in the remedial band in particular.

Table 4: Curriculum Changes 1977/78-1980/81 School A

Year	Fourth Year Curriculum		
	Core Subjects and Periods	Periods of Options*	Project Changes
1977/78	$E_5 M_6 Re_1 Ca_1 Pe_3$	6 x 4	
1978/79	$E_5 M_4 \boxed{\begin{array}{c} M \\ RPE \end{array}}_1 Re_1 Ca_2 Pe_3$	6 x 4	M reduced 6-5 Ca increased 1-2 M course for less able revised. RPE replaced one period of M for some of the less able. S option for less able revised.
1979/80	$E_6 M_5 \boxed{\begin{array}{c} M \\ RPE \end{array}}_1 Re_1 So_4 Pe_3$	5 x 4	E increased 5-6 M increased 5-6 So replaced Ca Number of options reduced 6-5
1980/81	$E_6 M_5 \boxed{\begin{array}{c} M \\ RPE \end{array}}_1 Re_1 So_4 Pe_3$	5 x 4	

---

* First figure = no. of option blocks;
Second figure = no. of ppw for each option.

Changes in curriculum structure

Table 4: Curriculum Changes 1977/78-1980/81 School A (contd.)

Year	Fifth Year Curriculum		
	Core Subjects and Periods	Periods of Options*	Project Changes
1977/78	E M Re Ca Pe 5 6 1 1 3	6 x 4	
1978/79	E M Re Ca Pe 5 5 1 2 3	6 x 4	M reduced 6-5 Ca increased 1-2
1979/80	E M [M / RPE]₁ Re Ca Pe 5 4 1 2 3	6 x 4	RPE continued into 5th year. 2nd year of new M and S courses for the less able.
1980/81	E M [M / RPE]₁ Re So Pe 6 5 1 4 3	5 x 4	E increased 5-6 M increased 5-6 Ca replaced by 2nd year of So. No. of options reduced 5-6

Key

E	= English	[M / RPE]₁	= 1 period M or RPE	
M	= mathematics			
S	= science			
Ca	= careers education			
Re	= religious education			
Pe	= physical education/games			
So	= sociology			
RPE	= record of personal experience			

Table 5: Curriculum Changes 1977/78-1980/81 School B

Year	Group	Fourth Year Curriculum	
		Core Subjects and Periods	Periods of Options*
1977/78	non-rem	$E_5M_5Ca_1Pe_4$	5 x 5
	rem	$E_8M_8Re_2Ca_2Se_2Cy_2S_4Cr_6Mu_2Pe_4$	

Year	Group	Core Subjects and Periods			Periods of Options*
1978/79	non-TG	$E_5M_5Ca_1Pe_4$			5 x 5
	(non-rem	$E_7M_5Ca_1Pe_4$	Sc Ch He Cy	Ic Ev Ph Ca	3 x 5
	TG (				
	(				
	(rem	$E_8M_8Dr_2S_4Cr_6Pe_4$			

1979/80 non-TG $E_5M_5Ca_1Pe_4$ 5 x 5
         TG $E_6M_6S_4$ [Dr Mu E]$_2$ Cr_6Pe_4 [Se Ch He Cy]$_4$ [Ic Ev Ph Ca]$_4$ 1 x 4

| 1980/81 | non-rem | $E_5M_5Ca_1Pe_4$ | 5 x 5 |
| | rem | $E_5M_5Ca_1Pe_4$ | 5 x 5 |

Project Changes

From 1977/78 to 1978/79   Se, Ch, He, Cy, Ic, Ev, Ph, Ca
modules introduced as two blocked 4 ppw sessions.   Ph also
offered as full option.   E includes 2 ppw for pupils to
record significant project events.
From 1978/79 to 1979/80   In addition to the Ch module,
child care also available as a full option, Te as a full
option, RPE for remedial band pupils. Mv option established.
From 1979/80 to 1980/81   Options programme extended to
remedial band.   Former modular programme re-cast into
separate options available to all and a double option 'Life
in the 80s'.

---

*   First figure = no. of option blocks;
     Second figure = no. of ppw for each option.

Key

TG   = target group   rem   = remedial band pupils
non-TG = non-target group   non-rem = non-remedial band pupils

Table 5: Curriculum Changes 1977/78-1980/81 School B (contd.)

Year	Group	Fifth Year Curriculum	
		Core Subjects and Periods	Periods of Options*
1977/78	non-rem	$E_5 M_5 Ca_1 Pe_4$	5 x 5
	rem	$E_8 M_8 Ca_1 Ss_5$ $\begin{bmatrix} A \\ Dr \\ Mu \end{bmatrix}_5 Pe_4$	1 x 4
			1 x 5
1978/79	non-rem	$E_5 M_5 Ca_1 Pe_4$	5 x 5
	rem	$E_8 M_8 Ca_2 Ss_2 Re_2 Se_2 S_4 Cr_6 Mu_2 Pe_4$	
1979/80	non-TG	$E_5 M_5 Ca_1 Pe_4$	5 x 5
		($E_7^5 M_5^5 Ca_1 Pe_4$ $\begin{bmatrix} Se \\ Ch \\ He \\ Cy \end{bmatrix}_4$ $\begin{bmatrix} Ic \\ Ev \\ Ph \\ Ca \end{bmatrix}_4$	3 x 5
	TG	(	
		(	
		($E_8 M_8 Dr_2 S_4 Cr_6 Pe_4$	
1980/81	non-TG	$E_5 M_5 Ca_1 Pe_4$	5 x 5
	TG	$E_6^5 M_6^5 S_4^1 \begin{bmatrix} Dr \\ Mu \\ Cy \end{bmatrix}_2 Cr_6 Pe_4$ $\begin{bmatrix} Se \\ Ch \\ He \\ Cy \end{bmatrix}_4$ $\begin{bmatrix} Ic \\ Ev \\ Ph \\ Ca \end{bmatrix}_4$	1 x 4

Project Changes

From 1978/79 to 1979/80 Modular programme of Se, Ch, He, Cy, Ic, Ev, Ph, Ca continued from 4th year. Also full Ph option. Playgroup associated with Ch module.
From 1979/80 to 1980/81 Continuation of RPE and Ch, Te and Mv options.

Key		
E = English	A = art	⌐ rotation
Ev = environmental studies	Dr = drama	amongst
Mv = motor vehicle studies	Mu = music	several
Ic = introduction to industry	S = science	modules
Pe = games/physical education	Cr = craft(s)	
Ph = photography (art/photography)	M = mathematics	
Se = (personal &) social education	Ss = social studies	
RPE= record of personal experience	He = health education	
Cy = community (& leisure) education	Te = traffic education	
Ch = education for parenthood	Ca = careers education	
(parentcraft)	Re = religious education	

Table 6: Curriculum Changes 1977/78–1980/81 School C

Year	Fourth Year Curriculum		
	Core Subjects and Periods	Periods of Options*	Project Changes
1977/78	$E_6 M_5 Re_1 Ca_1 Pe_2$	5 x 5	
1978/79	$E_6 M_5 Ca_{1\cdot2} Se_{0\cdot9} Lp_{0\cdot7} Pe_{1\cdot2}$**	5 x 5	Re and Ca replaced by new Ca, Se and Lp courses. New science option for less able pupils.
1979/80	$E_6 M_6 \left\{ \begin{matrix} Se \\ Ca \end{matrix} \right\}_4 Lp_4$	4 x 5	M increased 5-6 Se/Ca increased 2.1-4 Lp increased 0.7-4 Pe replaced by Lp. Options reduced 5-4 Modifications in maths course for less able Modular humanities option for less able.
1980/81	$E_6 M_6 \left\{ \begin{matrix} Se \\ Ca \end{matrix} \right\}_4 Lp_4$	4 x 5	

*   First figure = no. of option blocks;
     Second figure = no. of ppw for each option.

**   The content and structure of the programme at school C changed somewhat from term to term. The periods shown here devoted to Ca, Se, Lp and Pe per week have been obtained by averaging out the total across the year as a whole. Hence the non-integral values.

Changes in curriculum structure

Table 6: Curriculum Changes 1977/78-1980/81 School C (contd.)

Year	Fifth Year Curriculum		
	Core Subjects and Periods	Periods of Options*	Project Changes
1977/78	$E_6 M_6 Re_1 Ca_1 Pe_4$	(4 x 4 (1 x 6	
1978/79	$E_6 M_5 Re_1 Ca_1 Pe_2$	5 x 5	
1979/80	$E_6 M_5 \begin{bmatrix} Se \\ Ca \\ Lp \end{bmatrix}_4$	5 x 5	Re, Ca and Pe replaced by new Ca, Se and Lp. 2nd year of new science option for less able.
1980/81	$E_6 M_6 \begin{bmatrix} Se \\ Ca \end{bmatrix}_4 Lp_4$	4 x 5	2nd year of modular humanities course for less able. GYSL geography established in CSE course and in humanities course.

Key

E	= English		= rotation amongst several modules
M	= mathematics		
Ca	= careers education		
Lp	= leisure pursuits		
Pe	= physical education/games		
Se	= social education (preparation for adult life course)		

Table 7: Curriculum Changes 1977/78-1980/81 School D

Year	Fourth Year Curriculum		
	Core Subjects and Periods**	Periods of Options*	Project Changes
1977/78	$E_{5.3}M_{5.3}Gs_{1.8}Pe_{1.8}Fp_{0.9}$ $As_{0.9}Ps_{1.8}$	(5 x 3.6 (1 x 4.4	
1978/79	$E_{6.2}M_{5.3}Gs_{1.8}Pe_{1.8}Fp_{0.9}$ $As_{0.9}Ps_{0.9}$	(5 x 3.6 (1 x 4.4	E increased 5.3-6.2 Ps decreased 1.8-0.9 New M course. Mv with College of FE. Mk with College of Fe. New De/Cr course.
1979/80	$E_{6.2}M_{5.3}Gs_{2.7}Pe_{1.8}Fp_{0.9}$ $As_{0.9}$	(5 x 3.6 (1 x 4.4	Gs increased 1.8-2.7 Ps decreased 0.9-0.0 New C course. New Hm course. New De/Cr course discontinued.
1980/81	$E_{6.2}M_{5.3}Gs_{2.7}Pe_{1.8}Fp_{0.9}$ $As_{0.9}$	(5 x 3.6 (1 x 4.4	

*   First figure = no. of option blocks;
    Second figure = no. of ppw for each option.

** The non-integral number of periods arises from converting a 45 ppw timetable into its 40 ppw equivalent.

Table 7: Curriculum Changes 1977/78-1980/81 School D (contd.)

Year	Fifth Year Curriculum		
	Core Subjects and Periods**	Periods of Options*	Project Changes
1977/78	$E_{5.3}M_{5.3}Gs_{1.8}Pe_{1.8}Fp_{0.9}$ $As_{0.9}Ps_{1.8}$	(5 x 3.6 (1 x 4.4	
1978/79	$E_{6.2}M_{5.3}Gs_{1.8}Pe_{1.8}Fp_{0.9}$ $As_{0.9}Ps_{0.9}$	(5 x 3.6 (1 x 4.4	E increased 5.3-6.2 Ps decreased 1.8-0.9
1979/80	$E_{6.2}M_{5.3}Gs_{2.7}Pe_{1.8}Fp_{0.9}$ $As_{0.9}$	(5 x 3.6 (1 x 4.4	Gs increased 1.8-2.7 Ps decreased 0.9-0.0 2nd year of new M, Mv, Mk and De/Cr courses.
1980/81	$E_{6.2}M_{5.3}Gs_{2.7}Pe_{1.8}Fp_{0.9}$ $As_{0.9}$	(5 x 3.6 (1 x 4.4	

Key

E	= English	As	= assembly
C	= chemistry	Ps	= private study
M	= mathematics	Mv	= motor vehicle studies
Gs	= general studies	Mk	= engineering metalwork
De/Cr	= design & craft	Fp	= form period
Hm	= home management	Pe	= physical education/games

In the first year of the project (1978/79) a target group was identified consisting of the pupils in the remedial band together with a somewhat larger number from the rest of the year who were regarded as having particularly poor attainment and/or motivation. A programme consisting of eight short modules was developed for the target group which operated within two blocked sessions, each of four ppw. The modules consisted of careers education and personal guidance, education for parenthood, health education, personal and social education, environmental education, community and leisure education, introduction to industry, and art/photography. Pupils took these courses on a rota basis of two per week over a 10 week period. The full complement of courses was taken over the year and each one was intended to extend over the two year period from S4 to S5. The module of careers education was additional to the careers education provided in the core curriculum (one ppw in the case of non-remedial target group pupils). As well as the art/photography module there was a more extended version offered as a full two year CSE option. Target group pupils also had two ppw set aside for them to discuss and record significant project events.

The effect of these changes was to produce two curriculum patterns for the target group according to whether or not pupils were in the remedial band. Those who were not followed basically the same core curriculum as the rest of the year group. The main difference was that non-remedial target group pupils had the equivalent of two of their five option blocks replaced by the project modular programme.

In the second year of the project (1979/80), the modular programme was again introduced into S4 as well as being continued into the new S5. In addition, full two year options were established in S4 for child care (in conjunction with an FE college), traffic education and motor vehicle studies (at another FE college). One ppw of RPE was available to fourth year remedial band pupils. In general pupils in the fourth year target group followed essentially the same core curriculum. A playgroup was also established and fifth year pupils from the education for parenthood module were able to help with this.

By the end of the second year of the project it was increasingly apparent that the relatively complex modular structure was particularly vulnerable to the high levels of pupil absenteeism. The numbers attending each module were often so small, particularly in the fifth year, that they were amalgamated to give a single viable teaching group. It was also felt that the identification of a separate target group with its own distinctive curriculum was unsatisfactory. One reason was that it gave a low status to all things done under the project's auspices. For the following year (1980/81) the S4 programme was recast to give a series of options which were made available, with those others normally on offer only to non-remedial pupils, to all pupils in the year group. The overall effect of this was to blur the boundary between pupils in the remedial band and those in the rest of the year. Thus, although remedial band pupils continued to have a core curriculum separate from that of the rest of the year group, the option blocks were technically open to all. Included in these blocks were the former 'project' options: art/photography, motor vehicle studies, parent-craft/health education and child care. Other former project courses and modules were subsumed within a new double, non-examination, option called 'Life in the 80s'. The main components of this were careers education, world religions (a new module), traffic education, RPE, community studies and environmental studies. In the case of the fifth year the separate modular programme for target group pupils was continued from the previous year.

Thus the main effects of the project over the three years (1978/79 to 1980/81) were to lessen the separation of the remedial band from the rest of the S4 year and to extend the options programme to all pupils. However, 'Life in the 80s' and the other project options were designed with the expectation that they would tend to be chosen by the less able.

School C

In 1977/78 both the fourth and fifth year groups consisted of mixed ability forms. English, mathematics, religious education, careers and physical education/games formed a common core occupying 15 ppw in the fourth year and 18 ppw in the fifth year. For the remaining periods the majority of pupils chose one subject from each of five option blocks.

In the fourth year a small group of pupils followed an integrated humanities course. This course had been instituted in September 1977 for pupils who were considered to be unable to cope with academic subjects and/or the normal classroom situation. Altogether 15 ppw were devoted to the course. For part of this time, one morning a week, pupils participated in a social education project (SEP) based on a nearby youth club. The SEP pre-dated the integrated humanities course having been introduced some years previously at the time of ROSLA.

In the first year of the project the fourth year curriculum was modified by effectively replacing the core provision for religious education, careers education and physical education by a new programme consisting of an enhanced careers programme, a social education course called 'Preparation for Adult Life', and a leisure pursuits element. The latter consisted of a series of short options covering craft, physical education and 'hobby type' topics. In addition a new science course for less able pupils was introduced.

Because of timetable constraints during the first year, the project programme occurred on the same afternoon as the pupils taking the integrated humanities course were attending SEP at the youth club. As a result some of those pupils who had been identified as falling within the target group criteria were unable to take part in the project programme of careers education, preparation for adult life and leisure activities. This problem was overcome to some extent in the second year by timetabling the SEP as an option within the leisure pursuits programme.

In the second year of the project the number of option blocks in the fourth year was reduced from five to four. This allowed the core to be expanded from 15 to 20 ppw. The main changes were the introduction of four ppw of careers education/preparation for adult life and four periods of leisure pursuits. In addition some modifications were made to the mathematics course for the less able and a revised version of the humanities course for the less able was introduced.

By the third year this pattern had been established across both the fourth and fifth years. Thus all pupils in their last two years at school followed a basic core consisting of English, mathematics, careers education, social education (preparation for adult life) and leisure pursuits. In addition the target group and the less able pupils generally were likely to take the new science and humanities courses as part of their options programme.

The leisure pursuits programme consisted of a wide range of mini options from which pupils could choose several over a two year period. The programme available included most outdoor games and athletics activities together with badminton, table tennis, indoor hockey, trampolining, swimming, skating and the use of the facilities of a sports centre. Other options were photography, jewellery making, concreting, computer studies, soft toy making, first aid, motor vehicle maintenance, pottery, embroidery, child care/youth action, fishing and the SEP.

School D

The curriculum of school D was based on a 45 ppw timetable. In order to be able to compare its curriculum with that of the other schools the number of periods per week devoted to each subject has been reworked so as to give equivalents on a 40 ppw basis. In 1977/78 the fourth and fifth year were organised as mixed ability registration groups. English, mathematics, general studies, a timetabled form period and an assembly, together with private study, constituted a common core for 17.8 equivalent ppw. For the remainder of the time pupils chose an option from each of six blocks. The general studies course was an integrated one which included careers education, social education, health education and religious education. The fourth and fifth year general studies lessons were part of a course which ran throughout every year group of the school from the second to the seventh. 1977/78 was also the year in which the school introduced a two year CSE option course entitled 'Understanding Industry and Commerce'.

In the first year of the project the above curriculum was modified slightly so as to increase the allocation of time to English with a consequent reduction in the allocation to private study. By the second and third year of the project the only main <u>structural</u> change in the curriculum was a modest increase in the time allotted to general studies, achieved at the expense of the former period or so of private study. This situation was generally consistent with the rationale for D's designation as an 'associate' school. The school was chosen to take part in the project because it was felt that it had already achieved some reputation in the preparation for work and adult life area of the curriculum. The role expected of it was one of making its experience more widely available to other schools rather than in increasing substantially its time allocation to the careers education and related areas of the curriculum.

The project was seen, perhaps more than in the other schools, as a means of developing the curriculum as a whole. Whilst this included a concern for the transition from school to work and adult life, it was by no means limited simply to that. In the headteacher's view his staff did not perceive the project as a specific entity but rather as a general opportunity to get resources for overall curriculum development. In the first year, project resources were used to develop further the following existing courses: general studies, understanding industry and commerce, English and drama, mathematics and computer studies, humanities, science, art, technical studies, and home economics. In addition several new two year CSE courses were introduced, i.e. a maths course based on practical work and arithmetic, FE link courses in motor vehicle studies, and engineering metalwork[2], and design and craft. This pattern continued into the second year of the project with further new courses established in chemistry, and home management (combination of former courses in housecraft and home economics). However the design and craft course introduced in the previous year proved to have limited success and was discontinued at the end of the year.

DISCUSSION

The main structural changes which took place in the fourth and fifth year curricula of schools A and C over the period 1977/78 to 1980/81 were: an increase in the number of periods allocated to the core and a consequent decrease in the number of option blocks available and the periods allotted to them. This allowed in both schools the introduction of four ppw of careers education and social education in place of the one ppw of careers education which obtained in 1977/78. In school A this change coincided with the disappearance of social studies (four ppw) which was previously available as an option. However, social studies was one of the elements included along with careers education and health education in the new core subject which was given the title 'Sociology'. Whereas previously social studies tended to be chosen by the less academic pupils, its inclusion, at least in part, within sociology brought it to the attention of all pupils. Although in school C an enhanced core provision was also associated with the disappearance of social studies from the options, the integrated humanities course still continued and, in fact, provided a double option for many of the target group.

The changes in the overall structure of the fourth and fifth year curriculum of school D were much less marked. Over the four year period the total number of ppw allotted to the core remained constant. There was, however, an increase in the allocation to the core subject general studies of approximately one ppw. It is important to recognise though that in school D approximately two ppw of general studies were available to all pupils in each year group throughout the school. This course provided the basis of a guidance programme which built up progressively as the pupil moved through the school. It was concerned with "personal growth and development, mental and physical health, religious and political understanding, careers and choices. In the later stages it is particularly concerned with the student's ambitions, with all types of work, preparation for working life, and the responsibilities of adult living" (Annual Project Report School D, 1978/79). In other words its concerns were similar to those of the sociology course in A and the careers/social education course in C. However, where these courses were developed over the last two years of compulsory schooling, general studies was phased over four years in school D. In fact, by the time pupils had reached the end of their fifth year in D, the cumulative amount of time they had received in this area of the curriculum over four years was very nearly the same as pupils in A and C had encountered over two.

The changes which occurred in school B were somewhat different from those in the other three schools. Unlike the latter the changes made in school B, as a result of the project, were largely confined to the curriculum of the target group rather than the year group as a whole. This was mainly the consequence of the school being organised on the basis of a remedial band having a curriculum separate from the rest of its year group. The introduction of the eight ppw modular programme in the first two years (1978/79 - 1979/80) had two main effects. It replaced the former '$Re_2 Ca_2 Se_2 Cy_2$' part of the curriculum of the remedial band. Secondly, non-remedial target group pupils had the number of option blocks available to them effectively reduced from five to three. As has already been noted, the modular structure was regarded as unsatisfactory and was replaced in the third year of the project by an arrangement in which, very largely, the modules were recast and dispersed amongst option blocks available across the whole year group. The consequence of this was to give a basic curriculum structure which was the same for all pupils, i.e. a core of $E_5 M_5 Ca_1 Pe_4$ and a choice of options from five blocks. However, it was still true that the nature of the core English and mathematics offered and the options actually chosen by remedial band pupils and target group pupils generally differed from those which the rest of the pupils received. Indeed the 'Life in the 80s' double option was specifically designed with the needs of the target group in mind.

By the third year of the project the distinction between the remedial band and the rest of the year group in school B had been somewhat blurred. In terms of the overall <u>structure</u> of the S4 curriculum the situation in school B was very similar to that in A and C <u>before</u> the project began, i.e. a single period of careers education was provided for all and options specifically geared to the preparation of pupils for adult and working life were available across the whole year group.

Provision of the PFL Aspect of the Curriculum

Careers education is often included in integrated subjects such as general studies, social studies, sociology and humanities. For this reason and also because of the substantial overlap between these subjects and others, such as health education, social education and personal and social development, they may be conveniently grouped together in any analysis of the overall curriculum structure of schools. The term 'life skills' has increasingly of late been applied to the concerns which these subjects represent (e.g. Hopson and Scally, 1981). The use of such a term may run the risk of encouraging the facile view that successful living can be reduced to the identification and acquisition of a number of unambiguous social skills. For this reason, and also in order to imply that insights, understandings and attitudes are just as important as skills, we prefer to use the less focused term 'preparation for life' or PFL to describe that part of the curriculum represented by careers education, social education etc. Some might argue that all subjects in the curriculum contribute to PFL. Whilst this is undoubtedly so, nevertheless it is the case that preparation for adult life is the central concern of some subjects, whilst for others it is a subsidiary one.

The development of the fourth and fifth year curriculum in the four schools over the period 1977/78 to 1980/81 can be thought of as representing one or more of five models for providing PFL (Table 8). In model 1 all pupils in the fourth and fifth year receive a period or so of careers education. In addition the options programme contains one or more integrated courses, such as social studies, which the less able pupils are generally expected to choose. This model is represented by A and C before the project and by the S4 curriculum of B in 1980/81. The main disadvantage of this model is that the less able pupils receive most PFL whereas the bulk of pupils are restricted to that which is represented in the core careers programme. In addition, where several integrated course options are on offer, the less able pupils may receive varying amounts of PFL according to their choice of options. Moreover if the careers education and integrated courses are taught by different staff it is important that the ground which they cover represents a coherent whole. There is therefore a need for careful coordination of the various types of course.

In model 2 the majority of pupils have careers education in the core whilst the less able are provided for by a separate curriculum, which may include careers education together with various integrated courses, forming a substantial core with few or no options. The situation in school B

Table 8: Models for Providing the Preparation for Life (PFL) Aspects of the Curriculum

Model	Core Provision		Options Provision	Example
1	all pupils receive careers education		humanities, social studies, etc.	A and C before project, B at year 3
2	most pupils	(careers (education		B before project
	less able	(careers (education (+ (integrated (courses		
3	most pupils	(careers (education		B at year 2
	less able	(enhanced (integrated (courses		
4	all pupils	(integrated (courses		A and C at year 3
5	all pupils	(integrated (courses (year 2 - 5		D before and at the end of the project

before the project is illustrative of this model. Whilst the provision for the less able is more uniform in this model, the majority of pupils still receive relatively little PFL.

Model 3 is a derivative of model 2 in which the degree of integration of PFL is enhanced. This is exemplified by school B in the second year of the project where the former Re_2 Ca_2 Se_2 Cy_2

arrangement was replaced by the two four ppw
modular blocks. Model 4 can be thought of as a development of
model 3 in which the enhanced integrated provision
is made available to the whole year group. This is
represented by the four ppw sociology block at A or
the similar time allocation to careers
education/social education at C.

Finally model 5 has an integrated core PFL
course which extends throughout each year group of
the school rather than simply being concentrated in
the fourth and fifth year. This was the case in
school D even before the project began, where two
periods or so of general studies were provided for
all pupils from the second to the seventh year.
Although at least one school (C) had considered the
introduction of some careers education in the third
year, this had not been realised and the provision
of an integrated PFL core throughout the age range
had not generally developed.

There are several advantages in the adoption
of model 5. First, it provides a PFL programme to
all pupils and, moreover, one in which all pupils
receive the same amount of PFL irrespective of
ability. Secondly, by introducing the programme in
the lower school and extending it throughout the
age range, it is possible to match more sensitively
the consideration of specific topics and concerns
to the stages of physical, intellectual and
emotional maturation of pupils. Thirdly, its
presence as a core subject in the curriculum of
each year group also demonstrates its importance
and parity with other subjects.

In secondary schools generally the curriculum,
particularly from the third year onwards, is
markedly differentiated by ability, i.e. the
subjects taken, and the way in which they are
studied, differ according to the ability levels of
pupils. Whilst a reasonable case may be made out
for organising learning in this way for some
subjects, it is perhaps less defensible for PFL.
All pupils have to cope with the basic demands of
adulthood - this is something which emphasises the
commonalty of individuals rather than their
differences. If PFL justifies its inclusion in the
curriculum on the grounds that it facilitates this
process of transition from adolescence to adulthood
then access to it in the form of some common
experience should be the right of all. If PFL is
to be a component of the core curriculum of all

pupils then the question inevitably arises whether or not a mixed ability mode of organisation for it is the most appropriate. If, in fact, the concerns of PFL are personal, social and behavioural, rather than cognitive, then the organisation of groups composed of pupils of different abilities may be both possible and appropriate. The general life experience of some pupils conventionally regarded as 'unacademic' may often be richer and more varied than their 'academic' peers. Indeed Keddie (1971) found that pupils from the less academic groups were often more willing and able to question the issues which arose in a social studies course than their more academic peers. If PFL is to make a serious contribution to a critical examination of personal and social issues then a pedagogy which encourages the debate of alternative views and experiences is educationally desirable. Such a pedagogy may be more likely to emerge if pupils are allocated to groups organised on a mixed ability basis than if they are concentrated in separate groups according to their ability.

Two further points worth emphasising emerge from the analysis of the S4 and S5 curriculum presented here. The first concerns the potential contribution of religious education to PFL. Its contribution to the project programmes however seems to have been a slight one. In fact, in school C the period of core RE previously provided in the fourth and fifth year was effectively appropriated in the process of creating the new integrated course. This is a pity for if one of the functions of PFL is to develop pupils' personal resources in facing the increasingly uncertain vicissitudes of life then the claims which religions have always made to helping such development need to be considered. Hopson and Scally (1981) identify a concern to discover values and beliefs and to take stock of life as two amongst their list of 49 life-skills. If in tackling such concerns their religious implications are not examined then pupils' understanding of them will be imperfect. This is certainly not to argue a case for the primacy of the religious perspective but to ensure that it has a place alongside those other perspectives, generally secular in nature, that PFL courses typically present.

The second point concerns the view that many hold that society is irrevocably moving to a situation where the availability of employment will continue to diminish and where enforced leisure will increasingly become the lot of the majority. If that is so, then perhaps the school curriculum should seriously take account of such trends by helping to elevate the whole status of leisure. The motivation behind the creation of the leisure pursuits programme of school C may, at least in part, reflect such a belief. It is interesting to note that the leisure pursuits programme replaced one of the traditional 'leisure' aspects of the conventional curriculum, i.e. physical education and games. Although the new programme included many of the familiar activities associated with the latter, it also provided an extended range of physical activities and brought in others of a craft or hobby nature.

This chapter has looked only at the 'surface' structure of the curriculum. Some of the questions which have been raised however can only be answered by extending the analysis to what may be termed (with apologies to Chomsky !) the 'deep structure' of the curriculum. This is the concern of the next few chapters.

NOTES

1 The convention of referring to the fourth year of secondary education (i.e. 14+) as S4 and the fifth year as S5 is used here.

2 This represented the reinstatement of the arrangements of a former link course.

Chapter 3

CONTENT OF PREPARATION FOR LIFE COURSES

As outlined in the previous chapter the main feature which characterised the changes in the curriculum pattern of the schools was the expansion of that part of the fourth and fifth year core curriculum which we have called Preparation for Life.

In this chapter we examine the range of topics which are taught under this rubric. The information presented here was obtained from a study carried out towards the end of the second year of the project (1979/80). Table 9 briefly summarises the PFL core provision of each school for that year.

The study involved asking the main teacher concerned with each course or module to complete a checklist of possible topics and themes. Each teacher completed the checklist in the light of the teaching covered in both the fourth and fifth years in 1979/80.

The checklist consisted of 46 items falling under one of six main sections:

- pre-employment;
- aspects of employment/adult life;
- aspects of industry/commerce;
- aspects of economics/politics;
- general personal issues;
- social/community issues.

Each item was rated in turn according to the emphasis given to it during the academic year. The rating scale consisted of five points:

Table 9: Preparation for Life: Core Provision (1979/80)

Fourth year 1979/80		Fifth year 1979/80	
School	Core subjects classified as PFL	Total PFL periods	Core subjects classified as PFL	Total PFL periods
A	Sociology (So_4)	4	Careers education (Ca_2)	2
B	Community/ Leisure (Cy_1), Art/Photography (Ph_1), Health Education (He_1), Understanding Industry (Ic_1), Environmental Studies (Ev_1), Social Education (Se_1), Parentcraft (Ch_1), Careers education (Ca_1)	8	Community/ Leisure (Cy_1), Art/Photography (Ph_1), Health Education (He_1), Understanding Industry (Ic_1), Environmental Studies (Ev_1), Social Education (Se_1), Parentcraft (Ch_1), Careers education (Ca_1)	8
C	Careers education (Ca_2), Social education (Se_2),	4	Careers education (Ca_1), Preparation for adult life ($Ss + He$)$_{08}$	1.8
D	General studies (GS_{27})	2.7	General studies (GS_{27})	2.7

1. not dealt with or given only an incidental mention;
2. dealt with in the equivalent of a period or so;
3. dealt with in the equivalent of 2 to 5 periods or so;
4. a minor theme dealt with in the equivalent of 6 to 10 periods or so;
5. a major theme dealt with in the equivalent of 10 or more periods.

The items composing the checklist were drawn up after a content analysis of a small sample of relevant syllabuses/schemes of work and in the light of current trends in this area of the curriculum. The comprehensiveness of the checklist was attested to by the fact that respondents did not, in the main, find it necessary to add more than three or so items to describe the content of their courses. Table 10 shows the items used in the checklist and the way in which they were grouped under the six sections.

The checklist returns from the schools were summarised in the following way. A single number which reflected the original emphasis was assigned to each category within the rating scale, thus:

category 1 = 0
category 2 = 1
category 3 = 4
category 4 = 7
category 5 = 10

It must be noted that these numbers do not indicate exactly the number of periods devoted to these topics, but provide a guide only to the degree of emphasis, as measured by the time spent on it, given to a topic by the school in question. The fourth year returns and the fifth year returns from a school were each converted into numbers in the way described above, and were then added together to form a composite number for each item of the checklist. This was done in order to try to show the total core PFL curriculum which a pupil would encounter over the last two years of compulsory schooling. It was felt that this was more satisfactory than looking at each year separately, since in the latter case the pattern of both years would be distorted if a topic which one school emphasised in, say year four, were

emphasised by another school in year five. The
method adopted, however, gives a less true picture
of the curriculum encountered by a pupil in School
A. This was because A was in the process of
changing from a two year core Careers programme of
two periods per week (and the fifth year return
described the second year of this) to a two year
Sociology (including Careers) programme of four
periods per week (and the fourth year return
described the first year of this).

The results obtained by this procedure are
summarised in Table 11. Each item of the checklist
is arranged in decreasing order of the average
emphasis given by the four schools.

It might be thought that the maximum possible
emphasis which could be given to any one item, if
it received the highest rating in each of two
years, would be twenty. This was exceeded in the
case of School B for two items (personal decision
making and adult relationships) because
contributions to these were made by several
teachers in different modules. It should be noted
when comparing the results of the four schools that
the PFL curriculum for school B shown here is that
for target group pupils only, whereas for the other
three schools the figures of Table 11 refer to the
pattern for all pupils. In addition it should be
remembered that the amount of time devoted to PFL
by B was substantially greater than for the other
schools. Nevertheless it is felt that it is
legitimate to use the raw ratings (rather than
ratings adjusted to take account of differences in
total time devoted to this curriculum area) to
compare schools one with another, since the total
amount of time a school devotes to any item must to
some degree reflect the importance accorded to this
curriculum area.

It also needs to be mentioned that the results
obtained relate only to the Preparation for Life
(PFL) components of the core curriculum. It may
well be that some aspects of PFL are also
incidentally incorporated into certain option
subjects taken by some rather than all pupils of a
year group. However it is perhaps reasonable to
suppose that the main coordinated thrust in PFL
will occur within the core curriculum.

Some of the similarities and differences
between the schools can be clearly seen in Table 12
which lists the dozen or so most highly rated items
for each school. All four schools gave high

Table 10: Items in the PFL Checklist

1. Pre-employment aspects	2. Aspects of employment/ adult life	3. Aspects of industry/ commerce
Self appraisal Personal decision making Local job opportunities Further education and training opportunities Knowledge of specific jobs Finding and applying for jobs Preparation for interviews Communication skills Changing world of work* Sources of help and guidance (e.g. careers service)*	Adapting to life at work Leisure and work Trade unions and industrial relations Unemployment Self employment Money management and budgeting personal lifestyle - expectations of adult life	Structure and location of industry Commercial services (banking, insurance etc.) Wholesale and retail distribution Manufacturing industry Organisation of companies/firms

* Items added by respondents

Table 10: Items in the PFL Checklist (contd.)

4. Aspects of economics/ politics	5. General personal issues	6. Social/ community issues
Basic economic concepts	Adult relationships	Population
Private and public sector	Home management	Conservation (e.g. food, energy, environment)
Local and national government	Personal hygiene and health	Pollution
Decision making and democracy	Abuses of the body (e.g. drugs, alcohol, smoking)	Protecting the community (police etc)
	Aspects of sexual behaviour (contraception, abortion etc.)	Impact of technology
	Personal safety (at home, work, leisure etc.)	Health and welfare services
	Mental health	Youth and youth culture
	Consumer education	Sex discrimination and stereotyping
	Child development	Racial discrimination and stereotyping
	Parentcraft*	Mass media
		The family and other social groups
		The handicapped
		The elderly and sick

Table 11: PFL Checklist Items Arranged in Order of
Average Rating

Item	Ave	A	B	C	D
Personal decision making ...	18.50	20	27	10	17
Self appraisal	15.25	20	13	11	17
Knowledge of specific jobs..	13.50	10	7	20	17
Adult relationships	13.25	7	24	14	8
Local job opportunities	12.00	12	8	11	17
Unemployment	11.75	15	19	8	5
Communication skills	11.50	14	17	11	4
Personal lifestyle	11.25	14	12	11	8
Structure and location of industry	9.75	8	20	7	4
Aspects of sexual behaviour.	9.50	0	20	14	4
Adapting to work	9.00	8	10	14	4
Child development	8.50	10	20	4	0
Preparation for interviews..	8.25	7	9	7	10
Manufacturing industry	7.25	8	11	5	5
Personal hygiene and health.	7.00	1	12	11	4
Finding and applying for jobs	7.00	8	3	7	10
FE training and opportunities	6.75	14	0	5	8
Money management/budgeting..	6.75	4	11	7	5
Local and national government	6.75	11	2	7	7
Abuses of the body	6.50	4	8	10	4
Leisure and work	6.00	9	10	1	4
Basic economic concepts	6.00	4	12	4	4
Mass media	5.75	10	12	1	0
Family and other social groups	5.75	10	10	2	1
Personal safety	5.25	4	5	4	8

PFL content

Table 11: PFL Checklist Items Arranged in Order of
Average Rating (contd.)

Item	Ave	A	B	C	D
Impact of technology	5.25	5	3	5	8
Parentcraft	4.75	0	19	0	0
Home management	4.50	1	12	1	4
Trades Unions and Industrial relationships ...	4.00	4	4	4	4
Youth and youth culture	3.75	7	8	0	0
Population	3.50	0	14	0	0
Conservation	3.50	0	14	0	0
Protecting the Community ...	3.50	4	4	5	1
Decision making/democracy ..	3.50	7	2	1	4
Organisation of companies/ firms	3.50	4	2	7	1
Sex discrimination/ stereotyping	3.25	8	2	1	2
Pollution	3.25	0	13	0	0
Private/public sector	3.00	4	7	1	0
Sources of help and guidance e.g. careers service	3.00	0	1	7	4
Wholesale/retail distribution	2.25	1	7	0	1
Consumer education	2.25	0	4	5	0
Racial discrimination/ stereotyping	1.50	0	6	0	0
The handicapped	1.50	4	1	1	0
Health/welfare services	1.25	1	2	2	0
Commercial services	1.25	0	0	4	1
Changing world of work	1.00	0	0	0	4
Self employment	1.00	4	0	0	0
Elderly and sick	0.50	0	1	1	0
Mental health	0.00	0	0	0	0

Note: Figures for B refer to the less able pupils
only.

43

Table 12:   The Top PFL Checklist Items for the Four Schools

A	B	C	D
Self appraisal	Personal decision making	Knowledge of specific jobs	Self appraisal
Personal decision making		Adapting to work	Personal decision making
	Adult relationships		Local job opportunities
Unemployment		Adult relationships	
	Structure/ location of industry		Knowledge of specific jobs
FE & training opportunities		Aspects of sexual behaviour	
			Finding and applying for jobs
Communicat- ional skills	Aspects of sexual behaviour	Self appraisal	
Personal lifestyle	Child development	Local job opportunities	Preparation for interviews
Local job opportunities	Unemployment	Communicat- ional skills	FE & training opportunities
Local/national government	Parentcraft	Personal lifestyle	Personal lifestyle
Knowledge of specific jobs	Communicat- ional skills		
		Personal hygiene and health	Adult relationships
Child development	Leisure and work		
		Personal dec- ision making	Personal safety
Mass media	Population		
	Conservation	Abuses of the body	Impact of technology
Family and other social groups	Pollution		
			Local/national government
	Self appraisal	Unemployment	

ratings to 'personal decision making' and 'self appraisal' and all but one to 'knowledge of specific jobs'. This largely reflects the fact that careers education was a major component of the PFL programmes of all four schools, the principle aims of which have been defined as follows:

1. to help pupils achieve an understanding of themselves and to be realistic about their strengths and weaknesses;
2. to extend the range of pupils' thinking about opportunities in work and life generally;
3. to prepare them to make considered choices (DES, 1973).

To these three aims, which may be termed 'self awareness', 'opportunity awareness' and 'decision learning' Watts and Herr (1976) add a fourth, 'transition learning', which is concerned with helping pupils to prepare for the demands of working life and adult life in general. This latter aim can be related particularly to the checklist items of 'adult relationships' and 'personal lifestyle' which are amongst the top rated checklist items in three of the schools. The specific transition item 'adapting to work' also appears in the list of top items of one of the schools (C).

Another 'transition' item which was emphasised in at least three of the schools was 'unemployment'. Some years ago Watts (1978) pointed out that this was a topic which was rarely considered in careers education. Indeed anything which smacks of education for unemployment is often an anathema to teachers. In fact this point was very clearly made at one school in a discussion with senior staff prior to commencement of the project. However the results of this survey would suggest that by the middle of the project the reluctance to tackle 'unemployment' as a topic had largely disappeared - indeed this was confirmed by our own observation of careers education lessons and discussions with teachers during the second half of the project's life.

Generally speaking the most marked difference in the emphases given in the various PFL programmes was that between B and the remaining schools. In B, greater stress was put on items such as 'parentcraft', 'leisure and work', 'population', 'conservation', 'pollution' and 'structure and location of industry' than was the case for A, C and D.

Comparing the top items for the three schools A, C and D we find that: 'mass media' and 'family and other social groups' were apparently given greater relative emphasis at A; 'abuses of the body' and 'personal hygiene and health' were stressed more at C, and 'finding and applying for jobs', 'preparing for interviews', 'personal safety' and 'impact of technology' were given greater attention at D.

Some differences between the schools are also apparent amongst the least emphasised PFL items (i.e. the bottom 12 items in Table 11). Thus although these items refer to PFL themes which were generally minor ones, some were apparently given greater emphasis by school B, e.g. 'wholesale/ retail distribution', 'racial discrimination/ stereotyping'. School D gave rather more emphasis to the 'changing world of work' - a theme which was probably related to 'impact of technology' which was also rated higher than in the other schools. School C gave somewhat greater emphasis to 'commercial services' whereas school A gave rather more attention to 'the handicapped' and 'self employment'. The latter topic is especially noteworthy since it generally appears to receive little consideration in careers education. Whilst careers education programmes concentrate very heavily on paid employment, the possibilities of self employment seem to be passed over. Self employment is a topic which apparently lies outside the careers education mainstream. And yet in a situation of high unemployment other alternatives to the conventional one of working for an employer need to be examined.

Its omission as a topic inevitably introduces a fundamental asymmetry into careers education with only one side of the employment coin being presented. The failure to consider the possibilities of self employment tends to reinforce the function of careers education operating as a placement mechanism for existing socio-economic and employment structures.

Knowing what is involved in 'setting up on one's own' would give pupils an important insight into aspects of finance and business matters which tend to be regarded as the arcane concerns of elite groups. Such knowledge would be valuable to all pupils, even if only a few were able seriously to consider self employment, since it would help to de-mystify a significant part of the business world.

The differences which exist between the PFL programmes of the four schools are more clearly shown in Fig. 1. Here the ratings for items have been aggregated under each of the six main sections of the checklist. The aggregated ratings have been expressed as a percentage of the total ratings for all items so as to indicate the relative emphasis given to each of the six sections.

As can be seen the PFL programme of school D gives greatest emphasis to 'pre-employment aspects' and school B least. Schools B and C give greater attention to general personal issues than do the other two schools. Social and community issues tend to receive greater stress in schools A and B. Compared to the other PFL sections 'aspects of industry/commerce' and 'aspects of economics/politics' generally receive the least emphasis in all four schools.

DISCUSSION

The study of PFL in the four schools illustrates several important points that are likely to hold for this aspect of the curriculum in other schools. First, where PFL is differentiated according to the ability levels of particular groups of pupils the content and emphasis of courses are likely to be significantly different from those which are provided as a core for all pupils irrespective of ability. This is clearly shown in Fig. 1 where the pattern of the PFL course for the target group of B can be compared with the courses for pupils in the other three schools.

Whilst it is appropriate to modify the teaching/learning methods used and their pace for pupils of different ability levels it is more difficult to justify differentiated content in an area such as PFL which deals with concerns which should be relevant to the needs of all pupils.

Second, as Table 11 indicates, PFL courses may cover a large number of individual topics. Although there appears to be a measure of agreement on what some of the main ones should be (notably those that relate to the process of job choice) there are important differences between courses even where these are not internally differentiated

Figure 1: Relative Emphases given to Various Aspects of PFL

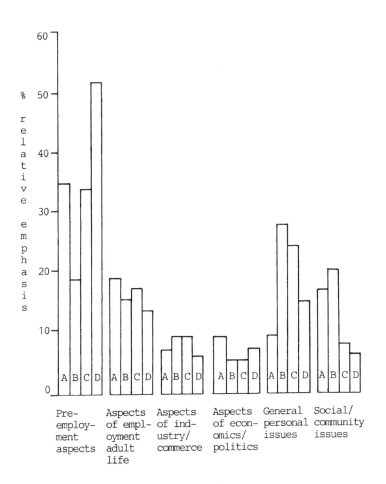

by ability. Thus knowing that schools have core
PFL courses, however they may be variously
labelled, does not tell you what is actually taught
in them. Whilst one might have a general idea of
what is taught in a fourth/fifth year course on
mathematics or French, say, what lurks beneath a
PFL label may be anyone's guess. To be able to
identify the internal structure of a PFL course and
to compare it with comparable courses in other
schools requires an analytic framework. This study
used one based on six global themes: pre-employment
aspects; aspects of employment/adult life; aspects
of industry/commerce; aspects of economics/
politics; general personal issues; and social and
community issues. Of these the two which were
given least emphasis across all four schools were
aspects of industry/commerce and aspects of
economics/politics (both under 10% on the scale of
relative emphasis of Fig. 1). Of course the
category system used here is just one amongst many
that could in principle be devised. It has the
disadvantage of being essentially one dimensional.
Thus although it enables a PFL course to be
analysed in terms of the emphasis given to broad
concepts or themes it provides, on its own, no
indication of what specifically is taught within
each of these nor, of course, how things are
taught. The APU Exploratory Group on Personal and
Social Development (APU, 1981) suggests a model
which examines each of ten possible themes in terms
of four dimensions: knowledge, understanding,
attitudes and practical application. However the
penetration of PFL courses to this extent is
probably best done by observing them in operation
seeing exactly how such topics as job choice,
unemployment and personal relationships are
actually taught. These and other examples of
classroom practice in the PFL area are considered
next.

Chapter 4

CAREERS EDUCATION: SOME CURRENT ISSUES

The content of this chapter and the six which
follow is based on data collected at the three
schools A, B and C. As indicated in the Appendix
on evaluation it was only possible to involve the
associate school (D) to a limited extent in the
research programme.

Careers education was a major component of
schools' programmes and one which teachers
generally felt the project had been influential in
developing (cf. Chapter 12). The importance given
to careers education in the project was reflected
in our own research activities in that nearly a
third of the 230 field notes collected over three
years was concerned with this aspect of the
curriculum.

The availability of extra funds from the
project enabled schools to increase the audio
visual basis of their careers education courses.
In all three project schools there was an increased
use of both commercial and teacher made materials.
The extra time allocated to careers education made
it easier to follow up films and other activities
than was the case previously within the
straitjacket of a single period. In general more
small group work had been possible than formerly as
a result of the availability of other staff e.g.
careers officer.

Whilst project funds could not be used for
capital developments, involvement in the project
had underlined the need for improving the physical
facilities for careers education and the LEA in
fact carried out such work in two of the schools (A
and C). During the time of the project there had
been an increase in the number of pupils

participating in visits and work experience schemes. In the case of the associate school nearly every fourth year pupil (90%) received one week's work experience in their summer term in 1981.

This chapter concentrates on three aspects of the careers education programmes: the job choice model; the treatment of unemployment as a topic; and the role of the careers officer. These three are chosen since they point up many of the crucial issues which careers teachers and others currently confront.

The first two of these aspects considered here provide an example of that kind of study, concerned with the exploration of careers education programmes in action, which Bates (1983) has noted is a rarity in the current literature.

THE JOB CHOICE MODEL

A feature common to the careers education programmes of the project schools, and indeed schools' generally, was the treatment of job choice. This was presented as a rational three stage process which may be expressed simply as find out about jobs, know yourself, and match the two. Such an approach is consistent with the view of careers education as reflecting a concern for opportunity awareness, self awareness and decision making (Watts and Herr, 1976).

Information about Jobs

One of the central notions which informs the teaching of careers education is that occupations can be ordered into job groups or families. In one system of classification the job families identified were: work with hands, figures, words, or people, and work which was active, artistic, or scientific. Another system which was used was based on the categories: scientific, social services, general services, organisational or persuasive, literary, artistic, practical, computational, nature and active/outdoor. The use of such categories is often recommended in careers education materials (e.g. COIC, 1975) [1]. They provide a way of dealing with the vast multitude of jobs which could be presented to pupils.

Careers Officer (teaching a class)	I want to give you a way of organising this, of making sense of it. At the moment it's just a long list. I want you to think about families of jobs which are somehow related to each other ...

While the good teacher does create meaning for pupils by providing them with organising structures, category systems can be used uncritically e.g.

Teacher	A typist - what does she need to do?
Pupil	Work with her hands
Pupil	Work with words
Teacher	Which is the most important?
Pupil	Words
Teacher	OK - a typist has to work with words.

This does seem to be a rather arbitrary designation - the main area of a typist's commitment might be justifiably assigned to either work with words, work with hands or both. More important, does either category adequately capture the essence of a typist's work? So while it is undeniably important to use some system for classifying jobs, there is a danger that pupils will perceive these categories as absolute and not as human designed and therefore modifiable devices for creating order and aiding understanding. Pupils might usefully be introduced to the rationale for categorising occupations while emphasising that there will often be inevitable overlap between categories and differences of view as to which category a particular activity should be consigned. In this way teachers and pupils could explore together their perceptions of the skills and activities which are important features in various occupations.

Another organising principle which was observed in use was that of job level. Four job levels were identified: technologist (or professional); technician; craftsman; and operative. These levels were presented as a hierarchy, determined by the qualifications required and the nature of the skills and responsibilities entailed. It is of course true that jobs can be differentiated in this kind of way. As a consequence it is imperative that pupils are made aware of this information so that their educational choices do not pre-empt possible vocational choices. Pupils do need to know the educational and other qualifications necessary for entry to particular jobs. The attempt to conceptualise all of this in terms of a set of four job levels however poses certain problems. First, do these levels apply to all career areas? Do they for example represent the most appropriate way of describing the hospital hierarchy, described in one lesson, as doctor, laboratory technician, nurse and ward orderly?

Secondly, the levels define a status hierarchy in which there is a top and a bottom. Teachers, perhaps to avoid the implication that the top is perceived as the most valuable or worthwhile, may stress the notion of equal importance.

Teacher   The technician is more skilled than the ward orderly - but not more important. All (staff) are important. All are important but all are separated - cannot have ward orderlies who say they would like to become nurses.

Teachers face a difficult dilemma. On the one hand they want to do the best they can for each pupil, e.g. as in one lesson observed, by emphasising the importance of qualifications and encouraging pupils to put in extra effort to improve their examination grades. On the other hand by presenting a description of job stratification as essentially unproblematic and helping pupils to slot into it at the 'appropriate' level they reinforce a tendency for careers education to become "an agent of social control adapting individuals to the careers opportunities which realistically are open to them." (Watts and Herr, 1976).

The justification for the use of job categories, as already mentioned, is to help pupils make sense of the enormously large number of jobs available from which they might theoretically choose. They may help to narrow down the possibilities and enable pupils to focus on some specific jobs which might be followed up in further work. An example of this was observed in one

lesson in which pupils were prepared for a
forthcoming careers convention at the school. The
pupils had a list of all the careers that were to
be represented at the convention and the list was
used as a stimulus to revise the job families which
had been introduced the year before. As the lesson
developed the various careers were listed on the
blackboard under the appropriate job families. The
focus was sharpened still further by asking pupils
to suggest questions that they would like to put to
convention representatives. Here pupils recalled
many of the important things about jobs which they
had been taught earlier in the course. These 'key
considerations' included: the nature of the work
involved; the variety of the work; training; pay
during training; qualifications needed; health
requirements; hours of work; career prospects;
conditions of work; 'perks' etc. Lists such as
this constitute a further frequently used method of
helping pupils to organise their understanding of
jobs.

Self Assessment and Decision Making

Questionnaire exercises provided the main
vehicle for pupil self assessment. One school, for
example, used a 19 page booklet covering the topics
'looking at myself', 'looking at work', 'job
satisfaction' and a section where general decisions
were made on job choice.
Such exercises were justified to pupils in
terms of the benefits of increased self knowledge,
e.g.

Teacher   You'll know more about yourself,
                 your interests and personality,
                 you'll know more about your ambition
                 ... The booklet, will help you find
                 out things not necessarily about
                 your job. When you leave school
                 you'll have more leisure time than
                 working time. What will you do in
                 this leisure time?

The information which such exercises provide
was also used by teachers.

Teacher   When the fifth year completed these
                 sheets last year, their tutors found
                 out more about them. Your tutor has

to write a report about you: what
sort of person you are; whether you
work hard; whether you take
initiative; whether you get on well
with your friends and adults; what
your attendance is like; what your
punctuality is like. These reports
come to me and with them and your
record card I write references - a
written comment which is sent to
your employer. You see how
important these sheets are.

When introduced to self assessment exercises
pupils may be told, "This is not a test, there are
no right or wrong answers", although the answers
given may be labelled 'strengths' and 'weaknesses'.
On their own such exercises implicitly communicate
the things about a person that are considered
important. Thus characteristics such as 'serious',
'quiet', 'tidy', are classified as 'strengths' and
'jokey', 'noisy' and 'untidy' as 'weaknesses'.
Pupils need to recognise that while certain
qualities may be valued by some employers when
people are in their work role, other qualities may
be of value in other roles, e.g. as a friend, in
the family, in leisure time etc.

Questionnaires, like those used in one school
where pupils were requested to rate themselves on a
scale from 'good' to 'bad', may lead to an
unwitting 'labelling'. Some pupils may get the
message 'they are x' which could constrain the way
they think of themselves and the things they are
prepared to try in life.

Approaches to encourage self assessment other
than through the use of questionnaires were
observed. In one school pupils wrote accounts of
themselves to compare with those written by
teachers. In another, pupils were asked to list
their ten most salient characteristics as part of a
simulation in which they had to imagine depositing
a computer record of themselves before leaving for
another planet. In one lesson the project careers
officer asked pupils to draw a picture putting in
some of the things that interested them as people.
Such approaches as these allow the emergence of
those qualities which pupils think to be the most
important before they are exposed to, and possibly
constrained by, questionnaire exercises.

Information about jobs and self knowledge were seen as the two necessary conditions for deciding on the choice of a job. Although much emphasis was placed on the importance of making sensible and responsible choices, exactly how this was to be done was not generally made explicit. The implication was that job choice arose from the matching of personal interests and abilities with the characteristics of different jobs. Although this seems straightforward enough, the process implied is dauntingly complex. Thus in some lessons pupils may be presented with long lists of factors about jobs which have to be evaluated against equally long lists of personal qualities. If this process is to be repeated with a range of possible jobs the task soon attains formidable proportions. In practice the time available, if not the pupil's ability to handle such complex matching tasks, necessitates some simplification e.g.

Teacher   You need to ask yourselves 'What kind of things am I interested in? Outdoor/Active?' Then you can single out the group and look at the jobs within it. Then you can go to the careers library and know which cards to turn to for help.

Job choice may be related to decision making seen as a generalisable skill. Thus a film shown in one lesson went through the different ways of making a decision ('gut reaction', 'leaving it to luck', 'leaving it to others' etc.) and strongly advocated 'working it out'.

Teacher   For the big decisions in our lives though, working it out helps us take more charge of our lives.

Individual pupils do not of course engage in job choice unaided, both the careers teacher and careers officer are involved in the process. In fact one of the explicit justifications for the inclusion of self assessment exercises, in at least one school, was to indicate the kind of person a pupil was so that the careers officer could suggest suitable jobs.

Computerisation of Job Choice

Recent applications of computer technology have now made it possible to accomplish the systematic matching of job factors with personal characteristics implicit in the job choice model. One such system, JIIG-CAL (Job Ideas and Information Generator: Computer Assisted Learning)[2] was used during the third year of the project by school A. The operation of JIIG-CAL can be summarised as follows. Pupils complete an occupational interest guide and copy their answers on to computer cards which are then sent off to the computer. In due course pupils receive back their individual interest profiles. In the second stage they complete a further questionnaire providing information about their preferences for school subjects and for a number of factors related to jobs. Answers are again copied on to cards and despatched to the computer. All of the information is matched by the computer against information stored on over 400 jobs. Finally the pupils receive a print out which records details of the 20 jobs most suitable for them, together with references to publications for follow up work. Print outs are also supplied for careers officers and teachers giving them appropriate technical information necessary when careers interviews are conducted (cf. Closs and Broderick, 1982).

The general response of the class to JIIG-CAL was favourable although several problems did emerge. Pupils' absenteeism, as in other aspects of the project programme, tended to vitiate the notion of continuity of work. The technology was not completely foolproof and occasional operator errors occurred. This meant that teachers had to spend time dealing with pupils who had job details missing in their print outs and occasionally cards had to be sent off a second time for reprocessing. As a result some pupils got out of phase with the main group and this involved teachers in extra work in helping them to catch up. Pupils also worked at very different rates in completing questionnaires and transferring answers to computer cards. This fact, and also because some of the class could move on to the next stage before all had completed the first, made it necessary to run several activities simultaneously in order to keep faster workers occupied while slower ones finished. However, these extra activities could often only run for

5-10 minutes before being interrupted by the next stage of JIIG-CAL. In addition the fast workers doing these extra activities tended to make further demands on the teacher which made it more difficult to attend to the slower ones and to discuss their print outs with them. Teachers considered that the system also generated extra work, i.e. keeping the cards separate, checking that they were filled in correctly, sending them off at the right time and sorting them out when they came back.

These difficulties are not of course insurmountable. In fact the teachers concluded in their report at the end of the trial that the system was "useful and worthwhile". Teachers' response to the organisational difficulties which emerged during the trial was to list several recommendations which would be put into effect during the next JIIG-CAL run. The difficulties were not thought to be of sufficient gravity to outweigh the positive features of the system. In fact the reaction of pupils of all ability levels to JIIG-CAL was very favourable. They also seemed to have a more developed understanding of the role of the careers officer following the officer's involvement in a complete 'run'. JIIG-CAL was also likely to have provided some pupils with their first contact with a computer system. A spin-off of the exercise was that pupils clearly became accustomed to handling computer cards and reading print outs.

UNEMPLOYMENT [3]

A major element of the careers education taught in the project schools, as in schools generally, was concerned with work and jobs, "a careers course is based on looking at work". It was implicitly assumed that the skills which the pupil developed through participation in the course would be related primarily to job finding.

"We will introduce lots of different ideas to you while you are at school, so that you'll not have as many problems finding a job when you leave."

When the project began in 1978 youth unemployment was already assuming worrying proportions. From the outset, project schools attempted to tackle the topic of unemployment, although it was regarded as being somewhere

outside the central focus of interest, i.e. looking
at aspects of work.

"We do not aim for unemployment - we think about it
separately."

As the project developed and the employment
situation worsened teachers had to reappraise how
the topic of unemployment was to be treated in
their general careers education programmes. By the
project's third year it was clearly a feature in
its own right in the programmes of at least two of
the schools. In addition a project working party
was established to develop teaching materials and
methods on unemployment. This activity continued
into the fourth year of the project.

Unemployment tended to be a topic which
teachers, perhaps understandably, had some anxiety
in handling.

Teacher (to researcher before beginning a lesson on unemployment)	I don't know how we'll begin it ... take it as it comes ... we're into the frontiers of knowledge.

In one lesson observed the teacher was able
to introduce the topic for discussion by direct
reference to his own experience of being an
unemployed teacher for a time. He described his
visits to the unemployment office, the amount of
unemployment benefit that he received, and his
reactions during that period.

This tendency to imply that unemployment is an
increasingly common occurrence may serve to dispel
the feeling of personal shame often associated with
it. This may be at least part of the motivation
behind such teacher comments as:

"We're coming to a theme called unemployment. At
the moment I don't know many people who don't
experience it one way or another. Even teachers
are unemployed. A lot of people have brothers or
parents who are unemployed - so it affects a lot of
other people."

Or again:

"If any of you are unemployed for a while it's
important to have understanding parents and know
it's not your fault."

Teachers may attempt to encourage a more positive approach towards unemployment by emphasising some of the productive alternatives to work which may exist, e.g. involvement in sport and hobbies.

"Almost any one can learn to do anything - you get good. In sports you practise and get good, get into a club, make friends and maybe get into competition."

Work may be stressed as being only one side of life.

Teacher   Paul is a good drummer. He can pot. He can ride. So even if Paul goes on a YOP scheme as a jockey and there's no job at the end of it - he does pottery in the evenings and practises drums. If someone came up to you then and said, 'Hi, Paul - what do you do? Who are you?' what would you say?

Paul   I'm unemployed but I make the most of my time.

Teacher   Wouldn't you say, 'I'm a horse rider, I do pottery'? What I'm trying to say is that you've got a lot more going for you - a job is not such a large part of your life.

The teacher here was consciously attempting to suggest that a person's identity and unique 'self' can be defined in ways other than by the job he does or might do. Choosing a career not only gives meaning to total reality and social structures but also gives identity to the individual. This is why the problem of youth unemployment is so acute in psychological terms (Roberts, 1980). What are the alternatives which can give the sense of order and predictability to life which work can? The potential of leisure activities in providing psychologically adequate alternatives is increasingly argued as the teacher was doing in the example just quoted.
    Classroom discussion also focused on the many practical matters that arise from being unemployed, e.g. how to locate the Job Centre, how to claim unemployment benefit or social security, how to

cope with the '21 hour rule', the range of YOP and
associated schemes available.

Some consideration was given to the reasons
for unemployment. These tended to be brief and
limited to giving a list of the economic factors
involved, e.g. "some trades ... are dying out; as
the economic climate is not healthy, recession
means there are fewer jobs in the building trade;
service industries are affected by adverse economic
conditions." This aspect of unemployment which
Watts (1978) identifies as <u>contextual awareness</u>
is one which was perhaps least developed in
lessons. It is also one which teachers may be less
confident in dealing with since it forces them to
confront the political nature of unemployment and
may challenge their notion of teacher neutrality.
As a result, the kind of critical analysis
suggested by Watts has, perhaps understandably,
been avoided. Watts' analysis of contextual
awareness identifies the following aspects:

a) awareness of possible alienating effects of
work;
b) awareness of effects of technological
change;
c) awareness of possible economic and political
solutions to unemployment;
d) awareness of possible alternative patterns
of work and leisure.

It could be argued that dealing with such
aspects might not only raise potentially sensitive
political issues but would also present conceptual
difficulties, particularly for less able pupils.
However, not to tackle them may leave the teacher
in the uncomfortable position of realising that, by
allowing the debate to go by default, he is helping
to buttress the status quo.

Thus the anxiety and uncertainty that some
teachers experience in dealing with unemployment
may be explained by the fact that it exposes a
harsh underlying political reality and edges them
towards political debate with their pupils. In
addition an analysis of the topic also strikes at
the heart of one of society's most deeply held
beliefs, 'laboro ergo sum' - I work therefore I am.

THE ROLE OF THE CAREERS OFFICER

One of the key staff appointed for the duration of the project was the careers officer. This appointment was in addition to the normal careers officer attached to each of the project schools. This section briefly describes the development of this specialist role, and draws mainly on interview data obtained from the careers officer and teachers as well as on the accounts provided by the former in her series of annual reports to the project director.

In the first year of the project (1978/79) the project careers officer (CO) worked, in the main, with fourth year pupils at all three schools except at school A where she had some involvement with fifth year pupils in the careers education course. The general pattern of her work consisted of a half day or so spent in each school as a member of the project <u>teaching</u> team. This often involved providing follow up to films or to contributions made by the careers teacher. Such 'follow ups' included consideration of the local job market, groups in society, the family, sex stereotypes, self awareness, job families and the structure of industry. When not in the schools, much of her time was taken up in the preparation of lesson materials. Other commitments included visits to firms, inter-office discussions, report writing and attending training courses.

The CO felt that the role she had developed had been marked by two major distinctive features. First, the strength of her relationship with pupils and her commitment to them was much greater than would be the case for a normal CO. Second, a feeling of a "crisis of identity" arising from not having, in this first year, an identifiable case load of fifth year pupils, and from having a multi-faceted involvement in learning/teaching, social education and traditional careers counselling. She felt that not many COs had had such an experience and that involvement in teaching and course preparation was very unusual.

The project CO left at the end of the summer term 1979 to take up a post in another authority. A new CO was therefore appointed for the second and subsequent years of the project.

In the second year of the project the CO spent on average a day a week in each school and continued the involvement in teaching pioneered by her predecessor. This consisted of not only being 'around' in careers lessons but also actually teaching a range of topics including self assessment, local industry, job information, job seeking skills etc. in small group and whole class situations. The main difference in the way of working this year compared to the previous one was the inclusion of a group of fifth year pupils for job interviews. The project CO's case load was composed of all fifth year target group pupils from schools B and C and a sample from the target group of school A. This gave a case load of 170 as against the average of 400 or so which most COs have. This meant that she was able to do much more follow up with pupils than is normally possible. This follow up mainly took the form of second interviews with pupils both in school and the careers office.

A particularly interesting partnership was established with the project education social worker (ESW) at school C. The ESW was able to go through the CO's target group list with her to identify those pupils with difficult home conditions. This helped the CO to appreciate more fully the total context of her clients. Joint visits with the ESW were also made to the homes of those pupils who had left at Easter but who had not registered with the careers office. As a result, the half dozen or so pupils involved subsequently turned up at the careers office. She was also concerned to get to know pupils outside the classroom situation and visited the youth club particularly associated with school C, as well as helping the ESW on a weekend residential trip for target group pupils from the same school. These activities reflected her belief that careers officers should become more 'community' based and more ready to meet youngsters on their own ground.

She continued the work of her predecessor on the project working party concerned with producing the 'Going Places' [4] guide and diary for school leavers. She also developed a 'jobs pack' for use with target group pupils. This was based on experience acquired in several days' field experience in Sheffield firms as part of her programme of liaison with industry.

In her annual report at the end of the year the CO considered that she had gone some way towards meeting the general objectives set by and for the careers officer in the project. However

she felt that she had been overtaken by the
dramatic rise in school leaver unemployment and
this had underscored an increasing realisation that
preparing young people for work was no longer
enough. She concluded her annual report by noting:

"I think I must look much more seriously at
preparing youngsters for significant living without
work."

The pattern of activity in the third year
(1980/81) changed again as a result of the decision
to follow the fifth year target group from the
previous year into employment and unemployment.
One facility offered was a 'casual caller day' once
a week when unemployed youngsters could call in to
see her at the careers office at any time. Work
with fourth year target group pupils was reduced,
partly as a consequence of this and also the
decision not to follow them into their fifth year
in the final year of the project. An exception to
this was represented by her involvement in the
JIIG-CAL trial. Fifth year work included the
introduction of the topic of unemployment in all
three schools, mock interviews at school B, and
using lifeskills materials in school A. Fifth year
interviews were changed somewhat by confronting
each youngster with the problem of what they would
do if there were no jobs. Guidance was given on
YOP schemes and '21 hour' courses. Other
initiatives included the use of groups and
individual interviews at the careers office as a
bid to reach school non-attenders, a parents
evening on the theme of unemployment and increased
contact with pupils and those who left school the
previous year by meeting them in the evenings at a
youth club. Much of this reflected the CO's belief
that she should be preparing young people for work,
leisure and times without work and also encouraging
them to take advantage of whatever was available
(further education, 21 hour courses, YOPs etc.).
By the end of the third year she felt that
events were impelling her towards a commitment to
change, both on an individual and a societal basis.
In her report for the year she commented that she
felt it was no longer enough to explain jobs and
YOPs to youngsters and that she needed to
participate in the process of change herself.
Examples of the latter included involvement in the
work of the Trades Council, helping to set up a

scheme to generate new jobs in one area of the city and encouraging young people to join careers officers on a 'People's March for Jobs'. The rationale for this increasing politicization of her role was that an acceptance of the status quo was not really a tenable approach: "unless we want young people to accept the appalling prospect of short or long term unemployment. The non directive approach is no good in careers guidance when the careers opportunities are becoming more and more limited", (careers officer's third annual report 1980/81).

Implications for the Careers Service

Compared to the usual role the project careers officer was able to develop one which:

- achieved a greater degree of involvement with school staff in both the teaching and planning of careers education;
- allowed a more thorough programme of guidance, counselling and follow up of those expected to be particularly at risk;
- fostered stronger links with other agencies, especially with the education social work service;
- took guidance and counselling into the community;

If the careers service establishment was increased by an extra one or two officers it would then be possible to second existing personnel to develop this kind of role more widely. Building on the experience gained by the project careers officer, it should be possible to foster a comparable degree of involvement with a further group of schools in a secondment lasting a year or so. Over a period of time different groups of schools could be covered, and the benefits of a closer partnership between careers officers, careers teachers, parents and community contacts would be available to all schools.

DISCUSSION

There are several reasons why the emphasis on job choice in careers education programmes is problematic. First, there is often insufficient time available to carry out the complex task of matching personal qualities and job characteristics which the model implies. Although the problem can be overcome by the application of computer technology this has the potential danger of reducing the individual's control and understanding of the process. Secondly, the structures by which 'careers' knowledge is typically organised tend to reinforce existing notions of job stratification so that careers education acts to reproduce the economic and social relationships of production. Thirdly, research evidence (including our own, cf. Chapter 10) suggests that for working class early school leavers, with few or no qualifications, the limitations of local opportunities and the influence of contact with family and friends are paramount in determining the type and level of first job entered. Both Willis (1977) and Corrigan (1979) have looked at the process of job 'choice' among working class boys. Willis concludes, "It is confusing and mystifying to pose the entry of disaffected working class boys into work as a matter of particular job choice ... the 'lads' are not choosing careers or particular jobs, they are committing themselves to a future of generalised labour." Similarly Corrigan comments, "There is no reasoned choice for these boys ... the picture is one of general cultural limitations of boys seeing their work as part of a chance configuration of family, careers and traditionally known jobs in the area." Finally the recent rise in the level of unemployment has also clearly reduced the validity of the notion of 'job choice'.

However, these difficulties do not mean that the idea of job choice in particular or careers education in general is irrelevant. Even if careers education is little more than a lubricant of marginal influence for the early school leaver as a class, real occupational choice can exist as a possibility for the individual. It is the individual, after all, who should be the concern of the careers officer and teacher. Moreover if job choice is treated as more than just a rational matching process, if the assumptions underlying it are examined, and if the influence of family and community on it are exposed, then pupils' understanding and potential control of their situation is increased.

As youth unemployment has risen it has increasingly brought into question the view held by many pupils that the principal justification for

careers education and school generally is job
acquisition. This has led to a debate as to what
should be the appropriate response to unemployment
of those engaged in careers education. Watts and
Herr (1976) have raised the possibility that, given
rising unemployment, one task of careers education
might be "to weaken the work ethic and emphasise
the satisfaction that can be achieved outside
work." They go on to argue that careers education
should be concerned with preparation for adult life
as a whole, looking not only at work roles but also
family, community and leisure roles. Watts (1978)
subsequently listed in more detail the range of
tasks which might now fall within careers
education, including 'survival' and 'leisure'
skills. Such an approach was broadly consistent
with the ways in which careers education, and the
PFL curriculum generally, had developed in the
project schools.

The existence of high levels of youth
unemployment not only strikes at the heart of a
belief in the work ethic, but it also forces
teachers and pupils to confront the question of
'why should unemployment be?' An answer in terms
of the personal inadequacy of individuals is less
and less convincing as the unemployment graph rises
ever more steeply. A consideration of the
political and economic factors associated with
unemployment is increasingly difficult to avoid.
It is not sufficient to tackle the topic of
unemployment simply in terms of 'coping strategies'
important though these be. Pupils also need to
have some understanding of the broader causes of
unemployment not least to free them from the
crushing, and more than often unjustified, sense of
personal blame. Careers education, probably more
than any other subject, increasingly raises
fundamental socio-political issues concerning the
relationship between schooling, the state and
economic production. It is perhaps the growing
realisation that this is the case that explains, at
least partly, the anxiety that teachers and other
professionals feel about tackling the topic of
unemployment.

Some may say that it is unrealistic and
perhaps even potentially dangerous for pupils,
particularly those judged as less able, to attempt
to understand these matters. We do not hold this
view since we believe that all pupils should be
given opportunities to understand those systems

which control their destinies - and this includes those of a socio-political nature. It is sad to note that the systematic development of economic and political concepts is a rarity in secondary education - at best dealt with as detached academic studies for a minority of pupils only. Careers education could provide a natural context for encouraging such development for all pupils.

Careers education then is a subject in the process of radical transformation. This transformation arises from an undermining of its basic assumptions, as a result of major changes occurring in the economy, and the attempt to establish a new rationale. This process can be usefully understood in terms of an analysis of careers education programmes put forward by Watts and Herr (1976). They suggest that programmes can serve any of four different socio-political functions:

1. As an agent of <u>social control</u>, adapting individuals to realistic career opportunities.
2. As an agent of <u>social change</u>, making individuals aware of the nature of the employment system and how it might be changed.
3. As an agent of <u>individual</u> change, accepting the employment system as it is but aiming to improve the life chances of the individual within it.
4. <u>Non directive</u>: making individuals aware of the range of opportunities and helping them to be more autonomous in choosing alternatives suited to their needs and preferences.

Although the rhetoric of careers education often seems to reflect a commitment to the non directive and individual change approaches, most programmes in <u>practice</u> are probably closer to the social control model. The development of careers education in the project schools over the three years 1978-81 represented some shift of emphasis towards individual and social change. This trend was likely to continue in the future particularly as the topic of unemployment became an established and substantial element within the programmes. Over the same period, careers education became somewhat less distinct as a separate entity and more a component of integrated PFL courses (e.g. sociology, preparation for adult life).

In some ways curriculum change is analogous to biological adaptation. Rather like an organism, a curriculum subject has a stable existence when it is functionally integrated with its external environment e.g. the functions of careers education in the past have been consistent with the demands of a stratified labour market under full employment. When major changes occur in the external environment (e.g. technological change, unemployment) the subject becomes dysfunctional and must adapt or perish. Careers education provides at the moment perhaps the most dramatic example of curricular adaptation.

NOTES

[1] This aspect is well illustrated in the Sponge Mix materials - a series of three related film strip/tape presentations which form an introduction to careers programmes - and also in Sign posts - a card index for use in the careers library - both produced by the Careers and Occupational Information Centre (COIC).

[2] An outline of the JIIG-CAL system and its associated software is given in JIIG-CAL Computer Assisted Career Guidance Release 3. Information Booklet obtainable from S. J. Closs, Department of Business Studies, Edinburgh University, William Robertson Building, George Square, Edinburgh, EH8 9JY, and W. R. Broderick, London Borough of Havering, Educational Computer Centre, Tring Gardens, Harold Hill, Romford, RM3 9QY.

[3] A highly structured approach to tackling the topic of unemployment with pupils is provided in Hopson, B. & Scally, M. (1982). Life Skills Teaching Programmes No. 2 Life Skills Associates: Leeds (particularly the chapter 'How to cope with unemployment', pp. 199-265).

[4] Information on this and other publications produced by the project may be obtained from Mr. M. Smith (Senior Adviser Secondary) Sheffield Education Department, PO Box 67, Leopold Street, Sheffield, S1 1RJ.

Chapter 5

DILEMMAS OF HEALTH EDUCATION

INTRODUCTION

The importance of providing health education in secondary schools has been stressed in most of the official recommendations on the curriculum from the Newsom Report (Ministry of Education, 1963) onwards. A recent document on the school curriculum from the DES provides a succinct definition of a rationale for health education which would probably be accepted by most in the field. "(It) should give pupils a basic knowledge and understanding of health matters both as they affect themselves and as they affect others, so that they are helped to make informed choices in their daily lives. It should also help them to become aware of those moral issues and value judgements which are inseparable from such choices." (DES, 1981a)

Health education has increasingly moved away from its original relatively narrow focus on health and hygiene to a broader notion which shades imperceptibly into a concern for individual development, personal relationships and social education. One result of this is that it is often difficult to locate health education precisely within the curriculum of most schools. Typically contributions to health education will be made by several subjects which may not necessarily be labelled as 'health education' or even have the topic as a major concern. In a survey of health education in Sheffield secondary schools some 20 or so different subjects or curriculum activities were identified as contributors to planned health education programmes. The six subjects most frequently involved were biology, science, home economics, social studies, physical education and religious education (Wilcox & Gillies, 1983).

Health education topics were components of the EEC programmes of all three project schools. They were to be found in the preparation for adult life (PAL) and modular science courses at school C, and in sociology and integrated science at school A (cf. Chapter 8). At school B there was a health education module in the fourth and fifth year rota which started in thefirst year of the project and formed a major part of the school's EEC programme. Some health education (mainly sex education) was also done in the social education module of that rota. Another relevant element of school B's programme was a two year child care course, leading to a CSE certificate, which began as a full option in the project's second year. This course was also associated with a playgroup which was originally run in conjunction with the earlier health education module. In the case of school B and school C no planned health education was included in the curriculum of pupils below the fourth year. In school A some health education was provided in the first three years through science and talks by the school nurse.

A search of the archive towards the end of the project's third year yielded a total of 40 field notes concerned, at least in part, with health education. Three quarters of the field notes (31) were based upon observation of individual lessons.

Table 13 lists the different topics covered in the lessons observed. Well over half of these were concerned with human development. Of these the great majority consisted of lessons on various aspects of sex education.

This chapter examines the field note data mainly in the light of the three features identified in the rationale for health education referred to above (DES, 1981a) i.e.

1. knowledge or content;
2. health choices;
3. moral issues and values.

KNOWLEDGE OR CONTENT

Much of the content of health education is of a scientific or, more specifically, biological nature. Not surprisingly then it is within science that much health education may be incidentally

Table 13: Topics Taught in the Health Education
Lessons Observed

Topic	School			
	A	B	C	Total
General Hygiene	0	1	2	3
Digestion/Nutrition	2	1	1	4
Skin	0	0	1	1
Teeth	0	1	0	1
Smoking	0	0	2	2
Sex Education	6	4	1	11
Male/Female Roles in Marriage/Family	1	0	1	2
Adolescence	1	0	0	1
Playgroup/Child Development	0	4	0	4
Health Services	0	1	0	1
External visit - not specifically health education related	0	1	0	1
Total	10	13	8	31

taught. This is illustrated in two lessons we
observed early on in the first year of the project
in one school (A). The first of the lessons was
concerned with the process by which food gets into
the bloodstream. The central feature here was a
demonstration experiment which simulated the action
of the intestine in letting food out through its
wall. This essentially science based lesson was
followed a week later by a more health education
oriented topic on calories and dieting. The lesson
began by revising the four main food groups.
Pupils then planned a day's menu from food lists
and calculated the number of calories involved.
The purpose of the lesson was explained quite
clearly to the class at the end by the teacher
stressing the importance that pupils monitored
their own diet. The basic message was the need for
sensible eating. Much the same content was
presented at another school (B) over two
consecutive double lessons with the difference that

a biology teacher dealt with four food types – their functions and the chemical methods for testing for their presence - and the home economist followed on with a consideration of the dietary implications.

Where health education is organised as a series of one off topics with a different one presented each week, the teacher may be faced with the task of introducing a considerable amount of technical detail in too short a time. This problem was particularly apparent in four double lessons on general hygiene observed in one school (C) as part of the preparation for adult life course. Generally the amount of biological knowledge introduced could have provided the basis for several lessons in a conventional biology course. The conceptual difficulties posed by such concentrated presentation, particularly for those pupils who may not be following a biology course, should not be underestimated. The pupil groups were also mixed ability ones and the problems of the less able members were likely to have been particularly acute. The difficulty is illustrated by one lesson taken by a non teacher which dealt in quick succession with the skeletal, respiratory, nervous, urinary, digestive, endocrine and circulatory systems.

These examples raise the important question of how much biology needs to be introduced in order to provide an understanding of health principles and practices. Although some pupils felt that the material had been covered in other subjects (notably biology) it has to be said that not everyone took biology at least in years 4 and 5.

The problems associated with the technical content of health education may partially explain the fairly common practice of inviting outside experts into schools to deal with various aspects of health education. All three project schools involved outsiders in the teaching of particular topics. Included amongst such personnel were a school nurse, health visitors, a school doctor and family planning staff. In the case of one school (C) the school nurse, who had been involved in the school's health education programme previously, also took part in planning the input to the project programme in its first year.

Health personnel are of course not trained teachers and it was clear that they had some difficulty, at least initially, in developing an appropriate teaching style. Because they did not generally know the pupils it was not so easy for them to encourage pupil involvement through questioning as it was for teachers. As a result there was a tendency to use a somewhat content packed lecture style of teaching. Of the eight lessons observed which generally conformed to this approach, five were in fact given by health personnel. Some evidence of pupil reaction to this style in one school (C) was provided in a follow up discussion observed early on in the first year of the project. A comment made by some of the pupils was that the material in the lectures (sic) was too complex and that it should be presented in simpler form. It is relevant to note however that the method of organisation - where half the year group at a time did health education - resulted in a combined teaching group of around 50 pupils. Faced with such a number it is more likely that a lecture approach will be adopted.

Not knowing pupils may pose difficulties for health personnel, particularly in the more sensitive areas of health education such as sex education. Thus one health visitor involved in teaching sex education commented that she got "landed" with the task and felt it would be better done by the school nurse who knew the children better. She said she hated doing tasks with pupils she did not know because "you get so little feedback".

Films were often used as a means of presenting content. In just over a third of the lessons seen, one or occasionally two films were used. They were generally used to complement and augment the teacher's exposition. Some of the films, generally ones concerned with sex education, were considered by teachers and health personnel to be somewhat dated either in terms of the images of adolescents that they portrayed or the mores they projected. One film, probably made in the 1950s, actually acted to reinforce traditional sex roles in a way that would be frowned on today, e.g. the film specified that no-one was capable of looking after a family except a woman. "Father can help, but only really by bringing in the wages to give to mother. Her task is to look after everyone and she has a special talent for doing this."

In watching films, particularly in one of the schools (C), we were reminded that the facilities for projection, particularly for sizeable groups, are often inadequate. Thus on one occasion pupils were seated on tables and chairs in a dining room which was adjacent to a noisy hall in which musical groups were practising. Sex education is one aspect of health education that may be taught by teachers who do not necessarily have detailed technical knowledge. This may be a particular disadvantage in dealing with such topics as contraception where the physiological and biochemical mechanisms underlying the use of such methods as the pill and coil are complex. In most of the lessons observed the teachers displayed a quite admirable command of the technicalities of the field. Occasionally, however, pupils' questions did outstrip the level of the teacher's knowledge.

HEALTH CHOICES

Clearly a major aim of health education is that pupils, by gaining an understanding of their bodies and how they work, will come to acquire appropriate habits for healthy living. In most of the lessons we observed the various health messages which the teacher intended to convey were quite apparent. In the lessons on general hygiene, health principles and practices were presented as logical outcomes of an understanding of appropriate physiological processes. Thus a lesson on the structure and function of skin provided the detailed context against which several desirable health habits were recommended, e.g. washing/ showering regularly to wash away impurities on the skin, the need to look after the skin in order to avoid chapping, sunburn, and to prevent infection penetrating it.

Several lessons on food and nutrition were seen which dealt with such matters as the mechanical and chemical processes of digestion, the nature of food types and their functions. The health messages stressed here included the need for sensible eating habits, the dangers of excessive dieting (particularly directed at the girls), problems associated with being overweight, the need for exercise, and the importance of cleanliness in the preparation of food.

The child care course at one school provided many examples of quite specific and generally unexceptionable health recommendations, e.g.

"Never let a baby suck a dinkie feeder containing a very sweet drink. Don't dip the dummy in sugar or jam."

"Give a baby a drink of cooled boiled water after feeding to help wash the sugar off its teeth."

"A baby should get used to seeing the dentist before he needs any treatment."

Messages could however be somewhat more controversial.

Teacher   I hope you will all breast feed.

Pupil   I shan't.

Teacher   Why?

Pupil   Well ... you'll have to get your ...,
           you know ..., out in public, if you're
           shopping.

Pupil   I think bottle feeding is better. Your
(another) breasts get all big otherwise ... ugh.

All health practices involve an element of choice by the individual. A dilemma inevitably implicit in health education is how far particular practices should be recommended by the teacher, and to what extent pupils should be encouraged to consider alternatives to them. The above exchange concerned with infant feeding illustrates this point well. The choice between breast and bottle feeding relates, to some extent, to social and cultural characteristics and a debate about their relative efficacies is entirely legitimate (Finch et al, 1981).
A lesson on smoking raises the same issue. In the first part of the lesson the Thames TV film "Dying for a Fag" was shown. This was a harrowing account of a 42 year old man who knows that he will die of lung cancer within the next three years as a result of smoking. The film accepts unequivocally a causal relationship between smoking, lung cancer and certain respiratory diseases. The school nurse who was also present stressed the detrimental effects of smoking on physical well being and, at the conclusion of the film, informed the class that the man had in fact died some months afterwards.

"Just when he should have been in the prime of life. By his age people are usually well established in their jobs, have a nice house and family around them, and all is going well. He has lost all of this."

The central message of the lesson was quite clear, i.e. that smoking is undesirable and harmful. Indeed the teacher present introduced the lesson before the film was shown by saying:

"My message to those of you who haven't yet started to smoke is quite simple - DON'T."

Perhaps, understandably, given the widely accepted link between smoking and cancer, there was no attempt to present any advantages for smoking - in fact are there any? It is however often claimed that smoking may relax one and facilitates social intercourse. Whilst one may not agree with this view it should perhaps be examined. The film did touch upon some social aspects, e.g. the man's identification, as an adolescent, with his screen heroes (Bogart, etc.) many of whom smoked. However, on the whole, smoking was presented as a negative and harmful activity. The principal issue of the lesson was not whether smoking was undesirable - it was clearly thought to be so - but to what extent people should be actively dissuaded from indulging the habit. In fact in the discussion which followed the film the teacher skilfully encouraged a debate about the pros and cons of prohibition.

Concern about pupils' own health practices, particularly smoking, were often expressed by the staff concerned with the child care course in school B, e.g.

Teacher (to health visitor)	It seems very sad to me that some of them (the pupils) can't manage to go from 9 to 4 without a cigarette. You should hear some of them coughing first thing in the morning.
Health visitor (obviously horrified)	Well, this sounds very serious. I can only say to those who smoke you are very silly and foolish. It can damage your health quite considerably, not to mention the unpleasant smells that come from

	your body and around you, from the nicotine.
Pupil	It can damage a baby too, Miss, can't it.
Health visitor	Oh yes, tests are indicating that all babies born of mothers who smoke are considerably underweight. You need to think hard about that.

Concern was also expressed at the girls' eating habits.

"They never stop eating. I suspect most of them don't bother with breakfast, and eat sweets and crisps throughout the day instead."

In the case of sex education the health messages ranged from simple recommendations, e.g. regular washing of the genitals, the desirability for females to avail themselves of the opportunities of cancer screening, etc., to injunctions which have more obviously moral implications, e.g. the increased danger of contracting cancer of the cervix and sexually transmitted diseases as a result of casual sex. These matters are discussed in more detail in the following section.

MORAL ISSUES AND VALUES

Moral issues and values inevitably lurk beneath any consideration of health education. This is perhaps most obvious in the case of sex education. This is a common topic in the fourth and fifth year curriculum of secondary schools and all three project schools gave some consideration to it in their project programmes (cf. Table 13). The inclusion of sex education in the curriculum can provoke controversy and parents are often anxious about the approach of schools to this topic. In fact, regulations made under Section 8 of the 1980 Education Act require LEAs to inform parents of the ways in which sex education will be provided in their schools.

The main topics covered in the lessons observed, the majority of which took place in two schools, included sexual intercourse, contraception, abortion, sexually transmitted diseases, conception and birth. In general the traditional view on sex was put forward, i.e. chastity before marriage and fidelity within. Thus a film shown in one lesson put the case quite explicitly, as shown by the following quotes:

"Our society has found that the only workable way is for men and women to pair off and bring up children in a family."

"Our society accepts marriage as right, and sexual intercourse outside marriage as irresponsible and perhaps disastrous."

"The sex act reaches its intended end - a baby: the result of the deeply satisfying relationship of man and wife."

In another lesson specifically concerned with the role of the family, the teacher read the following justification for marriage from a work sheet.

"(It is the) socially acceptable way of enjoying sexual relationships. Even though people can have sex outside marriage we agreed that it was easier in marriage as it saves embarrassment in society."

The notion of early intercourse was actively discouraged, particularly by reference to the potential health hazards. This is illustrated in the following extract of a lesson on family life and contraception. The lesson began with a film (ca 1960s) which came down heavily against sex before marriage: "Sex is only permissible in the context of a loving responsible marriage, one should not indulge wantonly one's mere animal appetites." After the film the class split into two groups and one was taken by a lady from the Family Planning Association. She began:

"I must stress that sex is illegal if you are under 16. There is only one way to get pregnant and seven ways to avoid it. But you need to be responsible. You don't want to have indiscriminate sex with every Tom, Dick or Harry. One of the consequences of indiscriminate sex is that you can get cancer of the womb. You also run the risk of getting VD - venereal disease. There are also STD - sexually transmitted diseases. You catch these

79

diseases through having sex with lots of people. They are sexually transmitted and are very unpleasant. They have long term effects - one of which is infertility in girls. You should think about sex within the concept of a loving relationship. It is only a small part of the relationship. However, you must think about the consequences of an unplanned pregnancy - boys as well. It takes two, although girls bear children the boy is also responsible..."

(The lesson went on to consider the various forms of contraception.)

In another lesson an attempt was made to discuss the case for and against sex before marriage. The lesson began by the teacher asking the group to read a short extract from a text book. This consisted of a dialogue between a youth leader and a couple of 18 who he had just discovered were sleeping together. The dialogue attempts to present both sides of the argument and the chapter ends with a series of questions for discussion. The teacher used these questions, supplemented by his own, to initiate a debate with pupils. Pupil response to the questions was however limited and in fact only two pupils out of the whole class spoke at all during the lesson.

The teacher presented the case for sleeping together as a means of getting to know each other and explained the notion of a 'trial marriage'. He then went on to outline the problems presented by the arrival of children.

Teacher   The thing is, if you have sex before marriage, the chances are you might get pregnant.

Teacher   Getting pregnant is a shaky reason for getting married ... how can a girl have a baby and still work?

He then presented the dilemma posed by readily available contraceptives.

Teacher   Many people say, therefore, that you should 'control yourself' until you get married. Is this good advice?

No response.

Teacher	Or would it be a better idea to make people have better education about contraception? Or will this merely <u>encourage</u> them to have sex?
Pupil	You should teach them about contraception.
Teacher	The trouble is, it is not 100% successful. Suppose it doesn't work. Is <u>that</u> a good reason for not doing it?

Then later:

Teacher	(reading a question from the book) Some people say that women are caught in the slavery of the Pill, rather than its freedom ... Do modern contraceptive facilities make it harder to find a reason for NOT having intercourse?
Teacher	It's harder in modern life for a girl to say 'no', and for a boy not to try. Do you agree?

No response.

Teacher	Well it's not easy to say no. But it's a free world. We should have the right to make our own minds up on these issues.

And later still ...

Teacher	People can ruin their lives if they don't know about contraception ... so should we just not do it?
Pupil	You can't just expect people to turn themselves on and off.
Teacher	No ... sex is natural and very enjoyable, so you can't tell people not to do it, but instead we ought to give them the right education about it.

Responsibility was a value explicitly stressed in some lessons.

"When you are an adult you have to take responsibility for your own bodies, you have to treat them well. You have to have reasons for doing things to your bodies and not do them just because everyone else is."

And again in a discussion of teenage pregnancies.

Teacher   ... If a boy and a girl make a baby at 14, its irresponsible. If she had the baby, what would you do?

Pupil   I'd go somewhere.

Teacher   You'd leave the girl?

Pupil 1   Yes.

Pupil 2   That's not right.

Teacher   Think about what you've done. You are 50% responsible for a new person - a baby who'll grow up. You've made a child. Is it the best thing to just run off? ...

And later:

Teacher   ... The baby needs love, care and attention. It stops you ... you're devoting your life to this person so that it grows up to be a responsible adult. If you have a child when you're a teenager, think what a difference it would make to your life.

Pupil 1   You couldn't learn your lessons right.

Pupil 2   People talk and it makes you depressed.

Teacher   The basic thing to remember is that in our society you're not expected to look after children until you're a good bit older than when you become physically capable of fathering children. You wouldn't be able to look after a child and manage life. You need money to live. So we've got to think very responsibly. You need to have lived your life and be mature enough to help your children grow up.

Methods of contraception were dealt with in all three schools. It was generally assumed that family planning was a topic on which there was no longer any substantial disagreement.

Health
visitor
Family planning is nothing new, it has been going for a long time. It's very expensive to have children - need to limit family to what you can afford.

Health
visitor
One of these days you'll all be going on the Pill won't you - it's a fact of life.

Teacher
(reading from the text book) ... It also says that a lot of people haven't really got to grips with contraception and the idea of planning families.

The Catholic Church's view on contraception was often mentioned, although the nature of its moral objections was not considered.

Teacher
(referring to rhythm method) It's very appropriate to certain kinds of people with particular beliefs.

Pupil
For Catholics, they can't use owt else, it's against their rules. The Pope says it's not natural. It doesn't always work - could make a slip-up in your dates.

Teacher
What else could Catholics use besides the rhythm method?

Pupil
Tie a knot in it.

Pupil
Withdrawal.

Teacher
Yes, but that's very unreliable. Will you get out your books and turn to the section on 'the family' ...

One health visitor in talking about methods of family planning clearly signalled her disapproval of young people practising it.

"It's worse having intercourse when you're young, you're much more likely to get pregnant. It's a rotten trick nature plays on the young. So the best family planning is not to have intercourse; don't go too far in your love making."

Abortion was a topic which was dealt with in two of the schools by means of a case study. In both cases a discussion with pupils was encouraged in which some of the views for and against abortion were brought out, e.g.

Teacher	Catholics do not believe in abortion, no matter what. But there are still some people who are Protestants who think this way ...
Teacher	The thing is, is having an abortion murder?
Pupil (boy)	No, 'cos the baby doesn't know does it?
Teacher	Well, even a 12 month old baby wouldn't realise you were going to murder it, would it?
Pupil (girl)	You aren't taking a life.
Pupil (boy)	You are ... but it's not ... in one sense.
Teacher	Surely, it depends on how you define life. When does it start? At fertilisation? Or when the heart starts? Or when it is breathing?
Pupil (boy)	When the heart starts beating.
Teacher	No doctor would abort if the heart was beating.
Pupil (boy)	Well, I've heard about abortions where the heart's been beating.
Teacher	No, there are special german measles cases (explains). Most doctors wouldn't do it after 18-20 weeks.

Teacher then discussed 'back street' abortion and outlined the Corrie Bill and what it would mean if it became law.

And again later.

Teacher   This is the vital point of issue. Now who is qualified to settle it?

Pupil (boy)   Doctors ... they have to do it.

Teacher   Remember no doctor <u>has</u> to do an abortion. So they have some say in the matter.

The teacher then cited a recent court case where a man tried legally to stop his wife having an abortion and the reasons why he lost the case. The teacher used this to illustrate the notion of a woman's right to choose.

Pupil (girl)   Why should he decide anyway? It's <u>you</u> who have to carry it for nine months - not him.

(Vehement discussion follows.)

Teacher   Don't forget, it's his baby too. He's also got a right. This has been taken away from him in this (court) case. The husband surely has the <u>right</u> to have a baby by a woman when he marries her.

Pupil (girl)   Well, let the husband have it then.

The teacher then continued with a consideration of the conditions for abortion under the 1967 Act and also referred briefly to the role of pressure groups such as SPUC.
At the end of the lesson the teacher commented to the observer on the difficulties of presenting a balanced view to a class, particularly on topics such as abortion.

"I am very anti-RC, but I am very careful not to appear so in front of a class, in case there are any Catholics in the class. I also am very pro-abortion. I suppose you could say I am left-wing on it. I believe in a woman's right to choose at all times, but I am nevertheless careful to present the SPUC side as well."

Sex education, given its moral connotations, is potentially a sensitive area for teachers to tackle. In the lessons we observed we were impressed with the general business-like and adult way in which the topic was treated. One teacher commented that he tried to keep himself as au fait as possible.

"It's important not to rush them. I try to get the words out first. Once you get one going it takes off and then it's very good."

He admitted to being a little nervous of what questions will come, but tries to give the impression that whatever they ask, it is all right and not shocking.
Several examples of sexual humour were observed as further evidence of a relaxed relationship between teacher and pupil.

Teacher   (showing a sample of contraceptives
                 as he talks) You usually get them
                 in packets of three.

Pupil   Sir, you can get packets of five.

Teacher   Yeah, well don't come begging for
                 them after the lesson as they're
                 past their sell-by date.

However, one health visitor talking to a group admitted:

"I feel awkward talking to you about this - I don't know you and you don't know me."

and the same person again:

"... it's very hard to teach you about this and not to moralise."

Some pupils may be embarrassed in asking questions openly in class. One way of minimising this was seen where pupils wrote down their questions anonymously. The staff then sorted them into broad categories and answered them during the lesson one week later.

TEACHING METHODOLOGY

The majority of lessons observed (81%) were characterised by a substantial element of teacher exposition. This is perhaps not surprising for a subject in which the presentation of a considerable amount of detailed information may be necessary. In just over half these lessons the exposition was punctuated by teacher questions directed to the class and in about a quarter a teaching aid or demonstration was also incorporated. In just over 70% of the lessons exposition was followed by a period of pupil activity. This most often took the form of teacher led discussion. The completion of notes, generally from the blackboard, or written exercises took place in approximately one third of the lessons observed. A few cases of pupil involvement in practical exercises were observed.[1]

The use of group or class discussion tended to follow a period of exposition by teacher or film or both. On occasions teachers felt that there had been too much input to a lesson as a result of which insufficient time was left for discussion. Group size, as one school nurse observed, was often too large to get children to talk openly. It is very difficult for schools to break down a whole year group into numbers less than those in normal teaching groups. However, the presence of one or more 'outsiders' can give extra adults who, together with the teachers present, enable more groups of smaller size to be formed. An occasion was observed when there were six adults[2] present to deal with 50 or so pupils. This meant that sub-groups of about eight pupils could be formed. This can be particularly helpful, as here, when the potentially sensitive issue of sex education is discussed. In one school especially there was some debate about the desirability of splitting groups by sex. This automatically happened for those aspects of health education covered in science, since the decision had been taken to organise the whole course on that basis. In the same school staff had tried both single and mixed sex groups in the sociology course where the sex education was largely covered. Staff felt that there was little indication that either method of organisation facilitated the asking of questions by pupils.

DISCUSSION

The health education we observed in the three schools was a sample of lessons from courses and modules in the fourth and fifth year project programme, i.e.

School A	School B	School C
Sociology	Social education	Preparation for adult life
Integrated science	Health education	Modular science
	Child care	

The sociology course at A and the preparation for adult life course at C were part of the curriculum of all pupils irrespective of ability. The others shown above were taken only by the less able pupils. It is, of course, possible that contributions to health education may have been made by other subjects outside the project but part of the general options programme of each school.

This kind of organisation for health education raises several questions which are likely to be significant for schools generally. Thus, where health education is an element of more than one course in the fourth and fifth year, do the staff concerned see their respective contributions forming a coherent whole? Do the pupils put the separate contributions together as a clearly perceived single experience? Such questions can be extended to include any health education covered in the lower school, e.g. Are the various contributions made in the first to the fifth year perceived as a single continuing theme transmitted through the agency of several different courses? Given the fact that some courses are taken by part of a total year group only, what can be said about the health education that all pupils encounter? Or, to put the matter another way - what constitutes the common core of health education for secondary pupils aged 11 to 16?

A dilemma which is faced by teachers of health education, particularly where the major input is made in the fourth or fifth year, is how to treat the associated technical content which is often of a largely biological nature. There are two questions here. First, how much information of the latter kind is needed in order to understand particular aspects of health? Second, how much knowledge can the teacher assume the pupil has already acquired from earlier courses in science? Whilst it may be desirable to recapitulate relevant earlier learned theory or sometimes to teach it 'de novo' there is a danger, particularly when the time allotted to health education is limited, in spending too long on this thereby leaving insufficient time for exploring the implications of health practices.

Dealing with health education within science lessons seems to be one possible solution to the problem. However, there is a danger that the health education theme in science courses, because it is merely one amongst many, may be obscured and go unrecognised by the pupils. Whilst science courses can play an important part it is unlikely that effective health education will occur if this is the sole curricular vehicle for it. It may be better to rely on science courses to lay the foundations for the prerequisite technical information necessary as a background to understanding health matters and leave to other teachers the task of exploring questions of health attitudes and behaviours. If health education is to become a part of the core curriculum, then a necessary concomitant may be that this should also be true of some elements of science generally, and biology in particular. Thus, in planning a health education programme, teachers would be advised to talk to their colleagues in the science department in order to find out what aspects of their courses are particularly relevant to health matters. It will be necessary to know whether or not all pupils encounter these and, if so, at what particular points in their school careers. A consequence of this may be the realisation that some aspects of the science course will need to be modified.

The fairly widespread practice of inviting outside 'experts' in to school to teach aspects of health education is also related to the issue of specialist or technical knowledge. It may also provide a safe way in which a school can deal with sensitive issues without directly exposing its own staff to potentially difficult situations. However, there can be problems since outsiders may

find it difficult to establish rapport with pupils
they do not know. They may also not be so able as
teachers in understanding the educational needs of
children. This may, in part, be the result of what
Engel (1979) sees as the difference in philosophy
which the medical and educational professions have
towards their respective clients. Thus, the main
medical imperative is to cure the patient and
whether he understands the treatment is largely
immaterial. The teacher however, if he is to
engage the pupil in an <u>educational</u> experience, is
under an obligation to ensure that the pupil
understands what is happening.
    This is not, of course, to say that health
professionals do not have a part to play in school
health education. They clearly do. Their
involvement is likely to be more effective however
if, as in some of the lessons we saw, it is a
collaborative one with teachers. Collaborative,
that is, not only in sharing the teaching but also
participating in the planning of the programme.
    Health educators have increasingly recognised
that the mere presentation of information is no
guarantee that the health attitudes and behaviours
of individuals are changed. They have also
stressed that the subject should conform to an
educational model rather than one which runs the
risk of being potentially indoctrinatory. As a
result notions of 'increased awareness',
'encouraging rational choices' have characterised
the rhetoric of health education in recent years.
If this rhetoric is to be matched by reality then
it is incumbent on health educators to encourage
pupils to confront the assumptions and values which
lurk beneath recommended health practices, health
education and indeed the notion of health
generally. The criteria of what constitutes
'health' or 'being healthy' are not absolutes but,
to some extent at least, culturally determined.
Included amongst such criteria are the desirability
of longevity, the minimisation of pain and
discomfort and the maximisation of pleasurable
sensations, and the development of bodily functions
and processes to maximum efficiency. Some of these
have secular origins and reflect the 20th century's
celebration of 'body'. Others, such as the notion
of responsibility, balanced development, may
reflect continuing adherence to older traditions.
    Teachers did in fact refer to the differing
views held on some health practices, most notably

those concerned with sexuality. Thus, in dealing
with abortion it was generally noted that some
people (e.g. Catholics) are opposed to the
practice. However, it is not sufficient just to
note the objection, it is also necessary to
present the reasons for it. The case against
abortion rests ultimately on several clear
assumptions, such as the nature of person,
continuity of life, the definition of life, etc.
To these, others might also add theological
assumptions, such as the sacredness of life. The
beginnings of what could have developed into an
exploration of such assumptions are illustrated in
the teacher/pupil exchange described previously.

The teacher's truly educational role in
dealing wih issues such as these is not to
recommend, as a result of his own authority, one
alternative over others but to present impartially,
and in as complete a way as possible, the reasons
behind the different views which are held.

If pupils are to confront and reflect upon
alternative courses of action they need both the
time to do this and the learning methodology
appropriate for it, e.g. small group discussion.
Discussion was actively encouraged in many of the
lessons we observed although often the time
available was inadequate. This was occasionally
the result of attempting to compress too much
content into a single lesson. This illustrates a
common failing at all levels of the educational
system, i.e. making over optimistic assumptions
about how much information individuals can
assimilate in a lesson or lecture. Where
discussion techniques are concerned, the health
educator might usefully examine the procedure
suggested by the Schools Council Humanities
Curriculum Project (Ruddock, 1976). This project
deliberately set out to examine controversial
issues using a group discussion approach focusing
on various pieces of presented 'evidence'. The
teacher was encouraged to adopt a position of
procedural neutrality. Although teachers
experienced difficulty in maintaining this role, it
is one which would be particularly appropriate for
examining at least some of the topics of health
education. Pupils often have an intense interest
in the views of their teachers and it may be unduly
artificial for these to be witheld from their
pupils. An approximation to the HCP approach could
be achieved by the teacher presenting his views as

yet another example of evidence to be considered alongside others which are available.

The aim of the teacher who adopts this approach is not to implant definite health attitudes and practices in his pupils but to make them aware of the possibilities and choices available and the assumptions underlying them. This requires the teacher to accept the fact that, at least sometimes, his pupils may make choices which are contrary to his own preference.

The aim of health education is, as Hopson and Scally (1981) hold for lifeskills teaching generally, one of self empowerment. Self empowerment means believing that there are always alternatives, that one can identify the alternatives in different situations and be able to choose one on the basis of one's values, priorities and commitments.

NOTES

[1] Nappy changing, food testing, taking blood pressure, etc.

[2] Three teachers, a Polytechnic lecturer and student, and a senior youth worker.

Chapter 6

SOCIAL EDUCATION

The PFL curriculum in all three project
schools can be conveniently analysed into three
elements. Two of these, health education and
careers education, have been the subjects of the
two previous chapters. The third lacks a commonly
agreed title and consists of a number of topics,
many of which are often found in social studies and
integrated humanities programmes. For want of a
better term we shall refer to this third element as
social education. This was a major feature of
the sociology course in school A and the PAL course
of school C. In the case of school B, aspects of
social education were dealt with in several
components of the modular programme. An
examination of course outlines and relevant field
notes indicates that much of what these courses
covered included such topics as: adolescence,
marriage and the family, groups, consumer rights,
local and national government, trades unionism (cf.
Table 11 Chapter 3).

This chapter considers some of the issues
involved in dealing with such topics in the
classroom, particularly those associated with the
organisation of effective pupil learning. These
issues are relevant to careers education and health
education as well as to social education. The
three elements careers education, health education
and social education are not, of course, completely
differentiated entities. They simply represent one
way of conceptualising the 'seamless robe' of PFL.

KNOWLEDGE BASED V. SKILLS BASED APPROACHES TO
SOCIAL EDUCATION

Probably the majority of the social studies
courses which were developed from the 1960s onwards

were essentially content based. Although such courses did not eschew the development of skills, indeed they often proclaimed a commitment to fostering enquiry methods, nevertheless the emphasis was on knowledge to be learned. The acquisition of skills was essentially incidental. Of course, knowledge v. skills, like all dichotomies, represents a considerable simplification of complex reality. No skill is possible without some knowledge, and no knowledge is so abstract that it leads to no increase in personal competence. The dichotomy simply represents the opposite ends of a continuum along which different courses can be placed according to their relative emphases.

If conventional social studies courses emphasised the knowledge end of the continuum then clearly the more recently emergent 'life and social skills' courses concentrate on the other end. Hopson and Scally (1981), for example, identify no less than 49 separate components in their lifeskills programme and these include such examples as: how to manage conflict; how to influence people and systems; how to set and achieve goals; how to cope with stress; how to use community resources.

In the project schools the social education aspects of PFL, and the PFL programmes generally, tended to reflect a knowledge rather than a skills base, e.g. schemes of work were set out more in topic than in skill terms. Moreover the lessons which we observed were ones in which content was explicit and skills in the main implicit only. In other words teachers, both in their formal conceptualisation of the area and their classroom practice, did not generally adopt a skills approach. However, it is important to stress that this is a description of the general state of affairs. Thus whilst the notion of skill was subordinate to knowledge or content as an organising principle, it was undeniably present on occasions. In one lesson dealing with problems which adolescents frequently face, the teacher concluded with the following remarks:

Teacher First of all, decide what you're aiming at - what you're trying to do. Unless you know where you're going, you'll be pushed with the tide and you won't be your own boss.

You need to have an aim in mind.
(Illustrates with situations dealt
with earlier in the lesson.)

OK, so you know what you want to do,
now you need to work out how to do
it. There may be very many
different ways of reacting.
(Illustrates different ways of
reacting to the situations discussed
earlier.)

In order to decide you need to think
about what will happen if I do each
of these things. Need to think and
weigh up the alternatives. Then the
last thing you have to do is to act
- and then learn from your
experience.

Teacher then wrote on the blackboard:-

1. Aim
2. How
3. Act

Teacher   You can spot the people who <u>think</u>
                   a mile off.

When asked by the researcher at the end of the
lesson what the main aim of the lesson was, the
teacher replied:

"The situations that happen to them are not unusual
- they happen to everyone and they can be overcome.
Need to develop skills (though I haven't used that
word yet), and you can <u>think</u> about them and
decide what to do. Everyone needs to learn to deal
with these situations."

The teacher here is explicitly recommending
thinking, and a particular way of tackling problem
situations, as a desirable skill to be learned.
This is similar to the generalised skill of
decision making which, as we noted in Chapter 4,
underpins much of careers education. Other
examples of skills oriented lessons were those in
careers education in which practice was given in
writing job application letters and in being
interviewed as one might be by an employer.

An important factor that can militate against the adoption of a skills approach and reinforce the trend towards a knowledge based one is whether or not a course is publicly examined. The public examination system is geared more towards the assessment of knowledge acquired than to skills mastered. Moreover in the field of social education the assessment of relevant skills would pose very considerable problems. In school A the PFL course (sociology) did in fact lead to CSE certification, although assessment was by conventional written tests and projects. As a result, teachers could feel themselves impelled to emphasise the knowledge content of their lessons. In one lesson we observed, in which the topic of adolescence was introduced in a 'fact' oriented manner, the teacher commented: "I'm trying to just get them to write some basic notes so that they stand a chance of revising something for exams."

An analysis of social education in skill terms can have the salutary effect of giving a sharper focus to what is often a somewhat vague and diffuse area. However, a taxonomy such as that advocated by Hopson and Scally (1981) tends to reinforce the view that there are in fact agreed and reliable ways of achieving social skills. The reality is, as Atkinson et al (1980) remind us, that "we know precious little about the nature of 'social and life skills' - about, that is, the awesomely detailed and subtle ways in which we organise our everyday social interaction. ... In the absence of any systematic body of knowledge there can be no adequate curriculum or pedagogy." (pp. 13-14) The uncritical application of skills analysis to this area of the curriculum may represent then little more than pedagogic legerdemain.

The teachers in the project schools may therefore have been on the right lines in developing programmes which were essentially an eclectic mix of the knowledge and skills approaches.

EXPOSITION V. EXPERIENTIAL LEARNING

This dichotomy is related to the one just considered. Thus a knowledge based approach will tend to be associated with an expository style of teaching whereas a skills based curriculum is likely to utilise actively the experience of the pupils.

The majority of lessons which we observed were
introduced by means of a content exposition by the
teacher. On occasions a film or video provided a
substitute for the teacher's introduction to the
lesson. In most cases however the teacher's
exposition was interspersed with a series of
questions which required short answers from pupils.
These served the purpose of maintaining pupil
attention and advancing the lesson in regular short
steps.

A few lessons were encountered which consisted
of relatively lengthy teacher expositions, fact
packed, and which allowed little opportunity for
pupil involvement. Two lessons on consumer rights,
each in a different school, illustrate this
approach. One was taken by a visiting speaker from
the local Consumer Protection Department and was
essentially in lecture format. In the other the
teacher listed ten Acts of Parliament relevant to
consumer protection on an overhead projector, and
talked in some detail on each as pupils copied down
the titles. The overall message of these lessons
appeared to be that if a customer was not satisfied
with a purchase he could take the goods back to the
shop. If he received no satisfaction he should go
to the Consumer Advice Centre. In the last resort
he had recourse to the County Court and could sue.
There was no hint that any of the stages in this
process might be difficult or unpleasant, or that
it would be an unusual experience for some pupils
to have the law on their side, and to be in a
situation where they were right and adults
officially in the wrong. If a main aim of these
lessons was to equip pupils with 'consumer
protection' skills, then perhaps role play/drama
might have been used as a means of exploration. In
actual fact after one of the 'lectures' the class
did break down into discussion groups and, in at
least one of these, pupils and teacher talked about
their respective experiences of changing goods
which they had previously purchased.

Many of the lessons involved pupils in copying
notes and doing worksheet exercises rather than
writing or talking about their own views and
experiences. The combination of exposition and
note taking may reflect the teachers' desire to
ensure that pupils had a permanent deposit of
knowledge for subsequent reproduction, perhaps for
assessment purposes. There is perhaps something
incongruous that in such lessons, particularly

those concerned with relationships and social situations, there should be a concern for formal note taking. This is likely to increase the possibility that pupils would view work in this area as just another school subject and therefore not personally relevant.

Since the experience of many social situations cannot, by their very nature, be enacted within the context of the classroom, some kind of simulation of them is necessary. The most common approach that we observed for doing this was one based on discussion using some appropriate stimulus material - examples of which included case studies, pictures and even music. An illustration is provided by one lesson where the class looked at a case study of an unmarried girl who finds that she is pregnant. The teacher first of all initiated discussion with the whole class on the options available to the girl: abortion; adoption; marriage; and bringing the baby up on her own. The class was then split into four groups, each of which was given one of the options to consider. The teacher went round each group asking the members what they thought and why. The groups were then brought together for a whole class discussion in which the teacher asked pupils to identify the pros and cons of all four options. Finally the pupils were asked to write a story about a girl who has a baby before she is married and who decides to keep it. It was suggested that they "take it up to when the child is ten years old or so. Think about all the problems. How will it feel, what sorts of things will happen when there's a baby and you and no-one else?"

One of the problems which teachers faced was that the number of pupils in the normal class was often too great for discussion and group work generally to be effective. Teachers sometimes attempted to overcome this by dividing pupils into several smaller groups, each of which discussed a separate topic. Some of the difficulties inherent in discussion activities are summarised by the teacher who said: "You can't leave them to discuss among themselves too long or it breaks down. And you can't discuss it with the whole group. They don't want to be seen coming up with ideas even if they have them, or else there are two or three trying to talk at once." This latter point suggests that pupils are generally inexperienced in taking part in discussions and that they need to be introduced to such approaches earlier in their

school careers. Another ploy which was used was to
assign pupils to one of several adults, each of
whom took a small group to a separate room for
follow up discussion. This was often possible
where the course involved a team of teachers or
where extra adults were present, e.g. the
headteacher or an external speaker.

As will be seen later (Chapter 11), the
attendance of pupils, particularly those in the
target group, tended to be poor. This sometimes
had the fortuitously beneficial effect of reducing
the numbers in a class to a level appropriate for
effective group work.

Group work, particularly that involving
discussion, needs to take place in an appropriate
environment. The serried ranks of seats which
characterise the typical secondary school classroom
do not help to engender the relaxed and intimate
atmosphere needed. Teachers often showed an
appreciation of the fact that the dynamics of a
group are potentially influenced by the seating
arrangements by rearranging tables before a
discussion lesson began, so that they faced each
other in groups of four, or by forming chairs into
a circle. The effects of an inappropriate seating
arrangement were observed on one occasion where
after a lecture by an external speaker the group
was split into three. Two of these left the class
to go to other rooms. The third group remained in
the room with the speaker in their original seats
as shown in Fig. 2.

Fig. 2: Arrangement of Pupils in a Discussion
Lesson

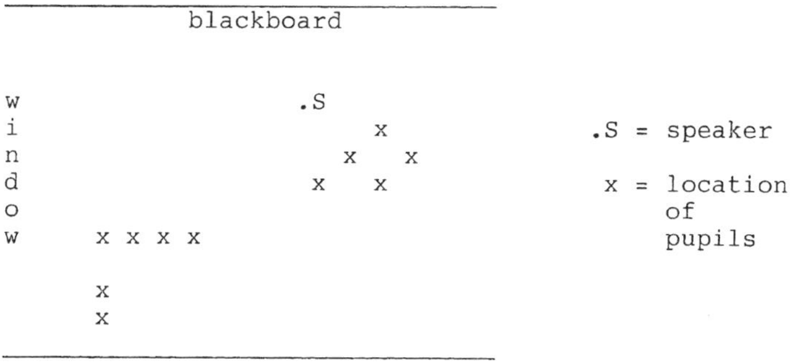

```
_____
                blackboard

w                      .S
i                           x            .S = speaker
n                      x    x
d                      x    x            x = location
o                                            of
w            x  x  x  x                   pupils

             x
             x
_____
```

The effect of this was that the speaker (S) concentrated his attention almost exclusively on the small group of pupils to his left - a group which was dominated by one pupil. The two pupils at the back of the room were uninvolved in the discussion which the speaker attempted to initiate, and chatted together on other matters throughout.

PASSIVE ACCEPTANCE V. CRITICAL DEBATE

Much of the rhetoric of the new social studies movement of the 1960s and 70s, and also that of the more recent 'life skills' one, implies a concern to encourage in pupils a critical approach to the social world and their relationships with it, rather than a passively accepting one. How far was this apparent in the PFL courses of project schools?

This question is related to the two issues just considered. If teaching is essentially didactic, concerned with facts, and oriented towards examination needs, then this is likely to minimise opportunities for critical debate. In contrast, a teaching method which draws on pupils' actual experiences and encourages discussion of them is more likely to lead to a consideration of possibilities and alternatives. Although such methods do not constitute a sufficient condition for critical debate, they most certainly are a necessary one.

Social education inevitably draws to some extent on the language and theories of the social sciences. However, if these are introduced at the beginning of a topic as a formal presentation of unproblematic facts it may foreclose debate rather than opening one up. Such an approach may also subtly reinforce the notion that the accounts of the social sciences are necessarily superior to those of everyday life and are therefore not open to question. This was apparent in a lesson which developed the familiar 'sturm und drang' theory of adolescence and culminated in pupils taking down the following definitive note.

"The transition from childhood to adulthood is not a matter of simple physical growth and intellectual development, it is a period of deep emotional and psychological upheaval, which shows itself in the tendency of adolescents to be moody or jealous, and either domineering or oversubmissive."

Such abstract technical definitions are likely to be repellent to less academically oriented pupils and may encourage, as our field notes seem to suggest, an obsessive pursuit by the teacher of the 'right' technical words, e.g.

Teacher   Can anyone tell me if we've used the word 'socialisation' before? Have we used that word?

and

Teacher   I want to teach you one word. Can you find it and explain it to me, what it means? Have you found it? This word 'function', as in 'functions of the family', means the things which the family does for the people in it.

This is not to say that theory has no place in social education courses. Theory does have the potential of providing pupils with succinct and elegant means of summarising the complexity of real life and helping them to make their own sense of it. In general however we believe that theory should grow out of the pupils' own experience and prior exploration of the phenomenon or issue concerned.

Although 'heavy' social science theory was not generally apparent in the lessons we observed, the predominant treatment of topics such as groups and marriage was one which reflected a structural functionalist perspective. This is perhaps not surprising since this is the one from which most authors of textbooks and teaching materials in this area write. Such a perspective tends to encourage a reification of social institutions characterised by unambiguous 'functions' which are somehow outside and beyond the action of individuals. Expository lessons which are implicitly or explicitly informed in this way may limit the likelihood of some options being aired. In a lesson on families the question "Why have families?" led to a list of positive aspects of having children. Any positive features of not having children and the disadvantages of both courses were not explored. Later in the same lesson the question "What factors make for success

101

in marriage?" was posed. The option of not getting married and being successful in personal relationships was not considered.

It was generally in group discussion sessions that the teacher seemed most free to depart from the straitjacket of presenting topics such as relationships as subjects with facts and rules to be learned. Thus in a follow up to a session in which separate groups had each discussed a specific problem situation which adolescents might face, the teacher presented relationships as being essentially rather messy, with no clear cut rules for success, no absolute rights and wrongs. The implication was that, even when one got older, one did not have all the issues and problems sorted out perfectly.

The drift of the argument presented so far is towards a view that, if the aims of social education programmes are to go beyond the simple acquisition of factual information, then they are more likely to be realised by approaches which are experiential rather than expository. Whilst experiential learning can take many forms, we consider that one of the most powerful and also one of the most natural to the classroom situation is that of small group discussion. In the next section we describe a sequence of lessons on political education which illustrates the effective use of experiential methods.

AN EXAMPLE OF EXPERIENTIAL LEARNING: POLITICAL EDUCATION IN SCHOOL C

A short module of political education was developed in 1979/80 for fourth year pupils in school C and consisted of three half day sessions over consecutive weeks. The module was noteworthy for several reasons. It was planned in conjunction with the LEA's adviser for political education, who, with the headteacher, also participated in the teaching. The module employed several experiential methods: a visit to the Town Hall, including informal discussion with the school's local councillor and attendance at a full Council meeting; simulation of a Council budget meeting; a film on local pressure groups; and group discussion. The staff team of head, adviser, and teacher enabled the 40 or so pupils to be organised into three separate small groups for discussion and simulation activities.

Observation of one of the discussion groups showed how the teacher and pupils together were able to debate a remarkably wide range of issues in the context of sometimes very different individual opinions on such subjects as political ideology, party politics, racism, population make up, educational organisation, traditional sex roles and voting patterns. These are often presented in a very biased way by the media, and the teacher was able to steer the discussion skilfully in such a way that the pupils themselves revealed the contradictions which often underlie people's taken-for-granted views of the world. Here is a sequence which illustrates how the teacher was able to tackle a sensitive issue and lead pupils at least to question their previously held views.

Pupil (National Front Supporter)	Them Paki's are all swarmin' us out. Your house goes down in price if they move in next door or down't street ...
Pupil	Ay, but think of the problems if we had no contacts abroad.
Pupil (National Front Supporter)	If you're going to have a mosque or summat in Bradford you may as well go back ...
Pupil	No ... the third world countries are not developed like ... we colonised 'em, so we should help 'em now.
Pupil	They can help each other too ...
Pupil	They can exchange things ...

Discussion then moved to the subject of South Africa, and white minority rule.

Pupil (National Front Supporter)	Blimey ... they'd batter us.
Pupil	Ay, but the whites have the army.
Teacher	The government also makes sure that it's the whites who have the best jobs.

Pupil   And clever blacks aren't allowed
                         to get on, are they ...?

(Pause)

Pupil   Well ... I'd still throw the
                         foreigners out anyway ...

Pupil   <u>You</u> should have said you voted
                         National Front, not Labour..

Pupil   Well, I'd chuck 'em all out ...

Teacher   What about the white non-English?

Pupil   Ay ... them too ... anyone who
                         weren't English, who weren't born
                         'ere.

Teacher   Well, ... you'd throw me out I
                         suppose?

(Blank looks)

Pupil   Why, sir? ... you're one of us
                         ...?

Pupil   You're not a Paki sir.

Teacher   No ... but I'm not English, I'm
                         South African.

(Consternation)

Pupil   No sir ... we wouldn't ...

Pupil   Not thee ...

Pupil   He's OK ... we couldn't chuck him
(to friend)   out.

Teacher   But I'm a foreigner ... I'm not
                         English.

(Much rapid thinking taking place among
pupils)

Pupil   Well sir ... we'd ... we could
                         make an exception like ... for
                         you ...

(Teacher went on to explain the tightness of the present immigration laws, leading to a more extended group discussion.)

DISCUSSION

The development of the social and personal competence of young people is a complex process, and one which is very far from being fully understood. The school is but one of several influences on this process, and not necessarily the most important - the family, peers and the media are amongst the others which may be at least as potent. Even within the school itself several influences are at work. The effects of the formal curriculum combine, in ways which are largely obscure, with those of the hidden curriculum and the extra curriculum to help shape pupils' social behaviour. Each of the many subjects of the formal curriculum can in turn claim, with varying degrees of justification, to contribute to this aspect of pupils' development. Given then the complex concatenation of potential influences involved, the effects which any <u>one</u> timetabled slot such as social education will have on pupils are likely to be slight and essentially unpredictable. The attempt to identify one to one correspondence between things done in social education programmes and the high level competences typically identified in the social and life skills taxonomies is likely to prove chimerical. Many of the skills identified by Hopson and Scally (1981) (e.g. how to discover my values and beliefs; how to take stock of my life; how to discover what makes me do the things I do; how to make effective decisions; how to express feelings constructively) are not skills in the strict sense at all, but awesomely complex characteristics of an idealised mature personality. The addition of the words 'how to' to these characteristics not only gives them a spurious status as apparently discrete competences but also encourages the view that there are known techniques which can reliably produce them. Whilst such statements may find a place amongst the general aims of education, it is a gesture of naive educational utopianism to tie them to a specific programme with the implication that they are potentially achievable (and by all pupils).

This is not to say that social education, and indeed PFL generally, has no place as a distinct curriculum element. We believe that it has. The justification for its inclusion is not that it can reliably produce specific skills but that it potentially heightens awareness of issues which might otherwise go unexplored. Social education as an element of the curriculum proclaims that its central concern is with personal and social development. In the case of many other subjects this is a subsidiary concern, and one which is often so subtly interwoven with others as to be invisible to many pupils. The existence of social education as a separate curriculum entity or as part of a broader PFL programme helps pupils to concentrate on a set of issues and concerns free of other distractions. It may also help pupils to recognise more fully the contribution made by other subjects and activities to their personal and social development.

In other words social education potentially provides pupils with opportunities to consider personal and social issues in a relatively single minded way. The outcomes of such exploration will seldom be predictable. The criteria for judging social education programmes are not in terms of the specific skills which they claim to foster but rather according to the learning experiences they provide. A 'good' social education programme is one which provides pupils with opportunities to explore the implications of a wide range of personal relationships and social situations.

In the past, social studies courses have been criticised as a means of keeping the masses in their place (Whitty, 1976) rather than of fulfilling their oft proclaimed liberating or radicalising aims. More recently social education, particularly as the social and life skills component of the MSC Youth Opportunities Programmes, has attracted similar criticism. Some would see such programmes as a response to the moral panic of youth unemployment, and social education in particular as a way of appropriately socialising a potentially dissident workforce (Atkinson et al, 1980).

The tendency for social education to function in this way is likely to be accentuated in courses where there is a heavy reliance on expository methods, the presentation of social 'facts', and an orientation to examination goals. A corrective to

this ever present danger is the greater use of a
pedagogy which is more reliant on experiential
rather than exposition learning. Much of the
former approach to learning can only take place
effectively, as our observation of some project
lessons confirm, in groups not only smaller than
the conventional class but organised on a different
kind of basis. Although we are critical of the
skills approach to social education, we do agree,
although for different reasons, with the view of
Hopson and Scally that learning will be best
accomplished in this area by pupils participating
alongside their peers and teachers in small groups.
The skills required of the teacher in such
situations are very different from those exercised
in the traditional lesson. Teachers wishing to
develop such skills would find the practical advice
offered by Hopson and Scally, and also that of the
earlier Humanities Curriculum Project (Ruddock,
1976) very worthy of their attention.

Chapter 7

CURRICULUM INTEGRATION

INTRODUCTION

An account is given here of the development of the sociology course at school A. This is based on information gathered in the main from individual interviews with each of the eight teachers who formed the sociology team conducted some 18 months after the introduction of the new course. The interviews were as far as possible held in private, lasted on average about an hour, and were tape recorded. While the interviewer was familiar with current practice on the sociology course [1] and had therefore been able to identify a number of questions which it was hoped to discuss with each member of the team, much time and encouragement was given to teachers to talk about their individual concerns relating to the course.

The decision to undertake this study arose from the realisation that the sociology course presented us with a particularly clear example of curriculum integration. The study attempts to describe some of the issues which teachers confronted in teaching the course. Since the study was completed many of the problems outlined have been resolved and much progress has been made. Its value therefore lies in its status as a 'snapshot' describing the initial experience of establishing a new course.

In September 1979 all fourth year pupils began the new course called sociology, timetabled for four periods per week and forming part of the core curriculum. Pupils were banded into groups of high, medium and low ability [2] and nearly 75% of the first cohort was entered for the mode 3 CSE examination in the summer 1981. The aim of the course was to integrate material formerly covered separately in social studies, careers and health education into a logical scheme providing the "skills and facts" required for young people "to lead full and active life in modern society". [3]

Ideas for the new course had been developing in the school for several years before the EEC project came into being. In 1972 the Humanities Curriculum Project (HCP) was established in the school and several of the staff involved in that subsequently became members of the sociology team. The HCP was originally intended for pupils of average and below average ability and the philosophy on which it was based had some similarity to that underlying the new sociology course. When the HCP came to an end in school A in 1977, an unsuccessful attempt was made to set up a course in social education that would be part of the core curriculum for all fourth and fifth year pupils. This meant however that, when later the EEC project made additional resources available, existing plans for the integrated course could be quickly re-introduced. Thus by December 1978 a coordinator of the new course had been appointed and confirmation given that the course would begin in the following academic year.

Seven staff (all male) were involved in teaching the sociology course in its first year (1979-80). Each member of the team had sole responsibility for one or two pupil groups and taught all parts of the syllabus. An exception to this was an assistant head who, while having a teaching commitment to the course for the equivalent of four periods per week, did not have responsibility for a particular pupil group. The new course meant that most of the team were involved in teaching at least some subjects with which they were relatively unfamiliar. A variety of strategies was employed to help ease this process and these are described below. Some of the staff also attended an in-service course on group work together [4] since this was thought to be particularly relevant to the teaching approach envisaged for the course.

Staff absences due to ill health caused considerable difficulties during the first year of the course. The heads of careers and social studies were both absent for a term each, and another member of the social studies department was also away for a substantial period. This created some strain within the rest of the team and clearly hindered the development of the course during its first year.

At the beginning of the second year (1980-81) two staff from the geography department joined the sociology team, taking one group each in the fourth year, whilst the assistant head's commitment of four periods per week as a 'floater' was terminated. In addition the head of social studies was again absent for the autumn term due to ill health. [5]

ISSUES AND CONCERNS

Assessment

The course was designed to lead to CSE Mode 3 certification and in fact nearly 75% of the 1981 fifth year was entered for the examination. As a result pupils were required to provide pieces of work for assessment regularly throughout the five terms of the course. Some misgivings were expressed about this situation, i.e. whether assessment for CSE was having too much influence on the content and method of teaching particularly in the case of the less able. It is important however to appreciate the constraints which the examination system can impose on those who develop innovative courses - "The reason we started off as an exam course was to make it more acceptable to large numbers of influential staff - this is the politics of curriculum development." "Originally we said we'd only enter those who could pass easily, but ... once it's offered as a CSE subject it's difficult to say to individual pupils 'You cannot do it'."

Teaching Methods

During the planning of the sociology course it was decided that the classroom approach adopted would be based on that used in the Schools Council Humanities Curriculum Project, i.e. one which emphasised discussion rather than instruction and invited teachers to treat pupils as young adults. In a teacher's paper dated January 1981, the coordinator of the sociology course and the head of careers reported that over the first 18 months of the course an attempt had been made "to evolve classroom teaching strategies that will assist in

the personal development of pupils through closer and informal relationships between them and teachers, greater pupil participation in activities and a relaxed though structured encouragement to discuss, debate and question the course themes." They added, "The most crucial and vital element in the course is seen to be the class teacher and his relationship with the pupils." [6]
While thus outlining "the general direction in which we want to evolve", however, the sociology team took the view that "you can't lay down rules as to how to teach in the classroom", and therefore adopted "a fairly individualistic approach" to teaching methods. However, three themes related to teaching methods emerged in the interviews, each of which was given prominence by several teachers. Broadly then, the sociology team seemed concerned to foster:

    i.   a close personal relationship between teachers and pupils, "there's a change in emphasis in seeing the teacher not as an expert, but the teacher learning with the kids to some extent";

    ii. discussion skills, "schools put too much emphasis on writing I think. Talking is going to be much more important to most of them";

    iii. cooperative working, "we try to get the groups to think of themselves as a whole and work together ... so that they help each other".

The interviews suggested, however, that nearly all the teachers in the sociology team would welcome some help in developing their teaching styles in these directions. There was a very widespread demand for more meetings at which classroom approaches could be discussed and ideas shared, and it was felt that more opportunities could be created for putting two classes together so that teachers could learn from watching each other teach.

Banding

"This was a difficult question we had to make a decision on, and it wasn't clear cut ..." Originally the decision to band pupils in high,

111

medium and low ability groups for sociology was taken because careers education material was generally designed for pupils of a specific ability, and because banding would obviate the necessity to cover all types of careers work with each class. It was not felt to be feasible to set by ability for careers work only, because of a desire to maintain a strong group identity among each group of pupils.

Up to the time of the study pupils had been banded into broad ability groups on the basis of test results supplied by another member of staff in the school. However in one teacher's view the bands "aren't very strict because we don't really understand the test scores that accurately and it turns out some of them aren't that accurate anyway. Also kids change a lot over two years and the groups are not reviewed." This means that there was likely to be considerable overlap between the groups in terms of ability. Thus to some degree there was already mixed ability teaching in the sociology course.

This led one teacher to argue strongly that tighter banding was essential. He felt that in a mixed ability class "you can't pitch lessons properly", and "it only tends to magnify the differences between (pupils)." This teacher would have liked to have seen pupils not entered for CSE grouped together and taught a course not tied to the examination syllabus, but geared to equipping less able pupils with basic life skills. However, most of the team favoured the introduction of mixed ability teaching. It was felt that banding pupils worked against many of the ideas being taught in the sociology course, and that mixed ability grouping provided a more appropriate context in which pupils could learn about some of the issues under discussion at first hand. "It's a class-conscious society. Neither side seems to understand the other. When you've got a degree of social mixing I don't see how you can avoid a loosening of these divisions, an improvement in the understanding between people. It's one way in which we can work in school towards ... a more egalitarian society."

Teachers also felt that mixed ability grouping could create more productive learning situations, providing a greater opportunity for cooperative working. One teacher also suggested that classes organised on the basis of friendship groups would,

in his opinion, enhance both the quality of
discussions and pupil confidence. Banding was seen
as having negative effects on the learning
situation. "If you put all that bottom group
together their ideas are very limited ... Maybe a
quarter of the group are anti-cooperative on almost
anything ... that problem of 20-25 incredibly
passive or hostile low ability children, all the
teaching problems you care to mention in one
classroom."

Teaching Low Ability Pupils

At the time of our study one teacher (head of
careers) had specialised in teaching sociology to
less able pupils, while three others taught both a
low ability group and one other. Teaching low
ability groups was not an issue that had been
discussed in team meetings, although the teachers
concerned had become aware that classes of less
able pupils created particular demands. "I'm
discovering you've got to have a different
approach. Virtually a different lesson on the same
theme will take place in each of the groups."
One teacher thought that with higher ability
pupils he could expect them to "do things a bit
more for themselves", and do "more written work",
whereas with low ability groups "I'd spend more
time talking to them and perhaps not be quite so
serious, and would ask them to do more practical
work." Another teacher felt it important with less
able children to "break up the morning" and to
ensure that any worksheets or reading were "at the
right level".
Teachers also talked about difficulties they
experienced in taking low ability classes. These
were often related to their arguments against
banding (see above). A high absence rate made
continuity of work and the development of group
identity difficult. Because projects were not
always taken home ("work folders get 'lost' "),
those taking CSE were under pressure of time to
complete work during lessons. Discussion was
difficult since the groups lacked verbal fluency
and pupils tend to have limited ideas. It was
difficult to make simple ideas interesting. In a
low ability class many teaching problems were
concentrated in one group making the task
particularly difficult for the teacher.

Teaching Materials

"A lot of stuff was produced individually in the first year but most of it is lost. A lot of it was perishable - for kids to use or put in their files. I don't think we realised at the time of producing it that it ought to be kept. What we have kept has not been systematically filed. I've got mine spread out in various rooms I use but there's no system in it. I'm sure other people have too. We're just getting the idea that we ought to be hanging on to this stuff we've produced." (Course coordinator)

This issue had been highlighted in the second year by the two new members of the team who found lack of support in the area of teaching materials very frustrating. It appears that a large percentage of the materials produced during the first 18 months of the course was developed on an ad hoc basis by individuals for use with their own groups only. The majority of teachers felt strongly that, given the limited time available, the system would be more effective if team members worked together on preparing materials instead of individually.

This state of affairs seems to have arisen partly due to the staff absences with which the course had been beset. From the beginning of the course efforts had been made to implement a system of 'topic leaders'. Under this system, if someone thought they had some specific expertise on a topic, or were personally interested in it, then they would undertake to prepare the materials on it. These would then be available to the rest of the team for them to use if they wished. In many instances, however, the topic leaders were the heads of careers and social studies and so the system suffered during their absences. Where other members of the team had undertaken the role of topic leader they had often found it difficult to put in the necessary amount of preparation. As a result, some teachers felt that what had been produced had been inadequate, "some information sheets, not more than that", "they need a great deal more work before they can be used in the classroom". Frustration was also expressed by several teachers at the lack of time available at meetings to present materials they had prepared for discussion. It sometimes happened that no such time was available and that materials were handed out without the benefit of comments from the person who had produced them or any formal opportunity for discussion or feedback.

Reservations were also expressed at the appropriateness of the topic leader system where classes were banded. It was felt that the materials produced were only suitable for some pupils, and that it was necessary to rework these substantially before they could be used by other ability groups. It was also thought that better organisation would benefit the accessing and use of existing printed materials.

The single major wish expressed by virtually all the teachers was for team meetings, which could be used for: "reporting back on what we've done in the classroom, how people have succeeded, what materials they've used. And talking about what themes are coming up, what materials are available, and presenting and thrashing through materials for use in the coming lessons." It was hoped that this would lead to an accumulation of tried and tested material which could be systematically filed and made available as a resource bank for all members of the sociology team.

Provision for New Staff

The two teachers who joined the sociology team at the beginning of the second year were given a folder of information in advance. This contained details of the syllabus and test papers which it was hoped to give at the end of the autumn term. There was also information about the EEC Project, a text book, a list of references available in the departments of careers and social studies. Advice and discussion occurred on an informal basis only. When the new staff took their places in the team at the beginning of the autumn term, there were two procedures used at the beginning of the course, one year earlier, which might have been employed to ease their induction. Firstly, when the course began, each teacher with experience of social studies was 'paired' with a teacher experienced in careers. The idea was that each could tap the other's expertise in that area in which he was unfamiliar. The second strategy which might have helped was the system of 'topic leaders' described above.

So while individual teachers gave help on an ad hoc basis, systematic help was largely lacking for those two teachers during their first term as part of the sociology team. In retrospect there was a widespread awareness of this problem and several teachers contributed ideas as to how the situation might be improved in the future. For example, it was felt that the file given to new staff should focus less exhaustively on syllabus content and concentrate more on a consideration of teaching methods. This might be followed up by some introduction to different teaching techniques: "We've not had demonstration lessons. Sometimes two groups combine but not a lot."

Another idea was that the experience of the rest of the team could be made available to new teachers if, at the end of the summer term, they took part in a one or two day induction course. This might also be an opportunity for the team which had taught sociology during the year to get together and go through the syllabus, to find out what went well and what did not and to discuss the different techniques that were effective in the classroom. Worksheets could also be considered and redesigned. In this way it would be possible, by team discussion, to develop a resource bank of materials and a pool of ideas about how to use them in the classroom.

One member of the team pointed out that these strategies for passing on ideas, information and skills would be helpful even if a new teacher had considerable experience in this area: "The assumption tended to be that because I'd taught social studies for a long time, I knew what I was doing. It was true I knew what I was doing, but not the potential of other directions. Much of what I've done on this course is what I've done before."

An 'Integrated' Course?

Pring (1976) suggests that curricular activities referred to as 'integrated' frequently "have in common only the negative feature of being opposed to the division of the curriculum into discrete and unrelated units. Positively, they mean very different things." The Schools Council Integrated Studies project reflecting this diversity defined integrated studies broadly as "the exploration of any theme or problem which requires the help of more than one teacher in achieving this." (Schools Council, 1972) Under this definition the sociology course at school A is integrated in the sense that it comprises the content of both social studies and careers, formerly taught as separate subjects, and involves the teaching staff of these two subjects.

When asked what the term 'integration' meant in practice in relation to the social studies, careers and health education components of the sociology course, teachers talked of developing "a package that makes more sense", "trying to get some logic into the course", and the "importance of making connections between things". There seemed to be a widely shared definition of what such integration would mean for the day to day teaching of the course: "For example, if we were doing local government we would say 'this is the way local government works, how the rate money is spent, what a councillor does. These are the people who do the jobs, these are the kinds of jobs that are available and the training that is available. This is why not many of these jobs are available. That would be complete integration." Other staff gave similar accounts of what integration would mean, although this was coupled with an assertion that there were areas in which integration would be more difficult.

Two of the team specifically raised the issue of 'social class' (a topic on the social studies syllabus), and its relationship to banding. One felt strongly that "social class is really an integral part of all the careers stuff. Although we probably don't admit it, it's there all the time ... Streaming 7 makes it very difficult." Both these teachers suggested that with mixed ability it would be easier to link careers and social class: "You could say to kids in mixed ability, 'Well according to this (his careers choice) he's middle class. According to this, you're working class.' Does it make sense? What do we mean by that?"

The team were divided in the extent to which they thought integration had already been achieved in the sociology course. The coordinator felt that considerable progress had been made in this area despite staff absences. Other staff felt that much of the teaching of the two main components of the course i.e. careers education and social studies was still carried out in parallel. The fact that

the teaching resources for the two areas were located in different places tended to reinforce any tendency to see them as separate. [8]
An important aspect of the sociology course which perhaps facilitated integration was that each member of the team taught the whole of the syllabus to the group(s) allocated to him. (In many integrated courses it is the practice for specialist staff to take each group in turn for particular sections of the course.) Thus among the sociology team over the first 18 months of the course, each teacher had developed his knowledge of both the careers and social studies elements in the syllabus. This growing familiarity with all parts of the course made it more likely that areas in which an integrated approach might benefit pupils would be recognised.
Interestingly, the possibility of developing a modular approach [9] to the teaching of sociology was considered by the coordinator and head of careers but was rejected. It was argued that such an approach would be contrary to the "main principle" of the team "that teachers and pupils should get to know each other in a trusting and caring relationship. Five terms is hardly long enough to build this relationship and sustain it. The shorter time of a module would come nowhere near achieving our aims."

The Role of a Course Coordinator

The role of a course coordinator "never was closely defined" and is therefore of particular interest. Clearly the way in which the course coordinator viewed his role and the way in which it was perceived by the rest of the team was likely to influence substantially the way in which the course developed. "The job was put to me as exercising some control over two competing heads of department. The course was a mixture of careers and social studies and it was thought that both heads of department would want to get a lot of their work in. Part of the job was to be a sort of judge and to try to keep the correct balance, however 'correct' is defined, to keep it as a sociology course." (Course coordinator) From this it appears that the coordinator saw a major element of his role as being to oversee and arbitrate in decisions concerning the content of the sociology course.

During the first 18 months of the course however, this and other potential functions of the coordinator were severely hindered by prolonged absences among the sociology team. "When (the head of social studies) was away, (the coordinator) took over that area, and when (the head of careers) was away, he took over that area. It was very much a patch and mend situation." "We were surviving from week to week ... I don't really think (the coordinator's) role has evolved as it should have done ... the coordination has been left and (the coordinator) hasn't got back to his original role yet - he's a bit shell-shocked."

During the first 18 months of the course, therefore, the coordinator was able to devote relatively little energy to his official role and, for the most part, functioned in this capacity only to the extent of performing a minimum of organisational duties (for example allocating rooms and teaching groups; drawing up rotas). Among the team there was a general agreement that during this period "we've not had the meetings we ought to have done" and that such meetings as did take place were restricted to lunchtimes and were dominated by the discussion of practical arrangements. Nevertheless, during this initial period, the course continued to operate in the face of the consecutive absences of the two key heads of department and other sociology staff. Perhaps success in this was helped not only by the commitment and effort of all concerned, but also by the fact that most of the team knew each other quite well before the course began and had had some part in its planning. It seems more likely too that the task of the coordinator was eased by the mode of assessment used which, by its nature, ensured that each teacher covered roughly the same items of the syllabus each term.

However, at the beginning of the second year of the course, two new members joined the team. This not only increased its size but also introduced teachers who were unfamiliar with the course and the organisation of the departments concerned. At the same time the team as a whole was beginning to question strongly the mode of course assessment being used; an issue which again had major implications for the role of coordinator.

So at the time of this study the functions of the course coordinator were still largely to be worked out. Satisfactory procedures for managing

the team and its decisions had not been
established. Everyone in the team expressed views
as to how they would like to see the role of the
coordinator develop. An amalgamation of the views
of team members provides an outline of a possible
coordinator's role i.e. the coordinator would:

- arrange meetings so that there is
  opportunity for
    - exchanges of ideas on teaching
      methods and materials;
    - the views of the team on key issues
      to be given to the coordinator and
      heads of department;
- consult the team as to the agenda of
  meetings;
- take final decisions;
- maintain a balance in the course between
  careers and social studies;
- direct attention to exploring ways of
  further integrating the careers and social
  studies elements in the course;
- arrange for new teaching staff to have
  access to members' experience and materials
  in an organised way;
- coordinate the production of teaching
  materials by the team and keep a record and
  file of such materials;
- deal with practical arrangements.

The coordinator himself was aware of the need
to give attention to the role. "As a team we've
been muddling through rather than working
together." Two future concerns discussed by the
coordinator were the promotion of a greater
integration in the content of the course and
getting the teachers "working together as a team".
The coordinator felt that the part of his job which
involved "exercising some control over two
competing heads of department" and keeping a
balance of careers and social studies content in
the course would "cease to be a problem as time
goes on because it will just be a sociology course.
... We're getting to the stage now where (the head
of careers) is thinking of himself as a sociology
teacher, and the same with (the head of social
studies)."
    The composite role outlined above suggests
that members of the sociology team saw the
coordinator's role rather as a "super head of

department" with special emphasis on overseeing the balance of course content. Comments on the issues this raises are made in the discussion section below.

Perceptions of the Sociology Course among Other Staff in the School

Members of the sociology team were asked by what means the rest of the staff were informed about the course and how it was developing. Initially the first draft syllabus for the sociology course had been circulated and comments invited. The coordinator, however, reported that this had elicited only one response. He was also disappointed that staff had not tried to find out more about sociology. He noticed that some staff came informally at lunchtime and listened to members of the sociology team talking together in the staff room. He felt that other informal channels of communication also existed in that many of the sociology team also taught in other departments and so spread the word. He expected that pupils too talked in other lessons about what they had done in sociology. On a more formal basis, the reports produced by the sociology team were available to the rest of the staff, and there was an opportunity to present information about the sociology course at the Tuesday evening staff discussion group.

The sociology teachers were also asked what they considered other staff in the school thought about the sociology course. Discussion on this issue yielded a list of factors which were felt by different teachers to influence the degree to which a new course was accepted among the rest of the school. The status of the person who introduced a new subject to the school was felt to be an important factor. In the case of sociology the headteacher was involved in its planning from the early stages and this was thought to have contributed substantially to the current status of the subject. The original decision to make sociology a CSE course was taken mainly "to make it more acceptable to large numbers of influential members of staff". The percentage of the fifth year to obtain grade one at CSE was felt to be a measure of a subject's academic respectability, "unless people say 'but it's only sociology' ". A more subjective criterion, it was thought other

staff employed in assessing sociology, was its
perceived usefulness. One teacher suggested that
perhaps "many heads of department feel that their
department could cover some of the stuff we do, we
need to prove our worth and show we're covering
things in a different way, given our teaching style
and our relationship with the kids." Finally, a
factor helping to maintain a favourable view of the
sociology course was thought to be its timetabling
in half day blocks. This virtually eliminated
disruption to other classes when outings and other
special events were arranged.

DISCUSSION

Although this is only an account of an
integrated course in one school it does highlight a
number of issues which may be of a more general
interest. One concerns the difficulties
encountered in arriving at satisfactory procedures
for making policy decisions about a course, for
organising a large team in its practical tasks, and
for maintaining adequate communication among team
members when two departments are working together
for the first time on a joint venture. Awareness
of the importance of these aspects of organisation
among the teaching team was heightened in this case
by a series of prolonged absences among senior
staff involved in the sociology course.

At the time of this study (mid way through the
third year of the project) teachers involved in the
course expressed the hope that decision making
procedures could be made more formal, and a
situation created whereby decisions were based on
the experience and ideas of the whole team rather
than on those of its few senior members.

"The value of systematic consultation within a
department and the importance of agreed policies on
such matters as marking and assessment" was pointed
out by HM Inspectors of Schools (DES, 1979) in
their survey of the last two years of compulsory
secondary education. Similarly Marland (1971)
writing about the head of department as team
leader, suggests that "most important ... is the
creation of ... a climate of discussion" and
regular formal meetings "free from administration
and available for their central purpose:
educational discussion".

Other changes in organisation suggested by
the team arose from the wish to have more formal

opportunities to learn from each other's teaching styles and methods. Originally it was hoped that staff involved in the sociology course would use a less formal, less book based, more personal style of teaching. However, most of the teachers felt that their development in this direction would be greatly facilitated by regular meetings at which they shared their approaches to current and forthcoming topics and discussed what 'worked' in the classroom and what did not. A more frequent use of the occasional ad hoc practice of putting two classes together with two teachers working with them was also advocated. Such procedures would perhaps become even more valuable if a mixed ability grouping of pupils replaced the current practice of banding. Eavis (1980) in a study of an integrated humanities course in a Newcastle comprehensive asserts that: "The problems to overcome to teach effectively in mixed ability classes in city comprehensive schools are such that it cannot be done single handed ... an organisation which forces teachers to work together is essential. The mixture of expertise and experience in a large department is perhaps the richest resource for teacher development in a school, and often the least drawn upon."

The production of teaching materials and access to them was another aspect of organisation which emerged as a central concern during the interviews. A system for collaboratively preparing teaching materials, perhaps by the reintroduction of the 'topic leader' practice, together with a much higher level of team discussion of materials was favoured. Ensuring easy access to such materials as their volume grew was also seen as important but problematic. Teachers also indicated the desirability of providing some organisation to help new staff become familiar with the teacher produced materials available as well as the large number of sets of books held in the school for use in sociology. A list of titles was viewed as inadequate for this purpose.

However, the introduction of such changes raises interesting issues. In making concrete suggestions in these and other areas as to how the course might be more effectively organised, teachers frequently referred to the role of the course coordinator. The person in this role was originally appointed to arbitrate between the two heads of department on decisions as to course content. Unfortunately most of his energy was necessarily absorbed by the need to cover for absent staff despite pressure for him to become much more active in team management and decision making. This raises questions which must emerge in various forms whenever integrated courses are introduced: what is the coordinator's role vis a vis the heads of department involved? In particular, when the sociology course becomes so integrated that its careers and social studies elements are no longer distinct, what role will remain for those two heads of department? How far can the coordinator extend his activities in trying to alleviate some of the problems outlined above without intruding improperly into the responsibilities of those heads of department?

Other constraints on the activities of a coordinator arise from the availability of his own time, energy and enthusiasm. HM Inspectors found (in respect of heads of department) that "most schools had not been able to relate the allocation of non-teaching time to the special responsibilities which these teachers were expected to fulfil." (DES, 1979). In discussing this, Marland (1971) concludes that "in essence the head of department's personal problems are those of establishing a tolerable hold on priorities". However, prioritising is likely to be difficult where no detailed job specification exists.

The issues outlined above relate to working arrangements among the teaching team. Other aspects of the organisation of the sociology course are also likely to be of interest however. While neither the setting of pupil groups by ability nor teachers' use of different approaches with different ability groups were discussed in team meetings, the organisation of pupil groups was clearly an issue of concern to the majority of the teaching team. Mixed ability groups were favoured by most teachers as being more in keeping with the content and educational aims of the course, and with the need to provide a better learning situation for the less able.

Related to the organisation of pupil groups is the question of how a new course shall be assessed. This raises political as well as educational issues. For example, the possibility of CSE certification may influence how highly regarded the course will be both within and beyond the school. Questions which arise include: will this be a CSE subject and if so what form will the assessment take? If the pupils are in mixed ability groups will all follow the exam syllabus? If, however, pupils are setted will the less able be freed from the constraint of the examination syllabus and assessment procedures? How can provision be made to ensure that the broader objectives of the course are not lost in the pressure to complete work for assessment?

The organisation of content in an 'integrated' course such as sociology is also of interest. What is the nature of an 'integrated' course? Teachers involved with the sociology course shared a similar view of what the term integration meant, but disagreed about the extent to which they felt that this had been achieved. Some teachers also expressed a hope for more exploration among the team of ways in which specific topics could be integrated with other parts of the course.

There also seems to be a need to bear the objective of integration in mind in the production of teaching materials. Rather than a social studies 'specialist' producing materials for the 'social studies topics', and similarly for careers, a working together to produce materials reflecting the connections between the two components of the course seems desirable. Decisions as to the use of physical space in the school may also have important implications in this context. In school A the designation of a 'careers' room, and the separate locations of the social studies and careers teaching materials were thought to militate against integration. Eavis (1980) suggests that the operation of schemes for change in schools is often "hampered, if not effectively destroyed by building layout" and that plans must, therefore, take into account the nature of the existing building.

In order to set the sociology course at school A in context as a venture in integration it is interesting to contrast it with the content of an integrated careers programme as described by Law and Watts (Law and Watts, 1977; Law, 1981). Whereas in school A integration involved careers and one other course in the school, Law and Watts' integrated careers programme involves the coordination of specialised careers teaching not only with "a wide range of other curricular and extra-curricular activity in the school (but also) ... with the wide range of resources in the community." Law and Watts argue that the present "very heavy reliance placed on the skill, information and other resources available inside the school makes neither economic nor social sense."

Continued exploration of the various problems and successes outlined in this chapter took place in the year following the fieldwork. Much has been done in the further development of the course and in establishing it firmly within the school curriculum.

NOTES

1 The interviewer had been involved in regular classroom observation and informal discussion with staff involved in teaching sociology over the period October to December 1980.

2 Banding was based on results obtained by pupils in the NFER tests EH1-3.

3 Paper produced by course coordinator and head of careers, 1981.

4 Courses run by the Careers and Counselling Development Unit, University of Leeds.

5 Immediately after this study was undertaken another teacher in the social studies department left school A to take up a post elsewhere. He was replaced by a teacher new to the school who was the first female member of the team.

6 It is interesting to note that no mention is made by teachers, either in their papers or interviews of the HCP notion of 'neutrality'. This seems to have been part of the HCP philosophy which was not adopted by the sociology team.

7 The teacher use of 'streaming' here refers to banding.

8 The resources were subsequently centralised.

9 As, in fact, had been developed in school B.

Chapter 8

THE ORGANISATION OF SCIENCE COURSES FOR LESS ABLE PUPILS

INTRODUCTION

Although the main thrust of project related curriculum development was directed to the areas of careers education and preparation for life, the project also influenced other subjects. Two schools, for example, as a result of their involvement in the project developed new courses in science for less able pupils in general and those of the target group in particular.

In school C an applied science course was introduced in the first year of the project (1978/79) for a small number (12) of pupils forming the 'hard core' of the fourth year target group. The remainder of the target group was accommodated in the existing science options (physical science and biological science) or in parent craft. In the applied science courses pupils studied a number of short modules which included services to the home, materials, electricity, fuels, laboratory skills, health and hygiene, photography and pollution. Pupils who took the course could obtain a mode 3 CSE qualification at the end of two years.

The applied science course was in effect the precursor of a more developed modular course which was introduced in 1979/80 for the fourth year target group. This was also designed as a CSE mode 3 course and consisted of a selection from the following modules: flight, atmosphere and weather, astronomy, pollution, maintenance of the body, horticulture, colourful chemistry (dyes and pigments), human chemistry, plastics, heating and lighting, materials round the house, health and hygiene and laboratory skills. The rump of the target group took a somewhat truncated version of

127

this course, called the special modular course, in which certain modules were excluded (e.g. flight, colourful chemistry). The modular science and special modular courses were also available to target group pupils in the third year of the project (1980/81).

In school A a similar course, called integrated science, was introduced for a substantial proportion of the fourth year target group in 1978/79. This two year course continued over the three years of the project and, although it did not lead to a CSE qualification, its coverage was similar to that of the modular science course at school C.

Although school B did not produce any special course in science as a result of the project, target group pupils followed the combined science or integrated science courses which had already been in operation there for several years. The latter were not included in the programme of lesson observation carried out by the research team.

A search of the field note archive, carried out at the end of the third year of the project, yielded 16 items relating to science courses for target group pupils. These were equally divided between observation of lessons and interviews with teaching staff. The relatively small number of field notes reflects the decision taken by the research team to concentrate its efforts on careers education and related aspects of the EEC programme.

The field notes were mainly collected in the first and third years of the project. This pattern was consistent with the procedure adopted of identifying the main features of the courses early on in the project's life and then seeing how these had developed one or two years on. Rather more attention was given to school A in order to explore what was considered to be the particularly interesting feature of organising the teaching groups on a separate sex basis.

RATIONALE OF THE COURSES

The rationale of the courses at school A and C was one based on notions of relevance, interest and cooperation. These were explicitly stated in the official aims of the course at C as given in its CSE mode 3 syllabus, i.e.

Science courses for less able pupils

"1. To offer pupils - by means of a flexible
   series of modules - a science course having
   maximum relevance to them whilst they are
   still at school and also when they have
   left.
2. To stimulate interest and cooperation by
   having the pupils make their own choice
   about which modules they study (wherever
   possible) and to renew their interest each
   time they change to a different module.
3. To maximise this interest by having modules
   taught by teachers having special interest
   in them.
4. To transmit to the pupils knowledge and
   skills which may be of use to them in their
   leisure activities, both at school and
   home, and possibly in their future working
   life."

   The head of science at school A saw the course
as one based substantially on an experimental
approach in which the work had to be relevant and
meaningful to the needs of pupils. He felt it to
be important, however, that the course should not
simply become one of entertaining pupils to gain
interest and spoke of the need "to find a balance
between stimulating pupils whilst giving them work
with some intrinsic educational value." He hoped
to develop group work in order to give pupils some
experience of being in a cooperative situation. In
his view working in groups and learning how to
cooperate with people would be a feature of pupils'
subsequent working lives. When interviewed at the
end of the first year of the project he elaborated
the rationale in terms of two major sets of aims.
One set included such concerns as: encouraging
scientific thinking about life in general;
developing analytic thinking to encourage decision
making; seeing science in relation to themselves
and life in general; and awareness of the social
consequences of science. The second set was more
concerned with social aspects: achieving self
discipline in the laboratory; ability to work with
the teacher seen as an exemplar of an adult with
authority over them, and working together on
projects.
   Both heads of department saw their courses as
being different, both in content and methods of
approach, from those which the pupils would

129

normally have followed had these new ones not been developed.

The maintenance of pupil interest was seen as paramount. At school C one science teacher commented that the length of a module, approximately six weeks, was just right if pupil interest began to wane. In addition, since each module was taught by a different member of staff, pupils would have the variety of seeing several different faces during the course. The head of department at A also emphasised the importance of linking topics together to maintain the level of interest. He saw the general theme of 'energy', because of its centrality to life for the next few decades, as one way of linking the topics together.

The two department heads, however, differed in their views on whether or not the course should lead to CSE certification. In the first year of the project they had discussed the possibility of developing a joint syllabus for mode 3 CSE. The head of department at A had, however, moved away from this early intention. He agreed that some pupils would have got a low grade CSE pass if the course had been examined but he felt that the file of work produced by pupils would be of more use to them when being interviewed by a potential employer.

The course at C was designed to lead to a mode 3 CSE and was available to a greater proportion of the year group [1], and hence probably a wider ability range, than was the corresponding course at A.

CONTENT OF COURSES

Table 14 shows that the two courses in schools A and C were very similar in content. This was perhaps not surprising since the two heads of science had been in touch with each other and the course materials were derived in part from sources common to both (e.g. LAMP Project).[2]

A particular module common to both courses was one concerned with health education ('health and hygiene'). Health education was also a component of other courses in the EEC programmes of these two schools. In Chapter 5 we raised the issue of whether or not the contributions made to health education by separate courses formed a coherent whole. In one school, when asked how the health and hygiene module related to the health education

Table 14: Content of the Integrated Science Course (School A) and the Modular Science Course (School C)

School A Modules	School C Modules
Fuels Food Energy at home	Heating and lighting in home
Body mechanisms	Maintenance of the body
Health and hygiene	Health and hygiene Human chemistry
Transport Flight	Flight
Consumer science	
Paints and dyes	Colourful chemistry
Materials - Metals Glassmaking	Materials around the home
Plastics	Plastics
Fibres & Fabrics	
Pollution	Pollution
Cosmetics Electronics Sound Photography	
	Atmosphere and weather Astronomy Horticulture Laboratory skills

covered elsewhere in the programme, a science teacher said that he did not know exactly how, but commented that "we've got our module out first".

A small number of lessons concerned with some of the modules were observed by the research team (Table 15).

A brief description of the two lessons on food listed in Table 15 has already been given in Chapter 5. We shall refer later to the lessons on motor cycle safety and chromatography. Both courses were concerned to develop laboratory skills and these formed a specific module at school C and

Table 15:   Topics   Taught   in   the Science Lessons
Observed

Topic	School A	School C	Total
Food	2		2
Fuels	1		1
Motor cycle safety and Highway Code	2		2
Chromatography	2		2
Laboratory skills		1	1
Total	7	1	8

served as an introduction to the course as a whole.
The skills were developed through 20 experiments
involving such operations as mixing solutions,
using a thermometer and weighing, although it was
not expected that pupils would complete them all.
At school A the head of department had been given
a list of skills by a local firm which it expected
school leavers working at its laboratory benches to
have. His aim was to teach skills from the first
year onwards in order to emphasise craftsmanship in
the laboratory.

COLLABORATION   WITH   THE   REMEDIAL   EDUCATION
DEPARTMENT AT SCHOOL C

A unique feature of the course at C was the
collaboration between the science staff and those
from the remedial department. The idea for
collaboration pre-dated the EEC project although
the project was undoubtedly a significant influence
in bringing it to fruition. The initiative was
taken by the head of science who had become
increasingly aware that the traditional science
courses were failing to motivate the less able
pupils. He therefore sought the help of the head
of remedial education in planning a special course
for pupils of this type. The commencement of the
EEC project in 1978 provided the appropriate
context for doing this. The head of remedial

education was able to provide advice on teaching and presentation of materials. He also recommended more emphasis on practical work and pupil choice. Although the ideas for appropriate topics came, understandably, from the head of science, he indicated that the head of remedial education had also been able to suggest simpler experiments that pupils might do which he would not necessarily have thought of himself.

The head of remedial education commented that he welcomed this opportunity of helping colleagues to devise appropriate ways of presenting their materials. He felt it was also useful to have someone in the laboratory to help explain things to pupils and talk them through. In addition he was able to suggest alternative ways for pupils to record results, e.g. through the use of diagrams, by encouraging 'write-ups' in narrative form rather than in the traditional 'method/results' style. He considered that the technical content of the course presented no problems and that he was able "to take it in his stride". He had also been able to help in devising a course record system which ensured that assessments were made and recorded on a regular basis. This procedure was seen in use in a fourth year target group lesson on laboratory skills which we observed. At the start of the lesson pupils had their folders returned and looked at the marking of the previous piece of work. Pupils then began working on an experiment, either individually or in pairs, following instructions from a work sheet on which they recorded their observations. They then attempted to write a full account in their own words. This was discussed with the teacher and then copied up again, after corrections had been made, for insertion in their folders. After pupils' work had been marked the grade was entered on a task sheet. Grades were given against the group as a criterion rather than the whole year so there was a good number of A's and B+'s. As the teacher concerned remarked, this caused some difficulties when the work was submitted for CSE assessment when the grades had to be scaled down.

It was only the 'hard core' target group pupils, i.e. those taking the special modular course in the fourth and fifth year, who were taught by a member of the science staff and one of the two members of the remedial department. Thus in these groups, with two staff present, the teacher-pupil ratio could be as favourable as 7:1. The other groups, i.e. those taking the full modular course, were taught by science department staff only.

There is no doubt that this mode of collaboration was regarded favourably by science department staff. One teacher commented that the support of the remedial teacher was good and helped on the discipline side. It made it easier to correct pupils' work as they went along. He felt he had learnt useful techniques from his colleague for handling pupils and that the presence of a remedial teacher had effectively provided him with an in-service experience.

SEGREGATION OF TEACHING GROUPS BY SEX IN SCHOOL A

From the very beginning of the project it had been decided in school A to organise the course in two groups split by sex. There had been two main reasons for this decision. First, it was felt that the course content could be more precisely directed to the interests of pupils. Second, it was thought to create fewer discipline problems. In the teachers' view pupils seemed to be more secure in single sex groups and there had certainly been no indication of pupils wanting to work in mixed groups. In the first year of the project one group was taken by the head of science and the other by a male colleague.

In the second year the fourth year girls' group was taken by a female science teacher. Those beginning the course in the following year (1980/81) were initially taught as mixed groups and then split by sex after the autumn half term. Thereafter the boys were taught by the head of science and the girls by a female teacher. The head of department had decided to take the boys because there were more of them and they were potentially disruptive.

Although the split minimised disruption and bickering between the sexes, the disadvantage was that it could reinforce sex stereotyping since there was a tendency to pick out of the course that material which it was thought would interest one particular sex or the other. Fourth year target group girls apparently had one advantage in the first year of the project in that they went out on visits more often. This was the result of the teacher concerned being a mini bus driver.

In the middle of the third year of the project the head of department agreed to try the experiment of teaching the same topic separately to boys and girls with a researcher present observing the lessons. In fact two topics were chosen - motor cycle safety and the Highway Code with fourth year pupils and colouring agents in foodstuffs (using the technique of chromatography) with the fifth year groups. Examination of the detailed field notes produced on these lessons suggested that there were few differences in the way the teacher taught the topics according to whether the group was a boys' one or a girls' one - the same teaching sequence, questions and even jokes were followed. The only major difference was that in the chromatography lesson a different experiment was used for the girls because they had done the one used with the boys' group in an earlier lesson.

The really sharp contrast between the two groups was that the boys were potentially very difficult. The head of department, who was a very experienced teacher, admitted that he found them more difficult to handle than other groups. This was particularly so in a laboratory situation. "In ordinary lessons where they're glued to their seats there isn't the same opportunity to misbehave as in the lab." In talking of the group at the end of an earlier lesson he commented, "Some people feel that these kids are too clumsy and dangerous to work in a lab, but I feel that's even more reason why they should do it. They have very poor manipulative skills and so often they don't learn from their mistakes."

The organisation concerned with putting equipment out and away presented problems.

"I wish I didn't have to regiment them, lads of this age, but it's a major problem getting equipment organised with this size group and this size room." (The group size was 24 for the lesson referred to, and would be somewhat larger when all were present.)

In contrast he found the two groups of girls no problem to handle and he commented on the fact that they were so placid. He felt that he "could do a lot more advanced work" with such groups. In reflecting on the two lessons on motor cycles he felt that some of the questions he had asked did not seem as appropriate for the girls as for the boys and it made him realise how much prior knowledge he had assumed. "They didn't know what the basic things are, like a choke, throttle and so on." On the other hand, he was surprised that they seemed as interested as they did and some seemed to know a lot about motor cycles. He noted that even very timid girls were coming out with the right answers. The reason for this, he thought, was:

"In a big class of boys they'd have been lost in a corner - neglected I suppose ... In a boys' group the peer pressure is considerable and they (i.e. the girls) may have hidden it when they didn't know the terms. There's a lot of aggression. In the girls' group there's no aggression - they could easily admit it if they didn't know the terms."

However, it must be admitted, as the teacher recognised himself, that these differences might also be the result of having a much smaller group of girls than boys (both girls' groups had only nine pupils present for these two lessons) and one which probably contained the 'cream'.

The female science teacher who usually took the girls also agreed that it was better having the girls and boys separate. In her view, when they were mixed the girls used the boys. If they did not feel like doing an experiment they would let the boys do it for them. With a small group of girls she was able to give equipment to each of them and provide individual attention so they had to do the experiments. She also tended to keep those topics like cosmetics, which it was thought girls might find of particular interest, until the fifth year in order to try to keep attention and attendance up.

When the pupils were carrying out experiments in the chromatography lessons the researcher was able to ask each group of them working together what they thought about being taught separately by sex and why it was done. The majority of both boys and girls claimed that they preferred to be segregated and the remaider thought it was "all right" or "were not bothered" either way. There was no indication of anyone being opposed to the idea. The two sexes appeared to differ in the reasons they gave for segregation. The boys tended to justify it in terms of each sex preferring to do certain things which the others did not, e.g. "girls can do make-up 'n that and boys do motor bikes". Girls, on the other hand, tended to emphasise the point that boys cause trouble, e.g. "You don't have all the boys causing trouble with you - they call you names and all that." "I prefer it like this - I don't get stopped behind 'cos of them. It's a bit quieter."

These comments were consistent with the head of department's view that "some lads cause chaos when mixed with girls".

Pupils' views on this issue may, of course, simply reflect the justification for segregation that had been given to them by the teachers.

One interesting result of having a very small group of fifth year girls (due to absenteeism) noted by the head of department was that it had been possible to do photography with girls only and this had turned out to be a huge success. This he felt would have been difficult to do in a mixed sex group when they were all together in the dark room.

TEACHERS' ASSESSMENT OF THE COURSES

The head of science at school C, assessing his course towards the end of the spring term of the third year, considered that the EEC project had helped to establish a more experimental approach to science teaching for the less able. He felt the course would have taken longer to come into being without the funds which the project provided. He did consider, however, that it had been difficult to plan in advance. Because of the way funds had been allocated he had never felt quite sure until the last moment whether money would be forthcoming. He thought the course had been worthwhile and that pupils had benefited from the qualifications they had obtained. He was disappointed that not as many links had been established with industry as he would have liked. He felt that pupil motivation had fallen off though with the recognition of impending unemployment. Involvement with the remedial department had been particularly beneficial. He expected the course to carry on the following year with no major changes.

At school A the head of science, reviewing progress in the autumn term of the third year, commented that the opportunity of being involved in the EEC project had helped him to focus on particular problems and children. Project funds had represented something like a 10% addition to his normal capitation allowance and had enabled him to purchase appropriate equipment and materials. The main problem, as he saw it, was for the teacher to find the time to prepare appropriate materials. The extra teacher provided by the project had some effect on his course. It had released him for one week for course planning although another was needed to rewrite the course. In future he felt it would be better to concentrate resources more, e.g. to have some teachers on a half timetable to see what could be done when people really had the time. At the moment, he thought, teachers were being asked to revolutionise their curriculum with very little resources or time. The effect of one extra teacher in a school with a staff of 60 was so diluted as to be negligible.

As for the course itself he felt it was too school based. In common with his colleagues in school C he would have liked to have developed more visits and outside activities. The course was still based on traditional laboratory experiments just adapted slightly for target group pupils. Ideally he would have preferred to have tried a more open ended, problem solving approach, perhaps by providing "design opportunities". A dilemma was that such open ended situations needed more supervision given the potentially disruptive tendencies of some of the pupils. The course had not noticeably improved the generally poor attendance of the less able/motivated pupils. The attendance of boys had been reasonable (15 attending on average out of 25) but that of girls was less so (9 attending on average out of 25). He felt however that pupils would have "voted with their feet" more if the alternative had been a mode 3 CSE in one of the conventional sciences.

He tried to give pupils the idea that the course was specially developed for them by using phrases like "I think you'll be more suited to this course". It was very important in his view not to give the impression that pupils were on the course because they were no good at the other sciences. There was no mention, however, that it was a course associated with the EEC project and it was probable that pupils had never heard of the term.

He was particularly aware of the need to be careful of the language used, both in written form (e.g. work sheets) and in teacher talks, since "pupils don't know half of the words we assume they do." He had recently checked out with pupils if they knew the meaning of the word 'transport' and had got no coherent answer. In his view "If we believe that thinking is silent talking, if they can't talk about some things they probably don't have the words to think about them."

He considered that teacher commitment and job satisfaction were vital in dealing with pupils of the target group type. This needed senior and experienced teachers.

DISCUSSION

Teachers in the two schools were concerned to find ways of providing a more satisfactory experience of science for less able pupils than that offered by traditional single science courses oriented towards examination goals. The aim of both project courses was to maintain pupils' interest through a flexible laboratory based approach using a series of short modules which were relevant to their present and future lives. Although the content of the two courses was very similar they differed significantly in the way in which they were organised.

In school A teaching groups were organised on a separate sex basis. It was generally felt that this minimised disruption. The head of science mentioned two boys who were a particular nuisance in the class of a colleague "like a spark to a tinder box with the girls" but who were little trouble at all in the single sex science group. Despite this separation by sex the boys' group was somewhat over large in number (25 or so) and was potentially disruptive. "Keeping the lid on" such a number was not easy and required a high level of supervision and tightly organised laboratory routines. In the case of the girls, although this mode of organisation did not appear to ameliorate the high level of absenteeism, those that did attend probably gained from being in both a small group as well as a single sex one. Girls in mixed science lessons are often overawed by the presence of boys and may be reluctant to take an active part in the lesson (DES, 1980). At school A staff felt that girls often opted out of doing experiments, letting the boys do them and contenting themselves with watching and drawing pretty pictures. Working in separate groups may also have benefited the girls because the lessons could be directed more closely to their own experience. The danger is that the content of a course could become overly differentiated. The important point is not that the content should be different for girls than for boys but that teachers should take pains to ensure that they use examples from girls' experience whenever possible (DES, 1980).

Teachers also need to be sensitive to the fact that girls' experience may mean that they lack some of the basic concepts which are taken for granted where boys are concerned and that these may have to be directly taught. This will take time and it may be necessary to identify what the requisite precursor concepts are and teach these to girls prior to embarking on major parts of the course. This might be done at the beginning of the course and/or at convenient points during it. Whilst this provision is being made for the girls, the boys could be given special sessions dealing with those aspects in which they can encounter difficulties, e.g. working neatly, planning ahead, safety consciousness. These need not take place in the laboratory but could be done by discussion, classroom demonstration etc.

The HMI report on Girls and Science (DES, 1980) has recommended that school science departments should formulate a policy relating to girls and science. An essential prerequisite for doing this is that staff should be aware of the problems girls can face in science. One way of fostering that awareness might be for staff to carry out the kind of experiment that the head of science in school A did, i.e. to teach the same topic to a girls' group and to a boys' group. Even where classes are organised on the usual mixed sex basis a temporary reorganisation to make such experiments possible would not be difficult to effect.

The organisation of the science course in school C was based on the quite different principle of collaboration with the remedial department. Whilst it is not unknown for remedial teachers to act as a support to the teacher of English or mathematics in mixed ability classes it is rare indeed for this to happen in science. Collaboration in the planning of a science course and active involvement in the preparation of materials is perhaps rarer still. Science staff were convinced of the benefits of the partnership, not least of which was that it provided an informal in-service experience in the natural context of the classroom. The overall effect of providing two teachers for the 'hard core' target group was to boost the pupil teacher ratio very substantially and thus make possible a degree of personal attention which is uncommon in most laboratory situations. It could be that if the organisational strategies of both schools were combined, i.e. single sex groups and an improved pupil teacher ratio, as happened fortuitously at A in the case of girls because of high absenteeism, then more useful and interesting things could be done. Such a strategy would be one of double positive discrimination in favour of the less able and an attempt to eliminate some of the problems encountered by girls as opposed to boys in the learning of science.

Purely organisational initiatives are however not enough. They provide the framework within which the teacher acts but do not necessarily guarantee that the educational experience which pupils encounter is an appropriate one. Equipment and teaching materials need to be provided too. Although extra resources to enable these to be purchased can be, and indeed had been, found in a project of this kind it is also important to recognise that possibly the most important resource is teacher time. New courses can never be completely bought "off the peg" and this is particularly true when one has in mind the needs of the less able. Teachers are inevitably involved in creating new approaches and material and imaginatively adapting existing ones. The preparation of a course should be a creative task calling on the highest professionalism of the teacher. Like most creative work it requires a period of time away from the mundane but pressing demands of the day to day round. It is doubtful how far teachers can be creative in a situation in which they have to snatch little gobbets of time as and when they can. The provision of some extra staff resource is needed to allow teachers to have periods of 'release' from normal duties for curriculum development work.

The attachment of an extra teacher to each school for the duration of the project provided limited opportunity for this to happen. It did enable the head of science to be released at least for a short time (a week). However, it can be seen that the allocation of one extra teacher to a staff of 60 cannot make a great deal of difference within any one department. To make a really significant impact on curriculum development ways need to be found to make it possible for 'key' teachers to be released from normal teaching duties for more than one week in a year.

NOTES

1 Over 50% of the year group at C compared to approximately 30% at A.

2 Science for less academically motivated pupils. Published by the Association for Science Education (ASE).

Chapter 9

PUPIL RECORDS AND PUPIL SELF ASSESSMENT

A major priority which was identified early on in the project was the need to improve existing pupil assessment procedures and school record systems. An assessment working party, with representatives from all schools involved in the project, was established in the autumn term of 1978, and this resulted in a number of initiatives. The two main ones were the development and implementation of a new record system, and the adoption of the RPE (Record of Personal Experience) scheme of pupil self assessment. This chapter provides a brief evaluative account of each.

THE RECORD SYSTEM

The working party agreed that any new system should:

- be easy to maintain;
- be simple to update;
- be intelligible;
- contain information easily transferable to records and reports required by outside agencies;
- contain a continuous record of the pupil's academic progress, intellectual development, educational and career decisions and contributions to school;
- provide opportunities for the pupil to contribute to his/her own record and a basis for dialogue between pupil and teacher.

A record sheet system was then developed on the basis of these premises. Although the format was subsequently modified to some extent by each

143

school, a substantial common structure was retained which had the following contents:

- general information - name, date of birth, address, telephone number, date of entry, previous schools, details of parents or guardian, position in family, siblings, medical history with spaces for any special circumstances, date of leaving and destination;
- attendance and punctuality;
- academic potential - results of standardised tests etc., any referrals and outcomes;
- academic progress - grades for performance and effort in each subject for each year of the main school;
- a profile of basic skills and personal qualities;
- personal interests - to be completed by the pupil;
- career interests and placement;
- record of significant day to day incidents - behaviour, contact with parents.

The new record sheets were typed and duplicated at the central project office. Plastic file covers for the record sheets, and filing cabinets to hold them, were purchased from project funds.

The account[1] which follows is based on information obtained in each school by interviewing eight or nine staff particularly involved in using the system, and by examining a sample of the associated files. The interviewees included senior pastoral staff, the careers teacher, and form tutors. Since one school (C) had made considerable use of the extra part-time clerk appointed to the school as part of the support to the project, she was also interviewed.

Implementation of The System

Two of the three project schools (A and C) were able to introduce a new record system, based on the working party recommendations, throughout the main school. School A had already appointed a senior teacher with responsibility for assessment before the project began. In the first year of the project this teacher was allocated a half teaching timetable so that he could devote the rest of his time to setting up a new record system. The system was introduced in September 1979 for all pupils up to the fourth year, and in 1980/81 for the fifth. All told, it took about a term to get the new system operational. File sheets were put together in the introductory year by the three staff of the remedial department. In the following year the files for the new intake were assembled by staff in the school office.

In school C a decision had been taken as early as December 1978 to move to the new system and teachers passed notes through for recording in anticipation of adoption. These were held, and the physical introduction of the new files delayed, pending the appointment of a project funded clerk in January 1980. The installation of the new files was overseen by a senior member of the pastoral staff (who subsequently became an assistant head). The clerk put the files together and sorted out the volume of notes waiting to be filed and summarised on the record sheets. The first year was spent in catching up and getting the system operational. Once this was done the clerk felt that keeping the records up to date was not a particularly time consuming task. The process in the school relied almost totally on the clerk making the entries on the records - all information from staff was passed to her for recording. Clerical help in filling in the records was seen as essential, although the high dependence of school C on the project clerk did lead at least one form tutor to feel uninvolved in the process.

Teachers in school B felt that their existing system of keeping pupil records was working satisfactorily. However, during 1979-80 the fourth and fifth year tutors agreed to try a scheme based on the working party's recommendations. New records for S5 were introduced part way through the year, for target group pupils only. This involved copying on to the new files information already held on the old record. Little use, however, seems to have been made of the new records. In S4 the year tutor had attempted to incorporate the new system into the existing one for all pupils. She had maintained this system as pupils moved into S5, although most of the form teachers had been reluctant to contribute to the new record as it was not being introduced in other years. Teachers of remedial education did however fill in information in the new files for fourth and fifth year pupils in their department. Although attempts to introduce the new record system in other years had not met with success, they had led to useful staff discussion and senior staff had come to see the need for a unified approach to record keeping in the school. At the time of the interviews the four year tutors were meeting with the new headteacher to discuss the form this might take.

Teachers interviewed in schools A and C generally felt that the new system was working well and was an improvement on the old, being more flexible and more likely to store the information needed. Records were seen as most useful for fifth year pupils when references needed to be written; for other pupils at times of transition, e.g. at the end of the third year or when moving to a new tutor group; and when particular problems arose.

The physical location of the files to allow ready access to teachers was seen as a key issue. The ease or otherwise of inserting and extracting file sheets was an important consideration to teachers who had to do this for a whole form of pupils. Senior staff found it necessary to schedule the filling in of sections of the record at times when teachers were not already undertaking other administrative tasks, e.g. reports to parents.

Some Aspects of The Record System

Currently there is considerable interest nationally in pupil profiles and pupil self assessment (e.g. Balogh, 1982; OCEA, 1983). Since the new record system had two sections specifically related to these aspects, teachers' reactions to them will be briefly outlined.

The profile section of the record system consisted of a sheet which listed 22 skills and characteristics under the headings language skills, number skills, physical skills, mental skills and personal qualities. These could each be rated on an A to E scale for each year of the pupil's school career. Examples included speech, basic arithmetic, coordination, learning capacity and cooperativeness.

In school A some initial effort had been made to introduce this sheet, although it was felt that it was too complex, and the administration too time consuming and tedious. As a result the sheet had not been used. The assistant head in charge of the

record system felt that more thought needed to be
given to what was to be recorded and how it should
be assessed. The sheer practicalities of
collecting this type and amount of information
(presumably from several teachers) also presented
substantial problems. Remedial education staff in
school B however had more success and had modified
the sheet and used it with their pupils. They had
devised their own system of grades based either on
test scores or on a consensus amongst the three
teachers involved.

Work done on the development of profiles
elsehwere (e.g. SCRE, 1977) emphasises the
importance of agreed definitions both of the skills
to be rated and the associated levels of attainment
which are to receive particular grades. The staff
in the remedial department would appear to have
gone some way towards this approach.

The 'personal interest' sheet was designed to
be completed by pupils giving them opportunities
for recording their interests and activities both
in school and outside. In school A the sheets
could be completed in morning tutor time with
discussion if the group tutor so wished. In the
main, staff saw value in completing the sheet,
although this had not become normal practice for
older pupils. It was also thought not to be
effective for those pupils already resistant to
school. The personal interest sheet was one
practical outcome of the view held by senior staff
in school A that pupils should be more closely
involved in evaluating their own progress. School
A had also introduced a diary in which pupils were
asked to keep a record of their work, giving for
each subject a brief description of assignments,
their comments on them, marks or grades received,
any remarks made by the teacher, and their
reactions to them. Pupils were also encouraged to
make daily notes on work given and kept their own
weekly record of attendance and punctuality. After
piloting in 1980-81 the diary was reviewed and
revised with the aim of re-introducing it in S4
early in 1982. In school B the sheet had been
completed by some fifth year target group pupils in
1979-80. Form teachers in school C thought that
the use of the personal interest sheet had been
patchy - a few having used it with their pupils,
particularly when the new system was introduced.
Some fourth and fifth year forms had also discussed
the sheet in careers lessons when looking at what

they might mention in an interview or letter of application.

RPE

The second major initiative associated with the assessment working party was the adoption of the RPE scheme by two of the project schools. RPE, or the Record of Personal Experience, is a cumulative pupil record scheme devised by Don Stansbury (Stansbury 1976; 1980; Swales, 1979). The scheme is designed with the needs of 14-16 year old pupils, particularly the less able, in mind. Pupils are provided with a loose leaf file in which a personal record can be completed during the last two years in school. On leaving school the file becomes the pupil's own property and can be presented to prospective employers at job interviews. Records are made on loose leaf cards, each dealing with a different type of activity. All cards have a space on which an adult (teacher, parent etc.) can insert his/her signature indicating that the record (generally a brief description of the work or activity carried out) is true.

The record consists of three stages. In the first stage three cards must be completed: interest, work, and self chosen task. The second stage requires pupils to complete as many interest, work, and self chosen task cards as they like, and at least one of each of the following: attendance; craft; creative work; journey or visit; learning; physical activity; service to others; working with others. In the open stage pupils can make as many records as they require on cards which repeat the form of those previously used and also include some new ones. The rationale of the system requires that every item is freely chosen by pupils and the resulting records expressed in their own words.

RPE was incorporated into the project programmes of two schools (A and B). This section briefly summarises the experience of these two schools in using the scheme. It is based on information obtained from observational visits made to RPE sessions on several occasions throughout the project and semi-structured interviews with RPE tutors carried out in June 1980 and again in February and June 1981. In addition, in the interviews conducted with fifth year pupils in 1981 (cf. Chapter 10) it was possible to ask the small number who had taken RPE about their views of it.

RPE in Schools A and B

In both schools RPE was taken by about 40 pupils for one period per week in their fourth and fifth year. The pupils involved in school A were those in the two lowest mathematics sets (the period of RPE having been taken from the allocation for mathematics). In school B the pupils were all drawn from the remedial band and took RPE in place of one of the periods formally allocated for English. School A had sufficient staff available to ensure that each group of 40 pupils could be split into two separate groups each under the supervision of two tutors. This gave a staffing ratio of 10:1, which was considered to be desirable for this kind of activity. School B only had two staff involved (both assistant headteachers) and was not able to achieve such a favourable ratio. As a result groups were considered too large to handle effectively.

Tutors in both schools had found it difficult to get some of the pupils through the first stage of the system. The work and interest cards each required 30 hours of pupil commitment. One tutor remarked that the writing which was necesary could be somewhat repetitious and also implied skills of summarising which were often difficult for slow learners. One of the tutors in B considered that the self chosen task activity in the first stage gave a lot of difficulty and required a considerable amount of tutorial work (often from other staff). Tutors had found it necessary to modify the recommended procedures for using the system to make it work for their pupils, e.g. requiring pupils to build up notes in draft as they went along, rather than leaving all recording to be done at the end of the 30 hours; splitting up the package and dealing with it each sheet in turn rather than making it available as a whole.

Tutors considered that one of the main difficulties to overcome initially was to convince pupils that they had anything worthwhile to record.

Tutor   In the beginning they come in and say "I do nothing, so I've nothing to record." Very often when you get talking to them you find they've got all sorts that are worth recording and that give an insight into their personality.

Tutors in school A were generally pleased with their experience of using the scheme. This had prompted the decision to involve all fourth and fifth year pupils in keeping a diary (see above). At B the tutor who had originally initiated the scheme expressed some disappointment about how things had gone and felt that the scheme was too demanding for many remedial pupils. Poor pupil attendance was considered to be a major difficulty.

Tutor   Unless they come there's not much you can do. The stumbling block is the 30 hours they need to cover on work and interest. If they come you can push them - they do it as part of their homework so they have something to write about next week.

Tutors in school A reported that, because of the dire unemployment situation, they tended not to stress with pupils the value of the record to potential employers. The emphasis was on its use in helping pupils to assess themselves and to develop their personal qualities. Some pupils were keen to bring their record to prospective employers, and tutors undertook to contact them to explain the system if the pupils wished it. One tutor thought that the record helped in the interview situation but doubted whether employers understood its deeper significance.

Pupils' Views

The majority of the small sample of pupils we interviewed at A saw the sole purpose of RPE as being to provide them with something they could take to a job interview so that employers "can read what sort of person you are" and "to make ... an interview easier, more talking". While some pupils felt happy with this idea and were prepared to take their RPE work to interviews, a number had reservations about using their RPE files in this way: "I think it's boring", "you think, God, why do I want to take that to a job? If you're not going to take it to a job, it's a waste of time doing it." Because of their narrow perceptions of the rationale of RPE, those pupils who felt unwilling to take their file to interview could see no other point to the activity. When asked "Do you think you've learned anything from doing RPE? Do you think you've got anything out of it for yourself?" the majority answered no to both questions. Only one pupil spoke of RPE as encouraging him to spend more time on activities and get better at them. Two pupils not only did not see any point to RPE but had acquired strongly negative perceptions of it. One boy felt "it's like they're prying into your life ... it's just like somebody spying into your life"; and a girl said she "felt daft" doing RPE "'cos I think it's only dunces who have it ... I daren't take it round with me." She felt that to take her RPE folder to a job interview would "show them what you're like. Show 'em you're not that brainy."

Thus the broader rationale for RPE seemed generally absent from these pupils' accounts, so that where pupils were reluctant to take their work to job interviews this rendered RPE of little value in the eyes of the majority.

DISCUSSION

Two of the schools were successful in implementing the new record system throughout the main school. The fact that school B only achieved partial implementation may be a reflection of the fact that the EEC project as a whole was oriented exclusively towards less able pupils and not to the complete ability range as was the case for schools A and C. As a result the generality of staff in school B were probably less committed to the various aspects of the project than those in the other two schools.

The adoption of a new record system represents a major administrative and organisational task for any school. Undoubtedly an important factor in the success of the operation, especially in school C, was the help which the additional part-time clerk was able to give to such tasks as transferring existing records from the old to the new system. In A the presence of a senior member of staff with a specific remit for pupil assessment, and a lighter than average teaching commitment in the first year of the project, was probably a significant factor in the system's relatively speedy adoption in that school. Whilst relatively minor changes in the internal organisation of schools can be smoothly accomplished within the on-going programme, it is very difficult without extra resources for major fundamental changes to occur. Additional resources released within the school (e.g. extra staff preparation time as in A), and also provided externally, may well yield benefits out of all proportion to the relatively modest financial outlay involved.

A substantial part of most record systems consists of a series of brief entries, made once or twice yearly throughout each pupil's school career, which purport to describe specific abilities and attributes. Many of these are expressed in quantitative form as grades or marks. The ultimate source from which these are derived is the very much larger number of assessments teachers make of individual pupils and which are kept in their heads and mark books. The processes by which these many assessments are transformed into the relatively few global grades or descriptions required by the central record system are seldom explicated and are likely to vary substantially from department to department and from teacher to teacher (cf. Wilcox, 1982). The criteria on which the original source assessments were made may also vary from teacher to teacher even for those within the same department. Do two teachers, for example, in an English department mean the same thing when they award a grade A to pieces of creative writing?

In other words, pupil records represent the final outcome of the usually obscure practice and procedures of individual teachers which are ultimately more important than the system's formal contents. An acceptable and credible record system can only really be based on a school wide effort which seriously confronts the fundamental issues of assessment, i.e. the establishment of consensus on the criteria on which assessments are to be made and the methods by which they are to be aggregated and transformed. These issues were not considered directly either by the assessment working party or the project schools generally. However, senior staff in the schools were encouraged to attend a major course on assessment methods which was offered on two occasions during the life of the project as part of the LEA's programme of in-service education.

The existing literature on record systems and assessment has been largely influenced by the psychometric tradition. This has inevitably emphasised technique and obscured the fundamental purposes which institutional records serve. Winter reminds us that schools, as bureaucratic organisations, maintain files so that "management decisions can be based ... on documentary evidence (the files) which ... are presented as objective and factual; thus the decisions which emerge when the appropriate official consults the appropriate files are assumed to be as rational as possible and thus fully competent. However, this rationality and objectivity ... is in many ways spurious: the files are used to 'justify' management decisions, of course, but clearly they can never 'guarantee' that those decisions will be wise or humane, let alone the best ones under the circumstances. Bureaucratic files, then, can be considered sociologically as ways of 'legitimating' the exercise of power. A file is an attempt to create a version of the client of an institution in terms of the purposes of that institution. (In the case of a school) ... the contents of pupils' files can thus be seen as a build-up to the justification of an estimate of the market value of the pupil." (Winter, 1976, pp. 83-84). Those who might be sceptical of such an analysis should reflect on the fact that much of the impetus behind the current interest in profiles has come from employers seeking reliable methods of identifying pupils with those characteristics considered appropriate for the jobs they offer.

Giving pupils the opportunity of contributing to their own record, as RPE in a sense allows, is one way of ensuring that the definition of the 'ruled' by the 'rulers' is rendered a little less than complete. However, as long as such schemes are largely confined to a less able minority, they are unlikely to have anything other than a very marginal effect on the assessment and record system. Perhaps when schools have more experience of involving the totality of their own staff in a critical analysis of their management systems generally, they may then be sufficiently confident to involve others - governors, parents and perhaps pupils - in the same process. Until such time comes, existing record systems might usefully be subjected to the criterion of parsimony by limiting, as Winter (op. cit. p. 85) suggests, what is recorded on pupils to that which is clearly of direct use to the next teacher. To which might also be added "or the prospective employer".

The interest in alternative methods of assessment at 16+ has accelerated apace in the last couple of years. One particularly well publicised initiative in this field arose from discussions which took place in the summer of 1982 between the University of Oxford Delegacy of Local Examinations, the Oxfordshire Education Authority, and the University of Oxford Department of Educational Studies on the development of an assessment system which would be more relevant to pupils' needs than the present examination system. This venture has attracted the involvement of several other LEAs and has resulted in the intention of producing an Oxford Certificate of Educational Achievement (OCEA) to be operational from September 1987. The Certificate will consist of three parts - a pupil record/report, a record of external examinations and graded assessments in English, mathematics, science and modern languages (OCEA, 1983).

At the present time, however, well established examples of such alternative methods in schools are rare. In the case of pupil profiles, Balogh (1982) argues that merely grafting such systems on to an existing curriculum is unlikely to be successful. A more promising way forward may be along the kind of lines recommended by Burgess and Adams (1980) where appropriate methods of assessment (which could include profiles) would be developed around a curriculum in the last two years of secondary education which had been individually negotiated between pupil, parents and school.

NOTES

1   This section is an abbreviated version of a fuller report of a study carried out by Joan Garforth, Adviser (Research and Evaluation), City of Sheffield Education Department, which we gratefully acknowledge.

POSTSCRIPT: Since writing this chapter it has been learned that the new record system adopted at school C (described above) allows pupils to have access, under staff supervision, to their individual files.

154

Chapter 10

PUPILS' VIEWS

INTRODUCTION

In this chapter we examine some activities in the project schools through pupils' eyes. We postulate that pupils' perceptions of their schooling are not necessarily immature or aberrant versions of the true reality (i.e. that of the teachers?), but represent a rational attempt to interpret their experiences in terms of structures of meaning relevant to them. In this respect our work in this area follows the kind of approach adopted in a number of recent studies (Corrigan, 1979; Willis, 1977; Woods, 1976(a); Woods, 1976(b)), whereby pupils' views are taken seriously as providing a valid perspective on events and processes in schools. However while standing in this tradition, the work reported in this chapter has a somewhat different emphasis to that of earlier studies, focusing as it does not on aspects of the hidden curriculum and pupils' responses thereto, but on pupils' perceptions of innovations in the overt curriculum undertaken as part of the EEC project. This study thus provides a pupil perspective which can be considered alongside the perceptions of teachers and project staff in thinking about curriculum changes facilitated by the project. It provides an indication as to pupils' structures of meaning and reminds teachers and others that the reality of the classroom and school which we take so much for granted may be perceived in alternative ways. It also suggests hypotheses for possible action by providing teachers with feed-back on current practices.

Table 16: Interviews undertaken with Pupils and School Leavers in each year of the Project

Pupil year group	Project year		
	1 1978/79	2 1979/80	3 1980/81
fourth year	/	/	
fifth year	/ school C only	/ schools B and C only	/
post school		/	/

In undertaking this research into pupils' views our aim was to interview intensively small samples of young people in both their fourth and fifth years at school. It was decided to concentrate interviews on those pupils who were least likely to identify with the aims and values of the schools, i.e. those in the target groups. As Table 16 shows, interviews were undertaken with samples of fourth year pupils from the three project schools during 1978/79 and 1979/80. In the case of fifth year interviews it was not possible to involve pupils from all three schools until 1980/81.

In each case the planned samples reflected the sex ratio in the target group for that year in each school. We aimed to interview approximately 15% of the target group in each school each year. This corresponded in the cases where the three schools were involved to a total sample of around 35 pupils.

Because of our lack of prior knowledge of the ways in which less academic pupils think about school, the pupil interview schedules employed in this study were essentially skeletal, consisting of open-ended questions designed to encourage reflection on a number of broad themes. We also wanted to hear pupils' authentic views, uninfluenced as far as possible by the prior constructs of the researchers and it was hoped that this approach would maximise the possibility of tapping pupils' own interpretive structures whereby they order and manage their experience. Our use of loosely structured interviews and small samples, however, contrasts with much research in the transition from school to work field involving large scale studies using highly structured questionnaires or interview schedules (Sawdon et al, 1979; Fogelman, 1979; Williams and Gordon, 1976).

The sequence and form of questions used in the interviews were devised in the light of discussions between the research team and senior school staff. In this way agreement was reached on a substantial core of themes and related questions, together with a small number of questions that represented specific interests of individual schools.

Pupil interviews took place in the schools themselves, in locations chosen primarily because of their neutrality in comparison with other in-school sites, and their availability on the day of the interviews. Interviews were carried out by the two female members of the research team, each of whom generally dealt with the pupils from a particular school. Interviewers attempted to play a responsive role, being prepared to digress from the sequence of themes in the interview schedule to follow up pupil comments.

The earlier sessions (up to one and a half hours in length) were tape recorded and transcribed in full for subsequent analysis. Later in the project a shortage of secretarial resources necessitated that the 1981 fifth year interviews were tape recorded but only partially transcribed.

It was also hoped to interview in both 1980 and 1981 a 15% sample of the target group pupils who had left school the previous Easter or summer. Because of the difficulty of arranging meetings with young people after they had left school, however, the number interviewed was substantially smaller than intended. In both years, therefore, a postal questionnaire was used to supplement the interview data, thus bringing the number of young people in two samples (21, 19) to just over half of those we had originally hoped to contact.

The interviews which took place in 1980 were tape recorded and loosely structured around a series of open questions concerning young people's experiences in the labour market and their retrospective evaluation of careers work in school. In 1981, however, the interviews were redesigned around a narrower range of topics, using mostly closed questions, and researchers recorded the responses by hand during the interviews on a prepared schedule. Interviews were conducted either in the project offices or in a centre for unemployed young people, both of which were located in the city centre. The same postal questionnaire was used in both 1980 and 1981.

As a result of the richness of the data and the smallness of our samples, no attempt has been made to analyse pupil responses into sharp categories for quantitative treatment. Instead we have attempted to suggest the range of responses received and to highlight the issues raised.

Pupils' Views on Aspects of the Project Programme

Among the pupils interviewed in school we were particularly interested in the views of the 1980/81 fifth year sample (25 pupils)[1], these being the cohort to have experienced the most developed form of the courses making up the EEC programme over the whole of their final two years at school. In this account of pupil views of school, therefore, we have drawn particularly on the responses of this group, using them to check hypotheses suggested by the earlier interview data which had been made available to schools in several reports throughout the project. We have focused on pupils' perceptions of those core courses in the EEC programme, including careers education and what we call 'preparation for life'. The objectives of these courses have much in common, emphasising as they do the development of self awareness among young people and their preparation for life as young adults. We have also examined the large amount of information offered by pupils throughout the research concerning their perceptions of lessons, looking particularly at our later deliberate exploration of their experiences of 'good learning situations'.

'Preparation for Life'

During the life of the project efforts have been made in all three schools to develop courses in what might broadly be termed 'preparation for life'. Teacher papers relating to these courses in each school describe similar aims, e.g. to provide the "skills and facts" for young people to "lead a full and active life in modern society". Despite some similarity, these courses differed in several important respects. In school A, an attempt was made to develop a wholly integrated course, 'social education', as part of the core curriculum, taught throughout by a single teacher per group, and block timetabled for a half day a week. In contrast in school B the course 'life in the 80s' comprised 11 separate components (some of which were optional), which was taken primarily by less able pupils, was taught by a group of specialist teachers and was timetabled in single and double periods throughout the school week. Provision in school C consisted of two core courses 'preparation for adult life' (PAL) course, taught by a single teacher per group and timetabled with careers education for a half day a week, and a 'leisure options' course one afternoon a week, involving a variety of specialist staff. Differences between schools were also apparent in the degree of assessment undertaken. In school A 75% of the first cohort to complete the course were entered for CSE mode 3, whereas in schools B and C the courses were not examined for CSE. These differences between the courses appear to have substantial effects on pupils' perceptions of this part of their curriculum.

Courses such as these are new to most schools, lack a common title, have no clearly agreed body of content and usually cover a very wide range of material which is either not part of the school curriculum or else is taught under separate subject headings. What overall perceptions do pupils have of such eclectic courses?

We asked fifth year pupils "What is this social education/life in the 80s/PAL you do in the fourth and fifth year? What's it all about?" The range of pupil responses between schools was considerable. In school B where the least integrated course was taught, none of the pupils interviewed was familiar with the official title by which the course was known among staff, and some denied having done it at all until teachers' names were mentioned. Other pupils tended to refer separately to their own names for the various course components, including the mysterious "rotation". The most coherent accounts of the course were given by a few pupils in school A where

a fully integrated course was being developed,
e.g.:

"It's looking at community life and ... what you've
got to look forward to ... when you go out into
life."

"... It's when you're young, working your way up
to what'll happen when you get older."

Such relatively lucid accounts were extremely
rare however. The majority of young people in
schools A and C responded by mentioning two or
three specific topics covered in the courses,
introducing no linking concepts at all. For
example:

Pupil   We've done about papers, courts,
                 groups of people ...

Interviewer   Anything else?

Pupil   No.

That such a response was typical raises
questions as to whether the range of topics covered
falls into any pattern discernible to the majority
of target group pupils, and whether they are aware
of links between components of the courses or their
overall shape and structure. The indication is
that awareness in these areas is typically low
among the target group and that teachers should
therefore beware of assuming that the overall plan
of work being covered in these courses is
unproblematic and easily understood by pupils.
During our interviews we also asked pupils
about their perceptions of the <u>rationale</u>
underlying the courses. These courses were
designed to be overtly relevant to pupils who are
rapidly approaching school leaving age and young
adulthood. However, when we asked young people "Is
there anything you've done at school over the past
two years which you think will be particularly
helpful to you when you've left school?" not one
pupil cited these 'preparation for life' courses or
work done on them. This is not to say that such
courses will not be of value to young people in
adult life, but it does suggest something of
pupils' perceptions of what is useful or not at
school. The young people in our samples

interpreted the 'use value' of courses almost
exclusively in terms of their perceived helpfulness
in obtaining a job.

When we asked young people why they thought
they had to do such courses and what they saw as
the point of them, responses again varied between
schools. In school A, by half way through their
fifth year the substantial majority of pupils could
give a generalised justification for the course:
"It's to help you in the world."; "It's to help you
know about life, about government, how to go about
it." In school C, where this provision is in two
parts, PAL and leisure education, about half the
pupils interviewed could see no point to the PAL
course however: "I can't stand it, it's a waste of
time, they can't find 'owt else to do." Although
virtually all the pupils responded positively to
leisure education, some mistakenly thought that its
purpose was to give variety to school activities:
"To give us a break in our lessons." In school B
where 'life in the 80s' was taught, pupils had
little or no conception of the overall structure of
the course and could not comment on what might be
its rationale.

It seems then that for a considerable
percentage of the target group the rationale
underlying courses of this type is far from clear,
and difficulties in perceiving their broad
justification seem to be substantially greater when
courses are fragmented as opposed to integrated;
timetabled in small blocks throughout the week as
opposed to half day sessions; and when taught by a
variety of specialist teachers rather than a single
teacher per group.

In looking at pupils' perceptions of these
courses, however, one is struck by the occasional
instances in which they seem to have made a
substantial impact on the lives of individual
pupils. In rare cases pupils spoke at length and
with enthusiasm about the importance of the course
for them. In school C, for example, one girl
reported:

"I went to a nursery and they showed you how to
look after little children. At home I've got
little brothers and sisters and when my mum's
cooking she wants someone to look after them. When
I tell them stories they're right happy and my
mum's happy 'cos I'm getting them off her hands.
And sewing - we've got two sewing machines at home,

had them a long time, and my mother wants somebody to sew clothes and I'm very interested - it's helped me the sewing ... I never used to do anything before, you know, apart from watch television and sometimes clean up, and now I've got all sorts of things to do, can't sit down a minute."

Perhaps more intensive teacher exploration of ways of communicating structure and rationale might help pupils to gain a better grasp of such courses and their personal relevance, and to make active use more often of what is offered.

Finally we were interested to ascertain whether pupils were aware of the different teaching styles advocated by staff involved in these courses. In fact pupils demonstrated their sensitivity to, and ability to talk about, variations in the social atmosphere and relationships of school elsewhere in their interviews, and so were clearly aware of, and able to articulate, observations in this area. However, when asked "Is doing PAL/social education/life in the 80s different in any ways from doing other subjects?" very few pupils suggested that they perceived differences between these and other courses in this respect. The exception here was the 'leisure option' course in school C, a course which was exceptionally activity based, provides for much pupil choice and involves low levels of teacher supervision:

"All the time you know you're ruled by teachers. Leisure activities is the one time you know you can do what you like sometimes."

"It's not like other lessons. It's your own choice, isn't it?"

"You enjoy doing it ... you're with all your mates. In most lessons you're not with your mates, they separate you."

Possibly the impact of moves towards new teaching methods and styles in other courses is diminished where, as for example in school A, formal written work for CSE assessment was required. There may also be some hesitancy on the part of teachers to introduce new teaching styles because of personal unfamiliarity with such approaches or because of a wish for the course to be seen as 'respectable' and not a 'skive' for 'dummies'.

Careers

In our interviews throughout the project we asked fourth and fifth year pupils what they thought careers lessons "were all about" and what they saw as the point of these activities. We also explored in some detail the process of occupational choice among target group pupils looking as well at the issue of unemployment, their views on what the experience of unemployment might be like, reasons for unemployment, and how rising unemployment affected their perceptions of careers lessons.

Our interviews throughout the project suggest that a large majority of pupils see careers education as 'very important'.

However, when asked "What is this careers education: what's it all about?" most pupils' accounts were brief and hazy, indicating a poor recall of careers lessons: "We do about jobs and things." This appears contradictory. However, on exploration, it seems that nearly all pupils see the importance of careers lessons largely in terms of their use value immediately after leaving school, i.e. in helping to find and obtain a job. Notions of the broader educational rationales underlying careers education were almost wholly absent from pupils' accounts. This perhaps explains why, in contrast to careers lessons, interviews with the project careers officer were often remembered in detail, and why many pupils expressed a strong wish for more work experience.

When interviewed after they had left school, young people were just as likely to rate the careers education programme in retrospect 'helpful' or 'very helpful' as 'not very' or 'not at all helpful'. The particular parts of the programme which were reported as being helpful were again those of an instrumental nature e.g. information about different jobs, what to expect when starting work, how to apply for jobs and in particular how to write letters.

It appears then that little impact is made on pupils by those substantial aspects of a careers course which focus on the development of self and opportunity awareness and decision making skills (Watts and Herr, 1976) which are seen as part of a process ideally culminating in an appropriate occupational choice. This raises questions as to how pupils see themselves as arriving at job choices. In our interviews in 1979/80 we explored this area in some detail. By the summer term of the fourth year it appears that boys had in almost all cases made a firm commitment to a particular type of work, their choices being confirmed during interviews a year later. Among girls however such early decision making was somewhat less apparent. Our findings suggest that the provision of information about the range of jobs available and the exploration of personal interests and aptitudes might make more impact on pupil choices if provided earlier than it normally is. Starting careers education in the third year also makes good sense given that subject options are chosen at the end of that year.

Other differences between the sexes in the process of occupational choice also emerged during our interviews.

Whereas there seems to be a substantial commitment from the male members of a boy's family to introduce him to particular jobs and to provide fallback, safety net occupations which can be taken up if they fail to secure their first choice of job, it seems that parental interest and involvement in this process was less strong for girls. Boys glean most of the information about appropriate occupational opportunities open to them from their (working) fathers, male relatives and friends. Most of the girls' mothers, however, were working either full time in the home or part time in routine domestic or factory work. There was less congruence between the occupational aspirations of girls and their mothers' current experience of work than that between the aspirations of boys and their fathers' work activities. Also whereas occupation provides the major source of identity and status for men in our society, girls may see occupational choice as less personally important:

"(I wanted to go in the) Navy, but I'll just get a job, get married and have a family."

Lack of parental interest in their job choices may also therefore reflect a belief that girls' major life commitments are to getting married and

having a family, with a job being only a means of
filling in time until this is achieved.
    Because boys enlist more family support in
their job search and are encouraged to make
enquiries in the community, they acquire a
knowledge of the conventional labour market and
also of the local 'black economy'. Their access to
informal local job networks is facilitated by the
greater freedom allowed them from an early age by
their parents: "All the boys are out at night.
They don't worry about them, my mum and dad." They
have the opportunity to establish links in the
community, to become known and to get to know
people who can help them secure work:

"I think I'd get a job ... I know some place
where we could get some jobs, a bit bad but better
than nowt. Primitive things - having to take cars
to bits, working in scrapyards, helping to stack
things ... I get them through me mates. I've got
one that works at a garage round here, one owns a
scrapyard, someone's father owns a garage."

    Girls seem to have less access to such
networks. They are allowed less freedom than their
brothers and have little opportunity to develop
contacts with their local community which could aid
their job search. Perhaps careers officers and
careers teachers might therefore reconsider their
respective approaches to take account of the
different situations in which girls find
themselves. Given current rapid technological
changes and rising unemployment, however,
professionals also need to take into account the
now diminishing efficacy of the family and informal
contacts until recently heavily relied upon by
boys. It may well be that careers education in
school will assume an increasingly crucial role for
both girls and boys as it becomes apparent that
parents and others lack influence and information
to help young people in this radically altered
situation.
    Increasing levels of unemployment raise
important questions concerning the appropriate
content of careers courses and their rationale.
Among some pupils it seems that awareness of the
possibility of unemployment is heightening their
view of careers lessons as being 'important'. Most
pupils seem to envisage only two possible responses
to the situation of not having a job however. The

165

first is to try to find work by frenetically
ransacking all the job sources open to them: the
second is to take any job available. While job
choice thus becomes an unrealistic concept for many
pupils, the acquisition of a job assumes paramount
importance and the components of a careers course
which focus on job search and acquisition are
therefore viewed as of over-riding significance.

Only a very small minority of pupils in
interviews later in the project had begun to
question these responses to unemployment,
expressing dissatisfaction with current provision:

"... but they teach you one minute that you're not
going to be able to get a job likely, and next
thing they say they put your hopes up ... I'm not
bothered about getting a job now 'cos I know I'm
not going to get one 'cos there's nowt going, no
job ... nowt that I'm interested in anyway."

Unemployment is seen by the very large
majority of pupils as a negative experience: they
expect that it would involve being "bored, idle,
fed-up; horrible when you're sat about not doing
'owt." Pupils were also aware of the importance of
obtaining employment as a way of achieving adult
status: unemployment indicates a failure to "get on
my own two feet". Pupils could apparently be
strongly influenced by parental feelings about
claiming 'dole': "None of our family have ever
been on the dole. You know we've been brought up
to work and if it comes to that I don't know what
I'll do." Pupils seemed to have almost no concept
of the broad economic and political issues
associated with rising unemployment, but felt that
reasons why they might not find work were grounded
in their own personal inadequacies and failures -
for example, not having enough educational
qualifications. Throughout, pupil comments about
the possibility of unemployment were redolent with
expressions of shame. It was also notable that
pupils had little clear or accurate idea of the
nature and function of schemes operating under the
government's Youth Opportunities Programme.

Regrettably some of the pupils interviewed
after they had left school had in fact experienced
unemployment. Their responses indicated that while
being unemployed during the first summer after
leaving school could be positively enjoyable, once
friends returned to school, began jobs or took up

places in further education and winter came, the honeymoon was over.

Pupil 1   I just were fed up really. Being at home all the time, nowhere to go, no-one to go with.

Pupil 2   It starts bugging you. It's having no money, it gets you down.

Pupil 3   It gets you mad - they're somewhere, but you can't find 'em.

Pupil 4   It's boring, you get pressured by your parents.

Pupil 5   Embarrassed. Disappointed when you don't hear from firms.

This selection of quotations from young people talking about their experiences of unemployment indicates the variety of factors underlying the overall negative impact: frustration of personal efforts to find a job; social isolation; lack of purposeful activity; social stigma and pressure from parents; lack of money.

Of those interviewed in 1981, four out of the six young people who had been unemployed for over a month could not remember having a good talk with anyone about what it was like being unemployed. One of the remaining young people had talked to a careers officer but "It didn't help really." Only one reported having had a good talk about being unemployed and feeling it had helped. Latterly, however, in all three project schools an effort had been made to incorporate some coverage of unemployment as part of their careers programmes.

Good Learning Situations for Low Attainment Pupils

Throughout our research, interviews with pupils have yielded a wealth of information about the ways in which young people who have been low attainers at school view lessons. In later interviews we attempted to explore explicitly with pupils both what they meant when they said that they liked or disliked a particular lesson, and what they perceived to be good learning situations for them. A number of interesting areas of consensus between pupils emerged.

In talking about lessons they disliked it was apparent that they often lacked a rationale for the activities involved:

Pupil   'Cos like once we were writing about newspapers, how many pages they've got and that. That's boring.

Interviewer Why is it so boring?

Pupil   What's the point of counting how many pages in the newspapers?

Pupils commonly described a particular lesson as "boring" and when questioned about their dislike of it said that they could not see the point of it. In particular pupils seemed to judge the usefulness of lessons solely in terms of their value in the job market.

"... You could get a job if you're good at woodwork ... as an apprentice. Same wi' metalwork ... but yer can't wi' English 'n that, it just gets you bored."

Other frequently cited factors which pupils described as accounting for their like or dislike of lessons may be grouped under the heading 'teacher style'. Pupils seemed to attach considerable value to teachers who were willing to talk to them on a friendly level: "You can talk to Mr. (-) like he were anybody, like he were a friend."; "You get on right well wi' 'im, have a right good conversation." This was contrasted with the teacher who "shouts at all of 'em half the time" and those who "think they own you, telling you what to do." A teacher's ability to maintain some discipline without imposing excessive restrictions was also appreciated, and in particular many fourth year pupils commented on the usefulness as well as the enjoyment of talking with friends while they worked: "You know, you can have a laugh when you're doing your work ... he makes you work, 'n you can talk 'n everything, but you're working 'n you're learning ... he's really good he is." In interviews with fifth year pupils preferences were also expressed for teaching methods which emphasised discussion and small group work, no objections being made to mixed sex groups even for subjects such as sex education.[2] As in

other studies of pupils' views a substantial number
talked about the importance of teachers who "really
explained things" as compared to those who "just
tell you to get on with it". Some pupils also much
preferred lessons in which teachers allowed an
element of pupil choice of both topics and pace of
work.

The comments on lessons summarised above thus
indicate broad agreement in some areas as to
variables under teachers' or school control which
are important to pupils and influence whether they
express like or dislike of particular lessons.
Such information may assist efforts to increase
pupil attendance since a reason frequently given
for "wagging it" is to avoid particular lessons.
However, while pupils' liking of a lesson is
important if they are not to 'vote with their
feet', it does not necessarily indicate that the
classroom is acting as an effective place of pupil
work and learning. Pupils' liking of some lessons
may reflect no more than their enjoyable social
atmosphere, rather than their quality as good
<u>learning</u> situations (see Woods, 1979, pp. 31-38).
We have therefore tried also to focus on those
factors which pupils feel have helped them work and
learn well.

Pupils interviewed in 1980 and 1981 were asked
if they could remember times when they felt they
had learned something really well. Most of those
interviewed were able to cite at least one
instance, and several gave two or three examples
including both subjects learned at school and the
learning of hobbies and skills outside school. In
exploring with pupils factors which they felt had
helped them to learn well on these occasions, a
recurring theme was the importance of pupils being
interested in and perhaps having chosen to learn in
the area concerned:

"'Cos it's summat that you <u>want</u> to learn, you got
a choice, you can pick any hobby you like, you're
learning it 'cos you want to learn it: it goes into
your head and you remember things."

Teacher activities that were found to be
helpful were explanation, demonstration and the
providing of opportunities for pupils to practise
on their own while still having access to someone
who could help them.

"They showed it you, told you how to do it, let you have a go and if you got it wrong they showed you again and told you how to do it again."

Learning by watching others perform skills need not necessarily involve a teacher, however: "I were mad on football ... going to matches, looking at players on't pitch - how they place the ball, how they control the ball." Pupils also suggested that in the good learning situations they were describing they had been able to choose their own pace of working: "He didn't push you, used to give you your own time to do it in." A final factor mentioned by pupils was the helpfulness of a teacher's friendliness, good humour and ability to give confidence and encouragement.

In another part of our interviews we also explored further with pupils the effect on the learning situation of being with friends. Fourth year pupils had expressed strong preferences for being with friends, finding it "more enjoyable", "a friendly atmosphere". When these pupils were put in classes where they had no friends (either because they were split into unfamiliar groups to do their chosen options, or for disciplinary reasons) it was "torture", there was "no-one to talk to", and they got "fed up" and "all on edge". But does this social element in the classroom influence the effectiveness of the learning situation? Some fourth year pupils strongly felt that it did:

"You say you do better work, but t' teachers don't. You think you get on with things quicker because yer can ask 'em 'Oh how do you spell so and so?' without feeling ashamed, or if you're sat next to somebody you don't know you don't like to ask them 'Oh how do you spell that?' or they think hey we've got a daft 'n here, 'n you'll have to sit there for about five minutes puzzling it out."

"They can talk to you and they can help you if you're having a bit of a struggle and you're ... like a sum or summat, they can help ... tell you how to do it."

It may be that with more academic or highly motivated pupils a strong argument can be made in favour of pupils having to sit alone and puzzle out difficulties encountered in their work for themselves. Perhaps with less academic pupils, however, access to help from friends "without feeling ashamed" may reduce the tendency for pupils to give up more difficult pieces of work before they are completed. Peer support may be a useful supplement to the teacher's resources in classes where pupils need a lot of individual attention, and help to maintain their concentration and interest.

DISCUSSION

We can summarise much of what has been said above in terms of three propositions:

Proposition 1: That parents of target group pupils still exert a major influence on the educational views and behaviour of their children.

Proposition 2: That pupils of the target group type may work better where a more permissive atmosphere or regime pertains than that which is typically encountered in the secondary school.

Proposition 3: That effective pupil learning is based on the extent to which pupils understand the rationale of the courses they take.

Whilst parental influence was clearly apparent early on in our research into pupils' views on the value of school, later interviews widened our perceptions to incorporate the significance of family and neighbourhood influences on pupils' career choice, job acquisition and attitudes to unemployment. It was found that amongst boys in particular, commitment to a particular type of job had frequently been made, with the advice and help of father and male relatives and friends, by the end of their fourth year at school. Such an early job choice structures the development of an adult identity congruent with the expectations of family and community - providing a means of acquiring 'nomos' or a sense of order and predictability to life (Roberts, 1980). However, in the fourth year, careers education generally focuses on the development of pupil strategies for making a reasoned assessment of their abilities and skills in relation to job choice. It is not usually until the fifth year that careers staff concentrate on 'hard' job information, encouraging pupils to make a firm choice of occupation. It is perhaps this misalignment that may help to explain why pupils rarely cite school influence as important in determining job choice and it suggests that a case can be made for introducing careers education in the third year.

The research adds to our knowledge of how girls are disadvantaged in the job stakes. Not only do girls seem to receive less parental support in the process of job choice than boys, they also do not have access to informal job networks comparable to those available to boys.

However, given technological changes and rising unemployment notions of job 'choice', whether based on information from family and community or school sources, and perhaps even initiative in job search activities may become less relevant. Of those interviewed in 1980 and 1981 after leaving school none of the girls in our sample and only one boy were actually in the occupation to which they had aspired while at school. It may no longer be valid therefore in careers education to put such a substantial emphasis on job choice and job acquisition skills.

It is now well recognised that periods of unemployment are likely to be among the experience of a large majority of young people in their first year after leaving school. This suggests that some preparation for unemployment has a valid place in careers education programmes. Pupils' views about unemployment and the unemployed, again strongly reflecting parental attitudes, indicate areas on which such preparation might focus. Watts (1978) in a seminal paper has put forward a set of suggested curriculum objectives relating to unemployment. These objectives may be usefully recast into an alternative formulation focusing on an individual's perceptions of the <u>causes</u> of unemployment and his or her anticipated <u>responses</u> to it.

As for <u>causes</u>, unemployment may be attributed to personal inadequacy and failure (e.g. lack of right qualifications, idleness, ineffective job search techniques), or to social and political factors outside the control of the individual. Now although both factors may account for a particular case of unemployment, the pupils in our sample clearly inclined to the former 'cause' rather than the latter. Young people who concur with parental and community views of the unemployed as "lazy", "layabouts" and "scroungers" may thus face <u>self</u> blame if they become unemployed. They are also likely to experience stigma and blame from their peers, many of whom also explain unemployment in terms of personal factors. Young people seem to have little understanding of the economic and political issues associated with rising unemployment. In part such incomplete perceptions are reinforced by teachers' continued emphasis on the importance of exams and school work for success in the job market. Such an emphasis seems less appropriate given the dramatic shrinking of job opportunities and the findings of a number of studies (i.e. Ashton and Maguire, 1980) which suggest, at least for the jobs which many pupils are likely to enter, employers put most emphasis on <u>non academic</u> criteria. Emphasis on examination performance and school work implies a <u>personal</u> responsibility for unemployment which needs to be balanced by education about those factors beyond the control of the individual which are also contributing to the likelihood of unemployment.

The <u>responses</u> which an individual might make at the prospect of being unemployed include:

1. developing job search and acquisition skills;
2. seeking jobs other than those which would initially be considered;
3. seeking jobs beyond the locality and perhaps away from home;
4. seeking to create self employment;
5. making increased use of leisure time whilst unemployed;
6. seeking official alternatives to employment and unemployment;
7. developing skills to cope with being unemployed.

Pupils' comments suggest that their responses to being unemployed would be enhanced job seeking and the willingness to take any job (1 and 2 above). There was no indication that pupils would contemplate either seeking jobs outside their own locality or away from home (3) or creating their own employment (4). Although the former may only be an appropriate option for a small proportion of pupils, perhaps thought ought to be given to preparing for such an eventuality. Probably many teachers would not see self employment as a realistic possibility for less academically motivated pupils such as the ones considered here. It may be that some such pupils do have latent entrepreneurial skills however, which could find an outlet in a range of service jobs in the community. Pupils characterised unemployment as a time of boredom and idleness. This suggests that the constructive use of leisure (5) may be of paramount importance when the individual is out of work. The vague idea that pupils had of the various government schemes (6) is also of concern and suggests that visits to such schemes might be included in careers education programmes. People who become unemployed ultimately have to learn to cope with it themselves (7) but contributions in careers programmes may help to make such coping something other than an unpredictable and distressing process of self discovery.

Our second proposition concerns an examination of classroom organisation and styles of working in an effort to identify effective learning situations for target group pupils. In our interviews, pupils identified the social relationships within classrooms as being of particular importance to their enjoyment of lessons and their ability to learn effectively from them. As has been found in other studies, they favoured friendly relationships with teachers in which the latter are willing to take time to talk with pupils individually and give careful explanations. Fourth year pupils especially also stressed the importance of working within friendship groups and having the freedom to talk with their peers while working. This suggests that schools might exploit more consciously the friendship group as the context for effective classroom activity. This may well mean however that teachers should be prepared to accept more readily certain consequences of social groupings, e.g. talking informally, joking etc. rather than assuming that they are inappropriate for, and potentially disruptive of, the learning situation.

There is no doubt that many pupils find the 'fairly quiet' atmosphere and apparent passivity of the classroom difficult to sustain. This study, like others, has shown the importance to pupils of "having a laugh" (e.g. Woods, 1976(b)). Several factors suggest that pupils' views about classroom method merit consideration. With less academic, perhaps less motivated pupils, some enjoyment of lessons may be a prerequisite for their attendance. Perhaps by giving attention to factors contributing to pupils' liking of lessons, absence rates may be reduced. Pupils' liking of lessons may contribute to a building of goodwill between teachers and pupils. Also organising lessons in such a way that pupils can help each other may assist less academic pupils who need extra attention and help. The friendship group may be actively employed as a supplement to the resources of the teacher.

As well as stressing the importance of social elements in classroom learning, pupils also reported enjoying class discussion as a teaching method, opportunities to choose topics of work, and situations in which pupils could choose their own pace of work. This type of classroom approach together with friendly, personal relationships with teachers would give young people opportunity to express their views, develop their skills in decision making and organising their time, and perhaps provide new experiences of relating to adults in authority. The development of such skills seem essential if pupils are to participate actively in school and post school life.

Our final proposition suggests that effective pupil learning is based upon the extent to which pupils understand the rationale of the courses they take. It emerged during our interviews that some pupils can see little reason for attending school at all. Others are confused by the implications of rising unemployment since it conflicts with their belief that the major, and perhaps only, purpose of school is to help them get a job. Many pupils are unclear as to the relevance of lessons not directly related to their choice of job, and most seem confused by the complex structure of some courses. A repeated theme throughout our interviews with pupils was a widespread discrepancy between teachers and pupils in their ideas about the purposes of the courses in which they were jointly engaged, pupils occasionally apparently lacking any rationale for some school activities. For example, the majority of pupils did not perceive 'preparation for life' type courses as being of direct use in obtaining a job, and hence reported seeing no point in them. This is especially poignant given that such courses are designed to be relevant to young people approaching adulthood, in their personal, social, and their working lives. These courses are also notable for their eclectic nature and complex structure. It seems that as well as having little or no grasp of the rationale of these courses, many pupils' awareness of the overall structure, pattern of topics, and links between different parts of the course is very low.

Ausubel's (1963) views on learning processes provide some useful insights as to how the rationale and structure of courses may be effectively communicated. He recommends the use of 'advance organisers' as a way of improving instructional effectiveness. Organisers are devices which give the learner a general overview of material in advance of actually encountering it and provide an aid to organising its conceptual content. Whilst Ausubel's ideas are particularly helpful in aiding the structuring of specific aspects of learning, it can also be argued that they are relevant to the task of developing pupils' understanding of the relationship between topics of a whole course. Organisers for this purpose might consist of short descriptions (perhaps a modified version of the syllabus) which indicate the relevance of each topic to be covered to the broad aims of the course and the inter-relations between topics. These would be given to pupils before a course begins. They might also, and perhaps more appropriately, be represented in other ways as charts, diagrams etc. It is likely too that, given high absence rates, pupils would benefit from reminders of the overall structure at key points during the course.

NOTES

[1] Due to the high levels of absence of target group pupils the samples actually interviewed were somewhat smaller than planned (approximately 10% of the target group rather than the 15% intended).

[2] The exception here was in the science course in school A, where single sex grouping occurred which pupils strongly supported (cf. Chapter 8).

Chapter 11

ABSENTEEISM

The main purpose of the project was "to
improve the preparation for adult/working life of
low achievers during the last two years of
compulsory education". We have already seen that
although all three project schools identified a low
achiever/low motivated target group, two of them
(A, C) made much of the project programme available
to all pupils. Schools differed in the criteria
which they used for designating their target
groups, and in the proportion of the year groups
which these represented. There was no guarantee,
in the absence of common objective measures, e.g.
test scores, that the target groups were broadly
comparable from school to school. Therefore, in
describing the development and effects of the
project, it is necessary to consider the year
groups as a whole as well as, where appropriate,
the identified target groups.
    If the project programmes were to help to
prepare pupils for adult/working life an essential
prerequisite was that pupils should be present in
school to experience them. However, this was a
major problem since a substantial proportion of all
pupils attended school irregularly. The first part
of this chapter examines the extent of absenteeism
across the project schools and the attempt to deal
with it by means of extra education social work
support.
    Pupil absenteeism is a perennial concern of
schools and one which was particularly highlighted
in the context of the project. In a survey of
fifth year pupils carried out in 1977, the year
before the project began, the three project schools
(A, B, C) were in the group of six schools with the
lowest average attendance (i.e. < 80%). The

associate school (D) had a slightly higher average
(82%) but was still amongst the 10 schools in the
LEA with the poorest attendance.

One of the objectives of the project was "to
help to ameliorate problems of persistent truancy
and absenteeism". It was hoped that the project
programme generally would be considered by pupils
to be of particular interest and relevance and thus
increase their willingness to attend school. In
addition, and more specifically, an education
social worker (ESW) was appointed to work
intensively with those pupils in the project
schools who presented the most severe instances of
non-attendance. This section describes then how
the project ESW developed his role and examines
some data relevant to attendance patterns in the
schools over the three years 1978/79 to 1980/81.

THE ROLE OF THE EDUCATION SOCIAL WORKER (ESW)

Education social work is the main support
service in an LEA with specific responsibility for
dealing with cases of poor school attendance.

Each of the three project schools, like all
schools in the LEA, had its own particular ESW. In
addition the project ESW had the task of developing
new ways of cooperating with teachers and parents
in these schools on matters of attendance and pupil
welfare generally. The description which now
follows of how this role developed is mainly based
on interviews carried out with the ESW and, to a
lesser extent, with teachers over the duration of
the project.

During the first year of the project (1978/79)
the ESW spent the equivalent of a day or so in each
of the three schools [1] and had a total fourth year
case load of 63 pupils. The main difficulty
experienced arose from the difficulties which
existed between the ESW's view of his role and the
expectations of the teachers. The ESW felt that
school staff rated the 'school bobby' aspect of his
role, i.e. getting children back into school, as
the most important. In his view, school attendance
was an important problem - but one amongst several
where pupils and parents were concerned.

At the end of the summer term it was decided
that the ESW would work in only one of the schools
(C) for the second year of the project. The idea
was that he would work intensively with a smaller
case load than previously so as to have more

opportunity to concern himself with a greater range
of pupil and parental problems and to identify ways
in which the pupil's situation in school could be
improved.

The ESW's case load for the year consisted of
45 pupils from 35 families. Pupils were drawn from
the fourth and fifth year target groups and, in the
case of a small number of third years, from those
pupils who were seen as potentially 'target group'
for the following year. Since the ESW's way of
working was essentially family oriented, his case
load also contained some younger siblings in the
first and second years. The breakdown of the total
case load, which was approximately evenly balanced
by sex, was as follows:

fifth year	23
fourth year	15
third year	5
second year	1
first year	1
	—
45 pupils	

A case load of 45 pupils represented
approximately one third of the normal commitment of
an ESW. The composition of the case load was
agreed after consultation with the head and senior
pastoral staff. The ESW considered that 80% of the
group were poor attenders although most had
behavioural problems as well, and some had
difficulties associated with home.

The ESW spent the greater part of his time
either in school or visiting homes and considered
that an important part of his work was getting to
know the children well so that, amongst other
things, "one can distinguish truth from lies". In
addition to informal contact with pupils, he was
able to sit in on some of the classes and also
participate in residential trips made by target
group pupils.

The ESW considered that parents were surprised
that he was prepared to take time off to chat and
to accompany pupils on school trips. This he felt
had probably helped to improve the relationship
with parents and increase trust. In his home
visits, the ESW was inevitably involved with

parents in other matters, e.g. giving advice on welfare benefits, behaviour problems, marital difficulties etc.

The school's normal ESW had a case load separate, of course, from that of the project ESW. However, there was a regular exchange of information between the two, and the project ESW was able, when necessary, to deal with the other's cases in her absence.

The ESW was able to identify several successes achieved during the year. These included greater contact and exchange of information with staff, more intensive work with pupils and the collation of more information on them for school uses (oral reports having been the norm in the past). He also felt he had a clearer perception of what was happening all the time and with whom he was working. Furthermore, having a smaller case load and area to cover than was normal meant that he had been able to make more visits. He felt that the duration of individual absences had diminished as a result of the enhanced opportunity to go out immediately and investigate particular cases. The process of bringing parents and teachers together to discuss cases where children had been excluded from school had been expedited. The ESW had been able to see parents beforehand, represent them in such situations and make them feel more comfortable in the presence of teachers.

The ESW identified several activities in which he had been involved which he considered to be relatively novel. Participation in residential situations was one such role which he thought had great value. He also welcomed the opportunity, not normally accorded to ESWs, of sitting in on lessons. Joint visits with the project careers officer (cf. chapter 4) had also proved to be beneficial and capable, in his view, of being developed further.

The opportunity of going into a school and being able to negotiate and define both a <u>role</u> and a <u>case load</u> was rare but one which recognised the professionalism of the ESW service. Another opportunity which the project gave him was to attend court with pupils who were in trouble <u>generally</u> and be able to "speak up for them" there.

For the third year of the project it was decided that the ESW should work exclusively in school A. Initially it was suggested, primarily on

the headteacher's instigation, that he should work
with the whole of the third year as a case load on
the assumption that this would give a firm
grounding for improved attendance when the pupils
reached the fourth and fifth years. The ESW felt
that this would be too large a case load and
subsequently a more manageable group of 29 pupils
and their families was agreed with the third year
tutor.

During the year the ESW was in the school for
some part of every working day, often twice a day,
and was able to discuss up to the minute situations
with the staff. He was also available at break
times in the staff room for general consultations.
He was invited to attend the welfare meetings held
by the school's pastoral care staff and found these
very helpful.

Although contact with the project careers
officer was less frequent than in the previous
year, he was able to work with her in the placement
of leavers on the work experience scheme for
unemployed teenagers. Other activities included
meeting small groups of children at lunch and break
times, and also after school and at weekends.

The ESW and the year tutor also spent some
time designing a new system for referring cases
from group tutor to year tutor and thence to ESW,
and also an 'early warning system' to inform
parents about poor attendance. The latter was
brought into operation in the following year when
the ESW worked with the same group of pupils, then
in their fourth year. The scheme involved three
types of letter. The first was a very informal
general enquiry letter. If this produced no
response, then the two follow up letters were sent.
These were couched in rather more formal terms
reminding parents of their legal responsibilities.
The result of this kind of approach was improved
contact with parents, especially with those who
would normally "have been content to give excuses
to the school bobby".

Also during this final year the ESW took part
in the fourth year sociology course, participating
in group discussions with pupils. This, he felt,
enabled him to develop a deeper understanding of
the pupils while at the same time giving them a
"broader and improved image of me and my work".

Summarising then, it would seem that over the
duration of the project he was able to develop a
role somewhat different from the usual one of an

ESW. The distinctive features were a case load which was much smaller than normal; selected in conjunction with senior school staff; and oriented towards families rather than exclusively towards individuals and therefore more in line with a generic social work approach. As a result he was able to work more intensively than usual with pupils, parents and other professionals, and to develop more effective follow up methods for pupils potentially at risk or already with well established absentee patterns. Contact and communication with teachers in schools and between school and home were also thought to have improved. Finally, better social relationships had been forged with pupils as a result of participating with them in a range of formal and informal situations.

ABSENTEEISM DATA FROM THE PROJECT SCHOOLS

At the beginning of the project, teachers and others expressed a need for information about the extent of pupil absenteeism in the project schools. As a result, the research team carried out an analysis of fourth and fifth year attendance registers in the three project schools for the autumn term of 1978/79. This analysis was later extended to cover the spring and summer terms of that year. Reports of these analyses were circulated to project schools where they aroused considerable interest. The exercise was repeated in the second year of the project for school C only (largely because it was the school in which the project ESW was working) and again in the third year (1980/81) for all three schools.
Table 17 summarises the attendance at the three project schools and also includes results from the fifth year survey carried out in 1977/78 referred to earlier. As can be seen, both fourth and fifth year attendance at school C was generally very much better than at the other two schools. The better overall performance of school C might be related to the size of the school - school C being very much smaller than the other two. In larger schools it is probably easier to be absent without attracting the attention of the staff and far harder to have good communication with parents and, therefore, more difficult to follow up cases of absenteeism. It should also be noted however that the catchment areas on which the schools drew were

Table 17: Comparison of Absence at the Three Project Schools

(a) Fourth Year

School	% absence			
	1977/78	1978/79	1979/80	1980/81
A	not available	24.6	not available	20.6
B	not available	28.5	not available	19.8
C	not available	16.2	13.3	9.6

(b) Fifth Year

School	% absence			
	1977/78	1978/79	1979/80	1980/81
A	32.0	34.3	not available	25.9
B	32.0	34.9	not available	33.6
C	27.0	15.8	16.4	11.3

almost certainly not equally disadvantaged. The indications (from such measures as proportions of pupils taking free school meals) were that school C had the more favourable catchment area.

Although differences between the years cannot be attributed unequivocally to the effect of the project, it is encouraging to note that in the case of all three schools the overall attendance was better in 1980/81 than it was in 1978/79 at the start. The improvement is proportionately greater in the case of C than for A and B.

It will be remembered that in 1979/80 school C had the project ESW working in it with a case load of pupils taken from the target groups of both the fourth and fifth years. As data were available for three years in the case of school C it is possible to examine these for any effect which the ESW may have had. Figures 3 and 4 [2] show respectively the absence pattern of pupils who were in their fourth year in 1978/79 and who finished school in the summer of 1980, and the fourth year of 1979/80 who left school in the summer of 1981. [3] Figure 3 shows the target group's attendance deteriorating in the fifth year. This 1979/80 fifth year target group included some of the pupils who were in the ESW's special case load during that year. However, the non-target group is shown to be improving since their attendance in the fifth year is generally better than it was in the fourth. This might be expected since pupils should be preparing to take examinations at the end of the fifth year. Figure 4 shows a great improvement in the 1979/80 fourth year target group, with the level of absence dropping to that of the non-target group girls by their fifth year in 1980/81, although the fourth year figures are also slightly lower than previously. Figure 4 also shows the non-target group as having a much steadier rate of attendance.

Thus the presence of extra ESW resource did not seem to be associated with an improvement in fifth year attendance. However, in the case of the fourth year pupils there may have been a beneficial effect which carried over so that the attendance of this group of pupils in their fifth year was greatly increased. It must, of course, be admitted that one cannot infer conclusively from such data that there was a causal link with the project generally or the ESW specifically.

Figure 3: Fourth Year Absence 1978/79 and Fifth Year Absence 1979/80 School C

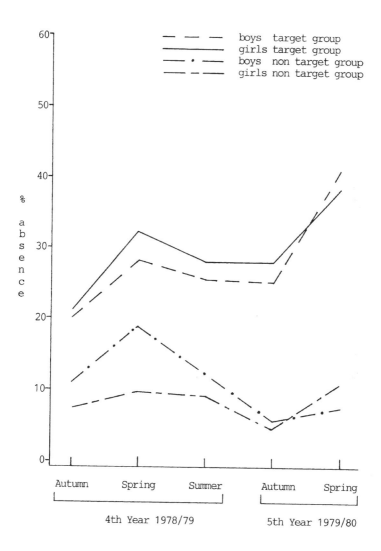

Figure 4: Fourth Year Absence 1979/80 and Fifth Year Absence 1980/81 School C

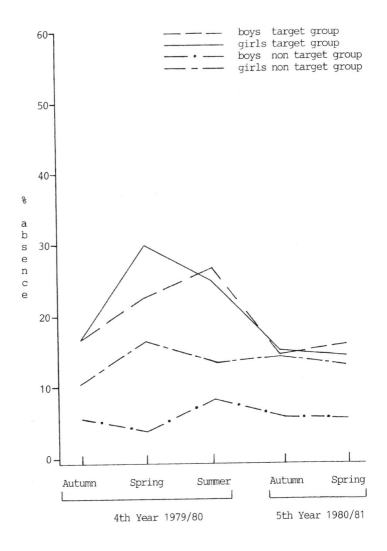

PUPILS' VIEWS OF ABSENTEEISM

During the course of our interviews with pupils over a three year period we had the opportunity of seeking their views on truanting or, in the Sheffield vernacular, 'wagging it'. From their comments it seemed that pupils who truanted organised themselves in the following ways:

- attended school but left after registration in the morning or afternoon;
- stayed at home without parental knowledge (if both parents worked);
- left home in the morning and went round to spend all or part of the day with a relative;
- telephoned a fellow pupil early in the morning, and suggested truanting, in various ways;
- pretended to be unwell and thus gained parental permission to stay away from school;
- arranged in advance of the day to meet one another (two or more) and go off for the day. This could be either to a local spot, or sometimes as far as London;
- 'borrowed' a car/motorbike and went off on a jaunt;
- met in town at a pre-decided point and wandered around the shops;
- came to school, and attempted to hide (in toilets etc.) for certain lessons;
- gained parental permission to truant when parents were at home or at work.

One particularly interesting feature appeared to be that, while some truanting is done on an individual basis, it is often a social or group activity, e.g. "Well before we go to lessons somebody'll say - or I'll ask him what he's got and he'll ask me what I've got - if he says 'Oh I don't like that' they wag it. If I say I've got social studies and I'll come wi' 'em."

Truanting pupils may engage in a variety of activities, e.g. staying at home, watching TV, hanging around places like betting offices or snooker halls and even shoplifting. Occasionally quasi-educational activities may be involved as in the case of the pupil who spent a day in the central library.

Interviewer   What do you do in the library?

Pupil   Read books.

Interviewer   So you wag school to go in the library and read books?

Pupil   Yes, <u>we</u> thought it were daft when we did it.

However truanting may become boring.

Pupil   Wagging gets right borin' after about two hours - then they come up here (i.e. to school).

It is then that pupils may return to school.

Interviewer   And why did you decide to start coming to school regularly?

Pupil   I don't know. All me other mates were coming and I didn't feel like waggin' it and I were getting right bored, so I thought, way, I might as well go, 'cos there were nowhere to go, so I come ...

It was interesting that several pupils expected to attend school more regularly in their fifth year, either because they saw the fifth form as important or because they expected it to be better in some way or other. However, whilst this may be the case for certain individuals, the evidence for pupils as a whole would seem to indicate the further deterioration of attendance levels in the fifth year (cf. Tables 16 and 17).

The two main reasons given for truancy are associated, i.e.

    1. dislike of components of the curriculum and/or the particular teachers involved in them; and
    2. general boredom.

Interviewer   Why do you think people wag it from school?

Pupil   'Cos they don't like school. Some days you have all good lessons like

> you might have got Craft all afternoon and you might have tutor - talking lessons in the morning; but if you've got maths, English, european studies and history all in one day, you think 'all them boring lessons; I think we'll go up the field and have the afternoon off'.

and

Pupil

> Most of the things (in school) are a waste of time. I think teachers don't know what you like and what you dislike. They just shove any old rubbish in your face.

and

Pupil

> I had yesterday morning off 'cos we'd got English.

The general epithet "boring" was perhaps the most frequently given description of school and reason for not attending. Even those pupils who did come to school often indicated that they found school boring. Two factors seemed to distinguish between those pupils who described school as boring, but nevertheless attended, from those who also saw school in this light but did not attend. The former group appeared to find the social contacts at school more satisfying and were also more subject to parental authority and influence to attend.

DISCUSSION

Much of the published research on truancy is based, as Brown (1983) has indicated, on one or a combination of four models of explanation which sees truancy arising from

1. the maladjustment of the pupil;
2. the inadequacy or wilful perversity of parents;
3. the reinforcement of truants' anti-social values by their wider working class community;
4. factors within the school.

189

A response to the problem of truancy based on the notion of individual and social pathologies inherent in the first three of these models will be one which emphasises the role of agencies such as the school psychological and education social work services.

The project provided an opportunity of exploring alternative ways of working for the latter of these two services. It is probably unrealistic, particularly in a time of economic constraint, to suppose that the extra education social work support which the project schools had could be made available to all secondary schools in an LEA. However, there may be a case for arguing that existing ESWs should be deployed on a basis which reflects more closely the extent of disadvantage in the catchment areas on which schools draw. This might mean that some secondary schools would be served by more than one ESW simply because the proportions of absentees and pupils with other social problems were greater than in the majority of schools. In order to deploy staff in this way it would be necessary to have a reliable measure of the social need of the school. An important component of such an index of need would be the level of absenteeism, however defined, in the school. Somewhat surprisingly, such measures are seldom computed either by schools or LEAs. The monitoring potential that is represented by the school attendance registers is rarely exploited. Very few schools appear to analyse their attendance data regularly and in any detailed manner. Whilst the analysis of attendance registers for a whole year group in a large school is a substantial task for one person to carry out, if subdivided amongst several staff it becomes a realistic possibility. With the increasing use of micro computers in schools the labour involved in analysis of this kind could be reduced substantially. A useful indicator that can be relatively easily obtained is that of persistent absenteeism. Galloway (1980) has used this measure, defined as the proportion of pupils absent for more than 50% of the time over a specified period, in a series of annual surveys carried out in Sheffield in the mid-1970s.

The experience gained in this project may also support the view that the work of ESWs should involve a greater degree of selectivity than is the case at the moment. This might mean concentrating on specific hard core cases for which, nevertheless, the prognosis for improvement is good. It might also imply focusing specifically on cases of persistent absenteeism which become apparent in the third year or below.

The indication, from the results briefly referred to above, that extra ESW effort applied in the fourth year might carry over as improved attendance when pupils entered their fifth year is worthy of further examination. The tendency to move down the school was apparent in the project's third year where the ESW concentrated his activities on a group largely composed of S3 pupils. It is unfortunate that the project came to an end before an assessment could be made of any effect which this intervention might have had on S4 or S5 attendance.

One of the benefits of greater selectivity and smaller case loads is that the ESW will have more time to facilitate communication and understanding between the school and the family. This will mean that the school will appreciate better any characteristics of the pupil or the home situation relevant to his performance in school. The parents will understand what the school is trying to do to help the pupil. In addition the pupil too may see more clearly how home and school form a cooperative partnership working for his benefit.

This kind of approach might be formalised as Galloway (1979) suggests into a system of contract based management (CBM), seen as a way of clarifying the responsibility of teachers, ESWs and other professionals, parents and pupils. An important point of CBM is that the contract can recognise the need for change not only in the child, and his parents, but also in the school. In such a situation the ESW might well act as honest broker between the main parties.

Our interview data from pupils also adds some support to the body of research (e.g. Reynolds et al, 1980); Cope and Gray, 1978; Reid, 1983) which inclines towards the last of Brown's four models (op. cit.) emphasising the contribution of the school to the creation of truancy. In particular our experience suggests that any systematic response to the problem of truancy must take seriously that many pupils appear to perceive much of their school work to be irrelevant to their needs. Indeed a detailed study of 52 truancy cases in Sheffield found that truants did not easily fall into the pathological typologies identified by other researchers but rather seemed "to be representatives of that perfectly 'normal' group of school children for whom the education currently available simply has no relevance to their immediate and future prospects in life." (Grimshaw and Pratt, 1983)

NOTES

[1] He did not work at any time in the associate school (D).

[2] These figures show the % absence for each of the three terms (autumn, spring and summer) in the fourth year. However, for the fifth year details are given only for the autumn and spring terms. Because some pupils leave at Easter and the remainder study for examinations, it is more difficult to interpret the register data for the summer term.

[3] We are indebted to Miss H. M. Carr, a third year statistics student at the City of Sheffield Polytechnic in 1981/82, for this section of the analysis.

Chapter 12

TEACHERS' VIEWS ON THE PROJECT AFTER THREE YEARS

INTRODUCTION

The project was in a sense what people perceived it to be. The director, the teachers, the pupils, the parents and others could all be expected to have views of the project which would differ somewhat one from the other. This chapter considers the views of the headteachers and teachers in the four participating schools. These were the views which they had of the project as it was in their school. Since programmes varied from school to school a picture of the project as a whole can only be obtained by aggregating the views of those in each of the schools. The director was perhaps uniquely placed to perceive the project as a totality and his views therefore are compared here with those from the schools.

School staff can be thought of in terms of three groups according to the nature of their involvement in the project:

1. those concerned with planning and implementing the project programme in their school, i.e. the headteacher, the project coordinator and other senior staff;

2. those involved in teaching certain aspects of the project programme - these included some of those in the group above;

3. those not involved in the organisation or teaching of the project.

A special questionnaire was designed for each of these three groups and distributed as a package to each school at the beginning of the autumn term 1981. The headteacher and senior staff questionnaire was designed to obtain a considered assessment of the effects which the project was thought to have had on the school over the three year period 1978-81.

Headteachers were encouraged to complete the questionnaire in consultation with senior staff. It was hoped thereby to obtain a consensus view of those principally concerned with the organisation of the programme since the project's inception.

Headteachers were asked to distribute a copy of a second questionnaire to the teacher principally concerned with each course, module or activity in the project programme. The aim of this questionnaire was to elicit teachers' views on their particular contribution to the project programme. In the case of the third questionnaire, headteachers were asked to make copies available to a one in ten random sample of teachers who had not been directly involved in the project at all.

The three questionnaires consisted of 11, 12 and 6 questions respectively. Some of these required a closed response although the majority allowed respondents to formulate their views freely on the general issues presented.

THE HEADTEACHER AND SENIOR STAFF QUESTIONNAIRE

Completed questionnaires were returned by the three project schools. In addition the director completed the same questionnaire looking at the project as a whole rather than in terms of any particular school. In the case of the associate school (D) the headteacher felt, after discussion with his senior colleagues, that a good deal of the questionnaire did not apply to his school because of its associate status. He therefore commented on each of the questions in the form of an extended letter. It proved possible however to use this letter to 'complete' the questionnaire on behalf of the school. However for two questions which required closed responses to a series of items a substantial number had to be coded as 'don't know' or 'not applicable' (see Tables 18, 19 and 21 following).

Effect of the Project on Various Aspects within and beyond the School

Respondents were presented with a list of 30 items covering different aspects of the school and its relationship with other bodies. The list was derived from an analysis and elaboration of the formal statement of project aims (cf. Chapter 1). Each item could be rated on a four to six point scale to indicate the extent to which it was thought there had been changes, increases or improvements since September 1978. The six point scales allowed ratings to be made in the negative sense, i.e. to indicate deterioration instead of improvement, or decrease instead of increase. In the event however the negative range was not used and so all the scales became four point ones permitting the extent of changes, improvements or increases to be rated as 'substantial', 'some', 'none' or 'don't know'. Ratings were made in the light of what was thought to be true for the respondents's own school. The items were then rated again on a six point scale to assess the extent to which any identified changes could be attributed to the effect of the EEC project. The scale spanned a 'helped' to 'hindered' range although the latter section was not used by any respondent. Thus the effective scale was a four point one: 'helped a lot', 'helped to some extent', 'had no effect', and 'don't know'.

The ratings of the four schools and the project director are summarised in Tables 18 and 19. Table 18 gives the perceived changes in each aspect since 1978 indicated as '2' for substantial, '1' for some and '0' for none or 'DK' (don't know). Table 19 uses a similar numerical scale '2' (helped a lot), '1' (helped to some extent), '0' (had no effect) and 'DK' (don't know) to show the effect the project was thought to have had on the changes which had occurred since 1978.

As can be seen, the ratings for individual items often differ somewhat from school to school. This is not surprising given the different project programmes and school backgrounds. Generally speaking school C gave more items a '2' rating and fewer a '0' in both tables, than did the other project schools.

In order to get an overall measure of the changes and effects of the project across the three schools the individual ratings were simply summed.

Table 18: Changes in Various School and Related Aspects
Since 1978

School and Related Aspects	Schools				Director	A+B+C
	A	B	C	D		
4th and 5th year curriculum (non target group)	2	2	2	1	2	6
4th and 5th year curriculum (target group)	2	1	2	DK	1	5
The post 16 curriculum	2	2	1	2	1	5

****

	A	B	C	D	Director	A+B+C
4th and 5th year careers education (target group)	1	1	2	DK	2	4
The lower school curriculum ..	2	1	1	1	1	4
School and FE college links ..	2	1	1	2	1	4
Preparation of pupils for employment (4th and 5th year target group).................	1	1	2	1	1	4
Provision of in-service opportunities (in the transition school to work area)....	2	1	1	1	2	4
Dissemination of curriculum innovations within the school	1	1	2	1	2	4
Contact between school and advisory service	2	1	1	1	1	4
Contact between school and parents	1	1	2	1	0	4
School and industrial/ commercial links	1	2	1	2	1	4
Contact between school and its governing body	2	2	0	1	0	4
4th and 5th year careers education (non target group)..	1	0	2	1	2	3
Pupil attitudes to industry and commerce (4th and 5th year target group)	1	1	1	1	1	3
Pupil attitudes to school (4th and 5th year non target group)	1	0	2	1	0	3

Table 18: Changes in Various School and Related Aspects Since 1978 (contd.)

School and Related Aspects	Schools				Director	A+B+C
	A	B	C	D		
Pupil attitudes to school (4th and 5th year target group) ...	1	0	2	1	1	3
Teacher attitudes to industry and commerce	1	1	1	1	1	3
Preparation of pupils for employment (4th and 5th year non target group).............	1	0	2	1	1	3
Provision of INSET opportunities (other than in the transition school to work area)	0	1	2	1	1	3
Contact between school and careers service	0	1	2	1	2	3

****

Employers' attitudes to the school	DK	1	1	1	2	2
Dissemination of curriculum innovations between the school and project schools ...	0	1	1	1	1	2
Contact between school and youth service	0	1	1	1	0	2
Pupil attitudes to industry and commerce (4th and 5th year non target group)	0	DK	1	1	1	1
Dissemination of curriculum innovations between the school and non project schools	0	1	0	1	1	1
School and Industrial Training Board links	0	DK	0	2	1	0
Schools influence on recruitment/training in industry/commerce	0	0	0	DK	1	0
Employers' influence on the school curriculum	0	0	0	1	1	0

Table 19: Extent to which the Project influenced Changes in Various School and Related Aspects

School and Related Aspects	Schools				Director	A+B+C
	A	B	C	D		
Provision of INSET Opportunities (in the transition school to work area)	2	2	2	DK	2	6
4th and 5th year careers education (target group)	2	2	2	DK	2	6
Pupil attitudes to industry and commerce (4th and 5th year target group)	1	2	2	DK	1	5
Preparation of pupils for employment (4th and 5th year target group)	1	2	2	DK	2	5
4th and 5th year curriculum (target group)	1	2	2	DK	2	5
School and industrial/ commercial links	1	2	2	1	2	5

****

School and Related Aspects	Schools				Director	A+B+C
Contact between school and careers service	0	2	2	DK	2	4
Dissemination of curriculum innovations within the schools	1	1	2	1	1	4
4th and 5th year careers education (non target group).	2	0	2	1	2	4
4th and 5th year curriculum (non target group)	1	1	2	1	1	4
Teacher attitudes to industry and commerce	DK	1	2	DK	2	3
Contact between school and advisory service	0	2	1	DK	1	3
Preparation of pupils for employment (4th and 5th year non target group)	1	0	2	1	2	3
Provision of INSET opportunities (other than in the transition school to work area) .	0	1	2	DK	1	3
Dissemination of curriculum innovations between school and project schools	0	1	2	1	2	3

Table 19: Extent to which the Project influenced Changes in Various School and Related Aspects (contd.)

School and Related Aspects	Schools				Director	A+B+C
	A	B	C	D		
The post 16 curriculum	1	2	0	1	1	3

****

School and Related Aspects	A	B	C	D	Director	A+B+C
Pupil attitudes to industry and commerce (4th and 5th year non target group)	0	0	2	DK	1	2
Pupil attitudes to school (4th and 5th year non target group)	DK	0	2	DK	1	2
Pupil attitudes to school (4th and 5th year target group)	DK	0	2	DK	1	2
Employers' attitudes to the school	DK	1	1	DK	2	2
Dissemination of curriculum innovations between the school and non project schools	0	1	1	DK	1	2
Contact between school and youth service	0	1	0	DK	1	1
School and FE college links .	0	1	0	1	1	1

****

School and Related Aspects	A	B	C	D	Director	A+B+C
Contact between school and its parents	0	0	0	DK	1	0
Contact between school and psychological service	0	0	0	0	0	0
Contact between school and its governing body	0	0	0	DK	1	0
The lower school curriculum .	0	0	0	1	0	0
The school and industrial training boards	0	DK	0	1	1	0
School's influence on recruitment/training/ procedures in industry/ commerce	0	0	0	DK	2	0
Employers' influence on the school curriculum	0	0	0	DK	2	0

This gave a scale ranging from 0 (i.e. 0, 0, 0) to 6 (i.e. 2, 2, 2). This scale can be recast to give a four point one defining two dimensions:

1. <u>overall</u> i.e. 'no overall change'   (0)
   <u>change</u>   'little overall change'   (1, 2)
                  'some overall change'   (3, 4)
                  'substantial overall change' (5, 6)

2. <u>overall</u> i.e. 'no overall influence'   (0)
   <u>project</u>   'little overall influence'   (1, 2)
   <u>influence</u> 'some overall influence'   (3, 4)
                  'substantial overall influence' (5, 6)

   The effect of these two dimensions can be examined simultaneously in Table 20. It was not possible to include the associate school in the analysis summarised in this Table. This was because of the large number of DK's (don't knows) recorded by the school particularly in Table 19. This reflects the fact that the school had utilised the additional resources made available by the project to assist its curriculum strategy generally rather than in developing a defined 'project programme'. As a result many of the items are less applicable and less easily assessed than they are for other schools.

   Table 20 ranks the overall effect of various aspects of the project from 'substantial overall change and influence' to 'no overall change and influence'.

   The director's ratings were broadly consistent with the pattern obtained except for those aspects in the last group. In general he was less likely than the schools to rate the project as having no effect on these aspects. The difference was most marked for 'school's influence on recruitment/training procedures in industry/commerce' and 'employer's influence on the school curriculum' which he rated as being 'helped a lot' by the project.

Influence of the Project on Curriculum Development throughout the School

   The project as originally conceived was principally concerned with the needs of the less able and motivated fourth and fifth year pupils (the target group). There is however some evidence that it had also stimulated curriculum development more widely. Table 19 shows that in all four schools the project had helped, at least to some extent, to bring about the changes which had occurred in the curriculum of non target group pupils. Three of the four schools (A, B and D) also indicated that the project had influenced the post 16 curriculum. This was attributed by two of the schools (A, D) to the funding of part-time post 16 courses which the project had allowed. The director and the schools also considered that the experience of developing new pre-16 courses had given staff the confidence and encouragement to develop appropriate courses for an older but similar clientele.

The effect of the project on the lower school curriculum was however nowhere nearly as marked. Only the associate school attributed any influence at all in this direction.

Successes of the Project

Schools generally agreed that one of the major successes of the project had been the opportunity it had provided to develop new courses and materials. Courses and activities which were specifically identified as successful were careers educaton, assessment (A); modular science, leisure options, careers education, work experience, record systems (C); work experience, further development of general studies and understanding industry courses (D).

The project was also thought to have had beneficial effects on staff. Involvement had raised the status of some staff (A), improved staff's understanding of pupil needs (B), and provided benefits through in-service training and project contacts (A). The director felt that the project had also shown that teachers and others can work together to produce curriculum materials in an effective manner.

Pupil effects mentioned were better social development (B), improved attendance and examination results of target group pupils (C) and better staff-pupil relationships (B, C).

Other successes identified included improved contact with industry (D), changes in the ways in which careers officers and education social workers worked with schools (director) and the way the

Table 20: Overall Change and Overall Project Influence across the Three Project Schools Since 1978

Change and Influence	School and Related Aspects
substantial overall change and substantial overall influence	- 4th and 5th year curriculum (target group)
some overall change and some overall influence	- 4th and 5th year careers education (target group) - Preparation of pupils for employment (4th and 5th year target group) - Provision of in-service opportunities (in the transition school to work area) - Pupil attitudes to industry and commerce (4th and 5th year target group) - School and industrial/commercial links
substantial overall change and some influence	- 4th and 5th year curriculum (non target group) - Post 16 curriculum
some overall change and some overall influence	- Dissemination of curriculum innovations within the school - Contact between school and advisory service - 4th and 5th year careers education (non target group) - Teacher attitudes to industry and commerce· - Preparation of pupils for employment (4th and 5th year non target group) - Provision of in-service opportunities (other than in the transition school to work area) - Contact between school and careers service

202

Table 20: Overall Change and Overall Project Influence across the Three Project Schools Since 1978 (contd.)

Change and Influence	School and Related Aspects
little overall change and some overall influence	- Dissemination of curriculum innovations between school and project schools
some overall change and little overall influence	- School and FE college links - Pupil attitudes to school (4th and 5th year non target group) - Pupil attitudes to school (4th and 5th year target group)
little overall change and little overall influence	- Employers' attitudes to school - Contact between school and youth service - Pupil attitudes to industry and commerce (4th and 5th year non target group) - Dissemination of curriculum innovations between school and non project school
some overall change but no overall influence	- Lower school curriculum - Contact between school and its parents - Contact between school and its governing body
little overall change but no overall influence	- Contact between school and psychological service
no overall change and no overall influence	- School and Industrial Training Board links - School's influence on recruitment/training procedures in industry and commerce - Employer's influence on the school curriculum

central project team acted as an effective force for many initiatives (director).

Aspects which did not go as well as hoped

Schools generally identified quite different aspects of the project with which they were less satisfied. School A was disappointed that the project had not had a greater influence on the staff not directly involved in it. School B commented on the failure of pupil attendance to improve, the need for a better flow of information between schools and the fact that there had been insufficient time at the beginning to prepare for the project. It was in fact the case that the period of time between schools agreeing to take part and the project actually commencing was only just over a term. Preparation for a major curriculum project probably requires at least a year for planning and development.

Two schools considered that greater links with commerce and industry could have been established and one (D) regretted that the MSC had not been involved to help in this. The disappointments of school C were concerned with specific courses. In the case of the preparation for adult life (PAL) course it was thought that, although certain modules were good, as a whole it had not gone so well as hoped because no-one had really taken overall responsibility for it. The social education project (SEP) option had not established a satisfactory sense of direction and methodology and the integrated humanities option had not really met the needs of the target group.

School D was conscious of the disadvantage of being an associate school and particularly in not having had an in-school coordinator concerned with the programme.

The director felt that the production of curriculum materials had gone more slowly than he expected. He also thought that the FE contribution had been slight although the collaboration between teachers and lecturers in the trades union working party and child care courses had been effective. His other concerns included the project's lack of effect on facilitating parental contact (cf. Table 19), the breadth of the in-service programme offered, and the level of teacher participation in it, and the extent of _inter_-project involvement of teachers.

Effect on the School and Staff Generally

School A felt that the project had had little impact on the bulk of staff and pupils although the activities of the education social worker had heightened attitudes towards attendance and the need for contact with parents over this. In school B the project was thought to have facilitated curriculum development by giving staff the opportunity to examine their purposes, methods and motivations.

School C gave the most positive evaluation of the project. It was felt that staff-pupil relationships had improved. Alongside this it was noted that the frequency of serious disciplinary problems seemed to have declined. Staff had become more sympathetic to the needs of target group pupils and the pupils themselves had developed a better self image. Involvement in the project had also helped to raise the confidence of staff which was thought to have declined in recent years as the school had moved from one leadership style to another. In the associate school the project had helped to increase staff's awareness of some of the problems facing young people and encouraged effort to provide suitable learning situations for them.

The director referred to the development of improved staff attitudes towards the careers and education social work service and also towards industry. He also thought that the project had provided an opportunity for a reconsideration of the curriculum. The project had encouraged readiness to work with others and helped the professional development of those involved in it.

Effects of Different Aspects of Project Structure and Organisation

Respondents were presented with a list of the main individuals, groups, facilities etc. which collectively constituted the project's structure and organisation. They were asked to estimate the contribution which each of these had made to the realisation of the project programme in their school. This was done by a rating on an eight point scale ranging from 'helped a very great deal' to 'hindered a very great deal' including a 'don't know' category. However, ratings were in all cases but one made on the positive side of this range[1] giving effectively the five point scale: 'helped a

very great deal', 'helped substantially', 'helped a
little', 'had no effect' and 'don't know'. The
results of the ratings are summarised in Table 21.
The associate school again had difficulty in
carrying out this exercise because it did not have
a defined 'project programme' in the sense that the
other schools did.

However it was again possible to attribute
ratings to the school from the comments made in the
extended letter. These other ratings may be taken
to represent the effect which each aspect had on
the school's <u>overall</u> curriculum development
strategy. Two aspects in particular were not
applicable to the associate school and have been
coded 'NA'. These were 'the extra teacher provided
by the project' and 'the school's project
coordinator'.

The aspects have been arranged in Table 21 in
decreasing order of their overall influence on the
three main project schools with ratings converted
to the numerical values 3, 2, 1 and 0. As can be
seen the top four facilitators were:

- Project clerical worker
- Project funds
- Project director
- Extra teacher provided by the project

Substantial curriculum development inevitably
throws an extra burden on a school's office staff.
Innovations invariably produce lots of paper:
syllabuses, minutes of meetings, worksheets etc.
The provision of an additional part-time clerk in
each school was recognition of this fact. There
was no doubt that this extra provision was greatly
appreciated by all schools.

Curriculum development on the scale in which
it had taken place in all of the project schools
would have made substantial in-roads into
capitation allowances had there been no external
funding. Funds provided by the project had enabled
schools to purchase not only equipment and
materials but also to extend their programmes of
visits to industry and elsewhere and increase the
level of in-service activity.

The high ranking given to the director
undoubtedly reflected the schools' appreciation of
the leadership which he had been able to give to
the project and the importance of having such a
role for a complex project of this kind.

Table 21: Extent to which Different Aspects of Project Structure Influenced the Project Programmes

School and Related Aspects	Schools				Director	A+B+C
	A	B	C	D		
Project clerical worker	3	3	3	3	3	9
Project funds	3	3	3	2	3	9
Project director	2	3	3	2	3	8
Extra teacher provided by the project	3	2	3	NA	2	8
In-service activities organised by non project agencies	2	2	3	2	1	7
Heads and senior staff meetings with the director .	2	3	2	0	2	7
Records and reporting working party	2	2	3	0	2	7
Project careers officer	2	2	3	0	2	7
Project in-service activities	3	DK	3	1	2	6
Project bulletins and publications	1	1	3	0	1	5
School's project coordinator	DK	3	2	NA	2	5
Contact with other project schools	1	2	1	2	2	4
Project conferences	2	2	0	0	1	4
Contact with other UK projects	3	0	1	0	1	4
Careers education working party	DK	1	3	2	1	4
Project research reports ...	1	1	2	0	2	4
Project advisory committee .	2	1	0	0	1	3
Project steering committee .	2	1	0	0	1	3
Residential education working party	DK	2	1	0	0	3
Research team	-1	1	1	0	2	2
Project education social worker	1	0	1	0	2	2
Contact with European projects	0	0	1	0	1	1
Trade unions working party .	DK	1	DK	2	1	1
Contact with other schools (non project)	0	0	0	0	1	0
In-service training working party	DK	0	DK	0	1	0

In all three project schools the extra teacher had been able, either directly or indirectly, to reduce the non-project teaching commitments of coordinators and other staff. The 'time release' that this allowed, although relatively small, was greatly valued and had a very significant impact. It made it much easier for staff to appraise relevant materials in their field, to develop new materials, to make visits and to engage in in-service activities.

Those aspects of the project next in order of influence were:

- In-service activities organised by non project agencies
- Heads and senior staff meetings with the director
- Records and reporting working party
- Project careers officer

Although no examples were given of influential in-service activities one school commented that the project acted as a means of bringing such to the attention of staff.

The occasional meetings between senior staff and the director were specifically described by one school as providing vital personal contact. It is interesting to note that the ranking of this type of meeting was somewhat higher than that achieved by the more formal advisory and steering committees. However one school did mention that the latter were valuable for sounding out ideas and obtaining support.

The records and reporting working party appeared to have been the most highly valued of the project working parties. Certainly one tangible outcome of its work was the adoption of a common record system by the project schools. The trades union working party was established later in the project and its activities were still underway at the time the survey was conducted. The expectations were that its influence would be more apparent in the fourth year when the materials it was producing were completed and in use.

The relatively high ranking of the project careers officer indicated the schools' appreciation of her contribution. One school commented that she had become important to many individuals in the target group. The somewhat lower ranking given to the project education social worker probably

reflected the fact that since the first year of the
project he had worked with only one school at a
time, i.e. with school C in the second year and
with school A in the third. The careers officer
however had maintained a presence in each school
throughout the duration of the project.
Perhaps not surprisingly the research team was
not rated as a major facilitator in the development
of project programmes. However 'research reports'
received a moderate overall rating and one school
referred specifically to the value of some reports.
'Contact with other project schools' seemed to
have been a moderate facilitator overall and one
which, in school B's view, was better developed at
senior staff level. 'Contact with other UK
projects' was rated highly by one school only (A)
and 'contact with European projects' was thought to
be helpful by only one school (C) and then only to
a limited extent. However the director commented
that although it was not always apparent, the
national and European project network had been
important in broadening horizons and in terms of
mutual influence.

Other Influences

    Respondents were also asked to comment on any
other factors or events which they thought had had
an important influence on their project programme.
Two schools and the director specifically mentioned
the worsening youth unemployment situation as a
significant influence. In a project like this one
lasting several years changes of key staff are
likely to occur. In two of the schools, for
example, there were changes of headteacher during
the life of the project. Significantly these two
schools (A, B) identified staff change, and in the
case of one of them specifically the change of
headteacher, as a major factor. Throughout the
duration of the project all secondary schools had
been encouraged by the LEA to develop collaborative
arrangements for the provision of post 16
education. This was thought by the director and
school D to have been an important influence - a
view that may reflect the fact that three project
schools (A, C and D) had been involved in the same
consortium arrangements.
    Other influences seemed to be specific to
individual schools. School B cited several
inhibitors: the lack of a clear timetable policy in

the early stages of the project, the disruptive effect of bad weather and bus strikes early on, and heavy teaching commitments which had the effect of reducing the creative effort that could be put into curriculum development. School C mentioned the involvement of the youth service in its social education project (SEP) option, the experience of using curriculum materials associated with the Schools Council GYSL and history projects and also an HMI visit made in the third year to look at the project programme. School D identified several diverse influences: assistance from industry/commerce, new appointments which had been made to the school staff and the support services of the LEA, the increasing multi ethnic character of the school, examination pressures and the introduction of the micro computer to the school.

Lessons Learned from the Experience of Running the Project

The answers respondents gave to the question "What lessons do you think you have learned from the experience of running the project?" were ones reflecting a concern with the process of curriculum development. The director felt that he had learned that there was much more potential in teacher expertise than was normally recognised although time, organisation and leadership were necessary to realise this. The importance of funds and the necessity of staff time to make changes possible was recognised (B, D). Two schools (C, D) stressed the importance of staff motivation if successful innovation was to occur. One (C) however also felt in retrospect that a stronger lead from head and senior staff was necessary and that it was not enough to leave curriculum development to the departments. The heads of two schools were particularly conscious of the many other calls on them and the difficulty experienced in finding the time to be fully involved in the project. Other 'lessons' cited included: the importance of a good school coordinator, the need for a tighter control over money, and the necessity for ancillary support. In addition the director stressed the benefits which accrued from a collaborative venture involving schools, including advisers, the careers service etc. and the importance of a good information system.

Main Developments in the Fourth Year of the Project (1981/82)

The main developments anticipated for the fourth and final year of the project centred on post 16 courses, further improvement of pupil record systems (possibly involving computerisation), alternative approaches to pupil assessment (e.g. RPE, profiling) and consolidation and extension of the new courses. The director also expected an increased production of curriculum materials (e.g. trade union studies) and their wider dissemination, the development of a more community oriented role by the careers officer and more effective communication between education social work service, the schools and the parents.

1982 and Beyond

It was anticipated that most of the new courses would continue when the project came to an end in August 1982. However cessation of the project funding meant that some courses might have to be curtailed (e.g. parentcraft (B); leisure options (C)). The loss of the extra clerical worker was expected to make further development difficult to sustain (C, D). The director hoped that the extended relationship of the education social work and careers services with the schools, and the developments within those services themselves would continue. He also expected that many of the materials produced by the project would be incorporated into general practice and that there would be a continuation of the industrial and trade union liaison work. He felt that the experience gained from the project could be a base for further development and that the 'central unit' notion could be applied to other curriculum areas.

VIEWS OF PROJECT TEACHERS

Completed questionnaires were returned by 29 project teachers (Table 22). The higher return from school C reflected the fact that a questionnaire was completed by each teacher concerned with particular options of the leisure pursuits part of the programme.

Most of the courses, modules or activities had been in operation, at least in some form, for three years, i.e. since the beginning of the

211

Table 22: Courses, Modules or Activities
Constituting Project Programmes

School	Project course, module or activity	Total courses, module or activities
A	Careers, sociology, integrated science, records and reporting	4
B	Careers/guidance, geography, parentcraft, art/photography (full option), art/photography (module), road traffic education, understanding industry and commerce	7
C	Careers/preparation for adult life, maths (for lower ability groups), modular science, humanities, (playgroup, concreting, jewellery, swimming, photography, hill walking, rock climbing)*	11
D	Art/design, chemistry, general studies, environmental/social studies, motor vehicle, control technology, understanding industry and commerce	7
Total		29

* leisure pursuits

project, and all but three were being offered in the fourth year (1981/82).

Nearly one third (10) of the programme items could lead to certification at the CSE level and a further 10 could do so in conjunction with other courses.

Factors Influencing Success

Respondents were asked to identify anything whether associated with the school, the central project organisation, or other agencies which they considered to have been very influential in helping them to realise the aims of their course, etc. The 29 teachers identified a wide range of influences of which the most frequently cited was 'project funds' (16 teachers).

The next most popular set of influences could be grouped under the heading 'help and resources from external agencies' (12 teachers). These included the police, FE colleges and the polytechnic, the careers service and project trident[2]. This was followed by three factors, each of which were cited by five teachers:

- the time which the project gave staff to research course and teaching possibilities;
- timetable and staffing arrangements;
- general backing and encouragement given (in three cases the role of the headteacher was specifically mentioned).

Table 23 summarises the complete range of factors cited.

Factors Inhibiting Success

The main factors which were considered to have hindered the realisation of course aims could be grouped under the head of 'organisational arrangements' and included inadequate timetabling (2), poor physical facilities (2), pupil groups which were too large (2), departmental reorganisation (1) and the imposition of CSE certification (1). The next two most frequent factors were 'problems of time' and 'staff'. The former included lack of time (4), delay in the first year of the project (1), searching for appropriate materials (1), other school commitments

Table 23:   Factors   Influencing Success of Project
Courses, Modules or Activities

Factors	No. of times cited
Project funds	... 16
Help and resources from external agencies	... 12
Time to research course and teaching possibilities	... 5
General backing and encouragement	... 5
Timetabling and staffing arrangements ...	... 5
Teacher attitudes/commitment	... 3
Pupil opportunities	... 3
Discussion with teachers in other schools	... 2
Clerical assistance	... 2
Teacher secondment to industry	... 1
Knowledge of economic trends	... 1
Total	55

Table 24:   Factors   Inhibiting Success of   Project
Courses, Modules or Activities

Factors	No. of times cited
Organisational arrangements	... 8
Problems of time	... 7
Staff (changes, attitudes, etc.)	... 7
Pupils' attitudes/attendance	... 5
Inappropriate length of course or module	... 5
Lack of financial resources	... 4
Economic situation in industry	... 1
Initial lack of understanding of scope of project	... 1
Total	38

(1). Under 'staff' were grouped staff changes (3), staff attitudes (3), and shortage of appropriate staff (1).

The next most frequent block of factors were 'pupils' attitudes/attendance' (5), 'inappropriate length of course or module' (5), and 'lack of financial resources' (4).

Main Achievements

The vast majority of answers (25 out of 40) which respondents gave to the question "What do you consider to have been the main achievements of your course, module or activity?" reflected a belief that there had been an improvement in one or more of the following: pupil motivation, attitudes, skills or concepts. The remaining examples were each given by one or two respondents only, i.e. better staff/student relationships (2), staff enjoyment (1), better self assessment (1), improved FE links (1), good exam results (1), bringing staff together (1), particular effect on girls (1), complete review of the syllabus (1), increased work experience (1), and opportunity for staff to promote their ideas (1).

Aspects which did not go as well as hoped

In total 25 aspects were cited as ones which did not go as well as hoped. Just under half of these (12) expressed disappointment with some of the materials produced. These were thought to have been either too difficult for pupils or to have lacked the necessary motivating qualities. Apart from a comment on visits to firms made by three teachers in one school all the rest were specific to individual schools.

Knowledge and Interest of Other Staff

Each project teacher was asked the two questions:

"Apart from those directly involved in the project, how much do you think the staff in general know about the project?"

"Apart from those directly involved in the
project like yourself, how much interest do
you think the staff in general have shown in
the project?"

Answers were given by a rating on a four point
scale and the results are summarised in Tables 25
and 26.

As can be seen, approximately two-thirds of
project teachers believed that staff as a whole
knew little about the project and had little
interest in it.

Despite this a number of project teachers were
able to cite beneficial effects which they believed
the project had on those staff not actively
involved in it. These effects included enhanced
interest in particular courses or modules (5),
recognition of the need for curriculum review and
change (2), "ripple effect" to other departments
(2), improved morale (1), greater access to
materials (1), effect on a comparable course in
other schools (1), facilitation of cooperation
between departments (1), and recognition of need
for community involvement. However, two negative
effects were also mentioned: envy of the
resources or time made available to project staff
(3) and occasional antagonism displayed by other
staff (3).

VIEWS OF NON PROJECT TEACHERS

A total of 12 questionnaires were returned by
non project teachers - two from school A, six from
school B, one from school C and three from school
D.

Responses to the two questions asking for
estimates of how much staff in general knew about
the project and how much interest they had shown in
it were very similar to those given by the project
teachers. The majority (10) thought that staff in
general knew little about the project and all
agreed that staff had little interest in it.

The main benefit of the project was thought to
be the extra money and resources which it made
available (10). Other benefits, each of which were
suggested by one respondent only, were initiating
curriculum review, facilitating a review of
assessment/records (A), opportunities for extra
curricular activities, variety in lesson content,

Table 25: Project Teachers' Ratings of the Amount of Knowledge Staff in General had of the Project

Schools	No. of staff giving a particular interest rating				
	none	a little	considerable	very considerable	Total
A		2	2		4
B		7			7
C		7	4		11
D		7			7
Total		23	6		29

Table 26: Project Teachers' Ratings of the Amount of Interest Staff in General had Shown in the Project

Schools	No. of staff giving a particular interest rating				
	none	a little	considerable	very considerable	Total
A		4			4
B	3	4			7
C		10	1		11
D	3	4			7
Total	6	22	1		29

217

more consideration of the needs of lower ability pupils, and encouragement of new ideas (B).

Half of the sample considered that there had been no disadvantages in being associated with the project. Those disadvantages that were mentioned by individuals were extra work load on certain staff, jealousy over allocation of cash, pupil return not commensurate with the effort involved, curriculum had become too 'work' oriented, and too much emphasis had been put on links with industry.

Only three teachers believed that the project had influenced them personally. One considered that his relationship with target group pupils had improved and two mentioned the opportunity the project had provided to purchase extra equipment. The majority (10) indicated that they did not know of any effects which the project had on other teachers. Only two examples were given - these implied that the project had influenced one teacher to change his syllabus and another to develop a more worthwhile curriculum for the less gifted.

DISCUSSION

As was to be expected, responses to the project differed somewhat from school to school. School C seemed to regard the project more favourably and to be the most certain of its effect. However, there was a general consensus that the project had influenced the preparation of fourth and fifth year pupils for employment, their attitudes to industry and commerce, and the curriculum provided for them, particularly careers education. This influence was most substantial in the case of the less able and/or motivated pupils (i.e. the target group). The project was also thought to have had a substantial influence on the development of school/industry links and in-service opportunities particularly those related to the transition from school to work area. The schools generally did not consider that the project had affected contacts with industrial training boards, the recruitment and training procedures of industry, and employers' influence on the school curriculum. However, the director was not in agreement with the schools' judgement on the latter and felt that the project had influenced these too.

The project was considered to have been a very effective stimulus for curriculum development in careers education, social education and related areas, and staff were generally pleased with the outcome of the opportunities which it provided to develop new courses. The staff involved in the project were thought to have particularly benefited in that their level of awareness of pupils' needs had been heightened, their confidence and knowledge increased, and a process of debate about the nature of the curriculum opened up amongst them.

Although the project had a fairly specific curriculum focus it was perceived as having influenced developments beyond this, particularly in the post 16 field. Staff however were somewhat disappointed that its influence had not spread wider to other staff and areas of the curriculum beyond the project's original remit.

Those in each school involved with the planning and teaching of the project programme had undoubtedly formed a coherent group united by a common interest in innovation. However, as had been noted before in similar situations (e.g. Shipman, 1974), this did not necessarily mean that it was seen as a concern of the remainder of the staff. Generally the indications were that the majority of staff had little interest in or knowledge of the project, indeed there were intimations of antagonism and cynicism towards the project in the case of a small minority of staff. This and the failure of the project to 'ripple outwards' may be discouraging to those closely involved with it. Jenkins (1974) suggests that theology is one of the sources which can provide guiding metaphors for understanding innovations - a project may be welcomed as an act of grace - there can be a feeling of certainty in belonging to an elect in the kingdom of curriculum development, etc. Those involved in innovation often reveal a messianic zeal and may be disappointed if the conversion of others does not follow. However, it is perhaps unrealistic to expect a specific innovation involving a relatively small number of staff to have such a total effect. In a secular and pluralist age curriculum conversion may be as rare as the religious variety. On the other hand, there may be a danger of underestimating the wider effects of the project. It must be admitted that it is difficult to isolate unequivocal causes for individual curriculum initiatives - an existing project is likely to be one amongst many potential influences. In the case of school A a significant development in the lower school curriculum was the introduction of a study skills programme which involved the participation of a number of departments. Whilst this was perceived as a distinct and separate initiative it is nevertheless significant to note that its originator was also deeply involved in the EEC project. It is pertinent therefore to ask the question "Would this initiative have happened, or happened so quickly, if there had not been this prior involvement in the EEC project?"

Interviews with staff earlier in the project had indicated that some of the initiatives had clearly been 'glints in the eye' some time before. The project was thought to have provided both the opportunity and the impetus to realise these in practice.

The main justification for the project was, of course, to benefit pupils and in particular those considered most disadvantaged by virtue of ability or motivation. As mentioned above, senior staff seemed confident that the project had substantially influenced pupils' attitudes to industry and commerce and their preparation for subsequent employment [3] of target group pupils. There was less agreement about the project's influence on these in the case of non target group pupils and also on the attitudes to school of pupils generally. Although senior staff in school C seemed convinced of the beneficial effects of the project on pupils' attitudes and social development those in other schools seemed less certain. School B was particularly disappointed because pupil attendance did not seem to have been influenced by the project. However, when the staff responsible for teaching the project programme were asked what they thought the main achievements of their courses were, a majority referred to improvement in pupil motivation, attitudes, skills or understanding. Where disappointments were expressed about their courses these were most often concerned with certain aspects of the materials used which were considered to be either too difficult or insufficiently interesting for pupils. Staff were also critical of some of their courses and felt that development had not always proceeded satisfactorily. An interesting example of this was the social education project (SEP) in school C. This had in fact pre-dated the EEC project by several years but had been incorporated within the programme from the very beginning. The SEP had a somewhat chequered career right from its inception and a substantial proportion of staff had been critical of its approach and in some cases distinctly hostile to it. Each year of the project senior staff expressed reservations about SEP and indicated that a special attempt would be made to overcome these in the following year. However these reservations continued to persist into the fourth year of the project. It seems as though some elements of the curriculum are singularly and stubbornly resistant to attempts to change them or make them more broadly acceptable.

The main facilitators of the project identified by senior staff were the project clerical worker - the loss of this resource would be particularly felt by schools when the project came to an end, project funds - also identified as a major influence by both project and non project teachers, the project director, the 'extra' teacher, in-service education - both that organised by the project and by other agencies, the project careers officer, the records and reporting working party, and the regular meetings of heads and senior staff with the project director. It is interesting to note that the latter were generally more highly regarded than the more formal meetings of the project steering and advisory committees. The project advisory committee had been the subject of a separate evaluation (Corbett, Parker and Shannon, 1981). This had indicated that few of the lay members of the body had a clear notion of its terms of reference or felt they had a deep involvement in the project. This highlights one of the problems of establishing a relatively large body composed of representatives from many different interests to oversee projects of this kind. The fact of long agendas, infrequent meetings and the difficulties which lay members may have in understanding the specialist and professional language of educators are familiar problems.

Contacts with other project schools both in Sheffield and the UK seemed to have been regarded as moderate facilitators. Contacts with European projects were generally seen as having had little influence. This was perhaps understandable since any influence they may have had was more likely to be discernible at the level of the director. Certainly he considered that such contacts had influenced his thinking and planning of the project. Individual project teachers also emphasised the help and resources they had received from external agencies - the range of these may well have been wider than some of the senior staff were aware.

Other factors which senior staff felt had influenced their programmes were: the fact of the increasingly severe juvenile unemployment situation; staff changes; the heavy teaching commitments of the staff involved; the problem of time generally; and the inhibiting effect of certain organisational arrangements, staff changes and attitudes. It was also noted that even in a well resourced project such as this one it was still possible for at least a minority of teachers to cite lack of funds as a major restriction.

There appear to be very few examples in the now extensive literature of curriculum development which are similar to the organisation and structure of the project described here. A recent exception is provided by the partnership set up in 1977 between schools in several LEAs and a group of HMI and advisers to review the secondary curriculum (DES, 1981b). In the report covering three years' work on this task, a list of recommendations are made to guide other authorities wishing to embark on any exercise of curricular reappraisal. Two of these are worthy of special mention:

> "An adviser with senior status, or perhaps a seconded head, should be designated to coordinate the exercise.
>
> It is important to consider the extent to which the work can be supported by secretarial and clerical staff and, within the schools, by supply teachers."

It is interesting to note that these two recommendations were prefigured in the establishment of the EEC project by the decisions to second the LEA's senior adviser for secondary education to the post of director and to provide the participating schools with additional clerical and teaching support.

What has been presented here is not, of course, an evaluation of the project. It is rather a partial contribution to an evaluation. Other chapters in this report dealing in more detail with particular aspects of the programme, including the views of pupils, constitute other such contributions. In the final chapter an attempt is made to fit the various contributions together to form a coherent critique of the project as a whole.

NOTES

1 The exception was school A's ratings of the contribution of the research team as having 'hindered slightly'. It was felt that some research interviews had come at an inconvenient time.

2 A local scheme coordinating the provision of work experience for pupils in schools.

3 Pupils' <u>preparation</u> for employment, not necessarily their chances of actually gaining employment.

Chapter 13

IMPLICATIONS OF THE PROJECT

INTRODUCTION

As is mentioned in the appendix, our aim has
been to produce an account of the project as a case
study of a major exercise in curriculum
development. It is moreover a case study of the
first three years of the project. These formed the
period in which most of the main developments took
place and were consolidated. We have not referred
to the project's fourth and final year where the
main emphasis was on disseminating, both within and
beyond the LEA, the lessons learned from the
project and the materials produced by it. In fact,
the dissemination of the 'results' of the project,
including this account, continued into a fifth
year.[1]

This chapter does not attempt an evaluation of
the project as a whole. Much more important, in
our view, is to set out a considered response to
the general question: How has experience of the
project and its effects influenced our general
understanding of certain aspects of education, and
our views on possible future action? An
appropriate criterion for judging a good case
study, or good research generally, is the extent to
which it transforms and expands understanding.
Ultimately the individual has to make 'sense' of
any piece of research - a process that involves
critical reflection on the research and its results
and an active interpretation of them. It is a
process which is inevitably tinged with
subjectivity. What we therefore present here is
the outcome of our own attempt to make sense of the
project. It is ultimately for readers to decide
whether 'our sense' is also 'their sense'. In this

224

chapter then we draw out what seems to us to be three major themes of the project. The first relates to the structure of the project and the extent to which this might inform LEA strategies for supporting curriculum development in schools. The second is concerned with the nature of that part of the curriculum, particularly apparent in the fourth and fifth year, which is appearing in a number of forms and to which we have given the title preparation for life (PFL). And finally the research model adopted in the project is presented as one method of conceptualising and carrying out the process of curriculum review.

THE PROJECT AS A MODEL FOR CURRICULUM DEVELOPMENT

Most of the literature on curriculum development has been concerned with large scale national projects (e.g. Stenhouse, 1980) and individual school based initiatives (e.g. Eggleston, 1980). There seems to be little documented of any substance on the kind of innovation which the Sheffield/EEC project exemplified. The project can be located somewhere on a possible continuum of curriculum development defined by the two extremes referred to above. On the one hand, it was part of a national (and indeed international) network of projects, and on the other, its development relied very heavily on local and individual school initiatives. The Sheffield project was defined by a set of very general aims which loosely linked it to other UK and European projects. However, working out the implications of these aims in terms of new courses, materials, and methods was largely the responsibility of the individual schools involved in the project. Unlike most school based development, the project was coordinated at the LEA level by a full-time director, who was able to provide substantial resources of money, staff, equipment, materials, and facilities to support appropriate school initiatives.
A significant feature of the Sheffield project was that the director was a senior educational adviser who had been seconded to the project for its duration. In a sense then the project was an LEA one, involving several of its schools, coordinated by one of its advisory staff, but funded externally (i.e. by the DES and EEC).

One aspect on which there was general agreement was the significant effect which various kinds of external resource had on facilitating project progress. Whilst the provision of funds was clearly important in enabling schools to purchase the requisite materials and equipment to realise their curricular aspirations, the provision of other types of resource was at least as valuable. The addition of an extra teacher had a 'knock on' effect throughout the school, enabling some time to be made available to those staff involved in project development. The extra time produced benefits out of all proportion to the comparatively modest amount available. Schools used this time in a variety of ways, e.g. to enable staff to visit other schools, attend meetings, participate in INSET activities, prepare materials etc.

As important as the effect of the extra teacher was the additional clerical support provided. Again a relatively modest addition to the staffing establishment (a part-time clerk in each of the three project schools) had substantial and significant effects. In the words of one teacher it "unclogged the whole system" and made it possible to carry out all the clerical and reprographic work that the project generated. The extra clerk was also an influential factor in the successful adoption of the new pupil record system in two of the schools.

At the present time schools are staffed on the implicit assumption of a static curriculum. If the notion of curriculum renewal at the individual school level is to be taken seriously, then teachers must be given the time and resources to do it properly. It is unrealistic to expect them to engage in the highly creative work of curriculum development - in effect to redraw the map of school knowledge - within the constraints of full teaching loads and low levels of clerical back-up. Curriculum development is a demanding task requiring time for reflecting, discussing, formulating ideas, and devising and testing new materials. These cannot be achieved in a situation of occasionally snatched free periods and by a 'grace and favour' relationship with office staff who already have their hands full in servicing the normal running of the school.

With falling rolls in secondary schools, staffing establishments are being increasingly scrutinised. It is important that when this occurs, and the staffing structures of schools readjusted, that consideration be given to the additional staffing increment necessary to make curriculum development a realistic possibility.

The director played an important part in the project. It was he who brought school staffs previously isolated into a closer, cooperative and creative partnership. Although staff were somewhat disappointed at the extent of the liaison which had occurred between them, there was, nevertheless, no other group of schools in the LEA at the time which were working together at anything like their level of intensity, at least on the curriculum of 14-16 year olds. The director was able, as a result of his connection with the advisory service, to make available to schools a wide range of opportunities, particularly through an enhanced in-service programme. The identification of the project with the advisory service had the added benefit that other advisers were also involved, particularly the careers education and political education advisers, either through invitation by the director, or by headteachers.

Another feature which distinguished the project from some other examples of school based development was the very close involvement of the headteachers of the participating schools. The headteachers not only represented their particular project programmes on the official committees and working parties of the project, they were also major influences on their planning and development. One head also took part in the teaching of the project programme of his school. Heads gave more than simply their endorsement to the project. They also invested a considerable amount of their own time, commitment and energies to it. Heads could thus talk about 'our project' in a very special sense. The head was seen, at least in one school, as the driving force for the project, capable of exerting considerable influence "to gee people up and cut red tape".

The project demonstrated how schools can work together cooperatively on an issue of common concern, supported and guided by a local structure which is adequately resourced. The presence of a director enabled the project to be continuously animated, its momentum to be maintained and its focus to be redirected as necessary. The project structure as a whole inevitably created certain expectations of staff (e.g. to formulate considered accounts of what they did, to assess them and to share their experience with others) which, although no doubt occasionally irksome, helped to maintain coherence and commitment and, at the same time, ensured a means of accountability to the project director.

The project can be regarded as an example of what we term the 'concentrated attack' model. This can be contrasted with the usual approach to curriculum development in an LEA which relies heavily on advisers, each of whom may be involved at any one time in a variety of curriculum activities, rather than dealing exclusively with one. The latter involves spreading resources thinly across many schools and many curriculum areas. A concentrated attack approach would focus some of those resources on a specific aspect of the curriculum as a development project involving a limited number of schools. It is interesting, as we noted briefly at the end of the previous chapter, that the recommendations made by HMI to LEAs wishing to establish collaborative projects with their schools (DES, 1981b) are very similar to aspects of the actual structure of the Sheffield project. Some of the main suggestions which were made by HMI included:

1. the appointment of an adviser as coordinator of the schools' work, with senior status and protected time;
2. a supporting team of advisers who also have time assigned, as a priority, to the needs of the schools;
3. provision of clerical and secretarial support for advisers, administrators and teachers in the participating schools;
4. the provision of reserved time to permit teachers to engage in sustained thinking about the curriculum;
5. a link with the Authority's running programme of in-service training for all its schools;
6. satisfactory means of communication, such as a regular newsletter or progress report to be circulated to all those involved;
7. the importance of evaluation.

In addition to what we have already said, it is worth commenting specifically on items 6 and 7.

Schools were kept regularly informed of developments throughout by means of the project bulletin, and a variety of other reports and papers. The project was also evaluated locally by a team under the direction of the Authority's senior adviser for research and evaluation. This activity generated its own series of interim research reports to the schools and added another link to the communication network. This feedback helped schools to change direction or correct perceived problems quickly when necessary.

The 'concentrated attack' strategy which the project represented is one which an LEA could, in principle, adopt within its own resources. Thus an LEA could decide to assign one or more of its advisory staff, perhaps even on a full-time basis, for a defined period of time, to work with a group of schools on a particular aspect of curriculum development. It could in addition decide to allocate to such a venture a proportion of the funds that it may have for encouraging curriculum development. This approach may often be the best way of spearheading new developments. To take an example, an LEA might give a special push for a year or so to preparation for life, and for the following year or two the emphasis might be on new technology and so on. A sequence of projects would thus be generated with each one generally associated with a fresh group of schools. An advantage of this would be that, over a number of years, a good proportion of schools would have had the opportunity of involvement in a major curriculum development exercise. The materials produced and lessons learned from these projects would not, of course, be confined to the groups of schools in which they took place, but would be disseminated to the other schools in the LEA.

PREPARATION FOR LIFE (PFL)

One of the recurring themes of the Great Debate and its aftermath has been the insistence that a fundamental aim of schools, and secondary schools in particular, is the preparation of their pupils for all aspects of adult life. A major preoccupation has been with ways of adapting the last two years of compulsory education so as to facilitate the transition to working life of those pupils who leave school at the earliest opportunity - especially those with poor academic attainments and little commitment to the values and demands of schools. This has led to an increased recognition of the need for more systematic careers education and guidance, enhanced programmes of work experience, and generally the establishment of better links between schools and the world of work.

As the youth unemployment situation has worsened, however, many teachers have come to the uncomfortable realisation that the 'promises' of careers education have an increasingly hollow ring. Careers teachers, perhaps more than their colleagues in other departments, are experiencing the trauma of having the basic assumptions of their subject rendered problematic as a result of major structural changes occurring in the economy. One response to this situation has been a switch of emphasis to preparing pupils for unemployment and enforced leisure and to the adoption of a rhetoric which refers to 'coping' and 'survival' skills.

In the face of such challenges many schools are restructuring their fourth and fifth year curricula, both in organisational and content terms. Some of the changes which can be discerned include: expanding the core curriculum with a consequent reduction in the amount of time devoted to 'options'; devising new approaches to pupil assessment with the needs of potential employers particularly in mind; and including careers education, health education and certain aspects of social studies programmes in new integrated courses under such titles as social education, personal education, and social and life skills. The emergence of such courses, to which we apply the generic name preparation for life (PFL), represented the main curriculum modification which occurred in the project schools.

This important area of the curriculum is not an easy one to describe. A currently influential way of attempting this is in terms of the notion of 'skills'. Hopson and Scally (1981), for example, identify some 49 'lifeskills' grouped under the four main headings of 'me', 'me and you', 'me and others', and 'me and specific situations'. Whilst such an analysis may be helpful in reminding the teacher of the range and complexity of the field and also useful as a curriculum planning tool, it does have the danger of encouraging the naive belief that such skills have been unambiguously identified and that, moreover, techniques and methods exist which can reliably develop them. The

230

word 'skill' is rapidly becoming the new curriculum talisman. It is "an incantatory word subduing critical reflection and engendering, simultaneously, narrow technicism of mind ... (It) feeds the automatic expectation of a technological civilisation that with the right techniques alone, things can be done, life yields positive results." (Abbs, 1981). The APU Exploratory Group Report on Personal and Social Development (APU, 1981) uses 'practical application' instead of 'skill' as one of four hypothesised dimensions for analysing the different aspects of the field - the others being 'knowledge', 'understanding' and 'attitudes'. The various aspects identified were: persons and personal relationships; morality; social awareness; religion and philosophies of life; occupational; political; legal; environmental; health; and community. Thus the field of personal and social development or PFL can be conceptualised as a matrix defined by the four dimensions and the ten aspects above, thus giving 4 x 10 = 40 cells. Such a matrix might be very helpful to a team of PFL teachers as a means of assessing the kind of emphases given in their lessons over a term or a whole year. This could help in identifying any omissions or undue concentration on certain aspects.

Our own analysis of the PFL area for the purposes of organising chapters 4, 5 and 6 was in terms of the categories careers education, health education and social education; although our field note archive indicated that virtually all of the APU aspects were dealt with in at least some lessons. Religion and philosophies of life was one, however, which seemed to be given little consideration within PFL programmes, although in one school (A) it was present as a separate core subject.

Of course, even where a school had a specific PFL course, e.g. sociology at school A, it would be naive to suppose that was the only aspect of the curriculum which contributed to this area. Most other subjects would claim to foster preparation for life since everything which a pupil may learn or experience in the classroom contributes in some way to his personal development. However, such contributions are typically incidental, implicit rather than explicit, subordinate to the notion of the 'subject', and often arise in a spontaneous

rather than in predictable manner. In addition to
the formal curriculum, extra curricular activities
will also have a contribution to make, as will the
nexus of formal and informal structures and
relationships which constitute the 'hidden
curriculum'. The organisation of pastoral care in
the school - whether in terms of houses, form
groups, tutor groups, year groups - will play a
part too. When to this is added the potential
influences outside the school we realise how
incredibly complex the whole process is. All the
more necessary then, one might think, to have a
specific timetabled slot which has PFL as a central
and explicit concern rather than as a peripheral
and implicit one.

Having PFL as a clearly separate entity within
the curriculum gives pupils the opportunity of
reflecting on the nature of personal and social
issues, and exploring their implications in a
relatively single minded manner. Where there is no
separate PFL course one of two possibilities can
exist. First is the situation where there is no
explicit PFL policy. The various subjects pursue
their own aims independently of each other. The
pupil is exposed to a variety of potential
messages, some of which he may be unaware of. The
onus is on the pupils to receive these messages and
integrate them in some kind of way meaningful to
themselves. The second possibility is where there
is a conscious policy to deal with PFL 'across the
curriculum'. This might take the form of certain
subjects dealing with specific topics. Such an
approach requires coordination in order to ensure
that the various 'bits' form a coherent whole. The
pattern of dispersal across the curriculum is often
characteristic of the provision of one PFL
component - health education. Evidence from one
study suggests that the coordination of dispersed
health education programmes may often be far from
satisfactorily achieved (Wilcox and Gillies, 1983).
Curriculum coordination is one of the least
satisfactorily developed functions of teachers and
surprisingly little has been written on it. A rare
exception is provided by the Schools Council Health
Project 13-18 which outlines practical ways to help
teachers in coordinating cross curricular practice
and in knowing 'what is going on and where'. Even
if a dispersed programme is coordinated at the
teacher level, there is no guarantee that it is
coordinated inside the pupil's head. Indeed the

evidence from our interviews of less able pupils suggests that many of them fail to understand the rationale for separate subjects and how they relate to each other. They are therefore likely to find a PFL programme which relies heavily on a policy of dispersal across the curriculum particularly hard to comprehend.

However making PFL a specific course does have inherent dangers. Concentrating what was hitherto a very disparate and scattered mass of information, attitudes, values and prescriptions for behaviour into one curriculum spot increases the chances that these will be 'picked up' by pupils in a much more predictable manner. Now, if we were talking about mathematics or science, that possibility would not be particularly worrying. But in the case of PFL we are concerned with personal and social issues and ultimately with the concept of person. In this area there are no unambiguous 'facts', although PFL courses may often imply that there are. The apparent unproblematic nature of much of the PFL curriculum, e.g. 'what is work?', 'factors for success in marriage', may mask an uncritical acceptance of conventional wisdom. If PFL is to be a distinct curriculum component it requires a pedagogy in which deceptively simple social and personal 'facts' are questioned, the range of alternative responses to human problems are considered, discussion and debate are the norm, and where the assumptions underlying the various models of man implicit in the PFL curriculum are examined.

If that is not done, then we risk at best perpetrating a benign form of social control and life adaptation. The appropriate pedagogy for the kind of approach that we see as desirable is one based upon small group work in general and discussion methods in particular. It is a pedagogy which sharply contrasts with the dominant one in most secondary schools, which is essentially expository in style and based on what Freire (1970) calls the 'banking' concept of education: "The teacher issues communiques and makes deposits which the students patiently receive, memorise, and repeat ... (and where) the scope of action allowed to the students extends only as far as receiving, filing and storing the deposits." Freire argues for an education where students "are increasingly posed with problems relating to themselves in the world and with the world, (and) will feel increasingly challenged and obliged to respond to

that challenge" and in which they are "critical
co-investigators in dialogue with the teacher ...
(who) presents the material to the students for
their consideration, and re-considers his earlier
consideration as the students express their own."
Freire's learning model here is one which has much
in common with that of the time honoured Socratic
method. Whilst it is one which is unlikely to be
adopted for the generality of the secondary
curriculum, it does seem to be particularly
appropriate for PFL. In our observation of project
lessons we did find examples where the teaching and
learning approximated to this ideal. Very often
however a number of factors militated against this
happening. An emphasis on exposition sometimes
left insufficient time for follow up discussion to
develop before the session came to an end. The
requirements of external examinations could
reinforce a concern for factual presentation at the
expense of open debate. Making PFL available to
all pupils, including the most able, together with
expectations that certification gives the seal of
credibility, puts teachers under considerable
pressure to link the activity with the public
examination system. The wisdom of doing this is
questionable. Allowing some pupils to take the
examination but not others may seem to be one way
out of the dilemma. Such a policy, however, is
likely to lead to the emergence of two PFL
curricula - one for those who take the examination
(the more able?) and one for those who do not (the
less able?). Such a distinction, particularly in
this area of the curriculum, would be undesirable.
It may be that, if an examination is needed, a form
of assessment might be negotiated with the local
CSE board which is less concerned with written work
and more appropriate to the kind of teacher-pupil
explorations outlined above. The presence of an
examination for PFL may lead to a decision to group
pupils by ability. It would seem that, given the
concerns of PFL, surely common to all pupils, the
case for mixed ability grouping is stronger here
than for many other subjects. Whilst teachers may
well differentiate how and what they teach
according to the perceptions of pupil ability, this
is likely to be less apparent in mixed ability than
in ability groups. To have a situation in which
there was one PFL curriculum for "the hewers of
wood and the drawers of water" and another for the
rest would provide yet a further example of the

school's tendency to reproduce the relations of economic production.

The results of our interviews with target group pupils indicated that few were able to give a satisfactory account of the purposes of PFL and the experiences which they encountered in it - a feature which was also characteristic of their perceptions of other aspects of the curriculum. There is a very substantial gap between teachers' rationales of their subjects and pupils' understanding of 'what's it all for'. Why is this so? Not because pupils, even those classified as less able, are unable to understand such matters. One reason is that it seems to be assumed that the different aspects which make up a subject, and the different subjects which make up the curriculum, automatically cohere in pupils' minds to form a meaningful whole. In fact little time, if any, is spent in the classroom actually showing how all the 'bits and pieces' fit together and indeed offering a sustained account of the curriculum purposes of the school. Part of the problem is that, given the complexity of the present organisation of secondary schools into separate subject departments, it is difficult for teachers to have a detailed understanding of the total curriculum which their pupils experience. The division of labour in the secondary school has resulted in a division of knowledge, each bit of which is appropriated by a particular group of specialist teachers. As a result it comes to be regarded as almost unprofessional to know what colleagues in another department actually teach. We, however, take it as axiomatic that if the individuals of any organisation are not to feel a sense of alienation from it then an essential prerequisite is that they should understand it in some way as a total enterprise. In the case of a school this means, for both teachers and pupils, having an understanding of the formal curriculum. If pupils could see the point of it all they would be better motivated to learn.

PFL is particularly well placed for encouraging such an understanding. Its concerns, because they are the very stuff of everyday life which do not require an arcane language for their expression, should be accessible to all, teacher and pupil alike. It is crucial that <u>all</u> teachers should know not only about the issues and topics with which PFL is concerned, but also how they are dealt with. This would enable them to establish relevant links with aspects of their own courses and thus help in tying the curriculum together. Opportunities for this process to occur need to be programmed. Occasions should be set aside when teachers actually explain why they are doing the kinds of things they are, how they relate to things being done in PFL and in other subjects. The headteacher should also attempt this from his unique position of being accountable for the activities of the school as a whole. This needs to be done, not as a one-off event, but regularly and in increasingly greater detail throughout the pupils' school career. The emphasis would not simply be on explication, but also on debate. Pupils' views would be encouraged, assumptions would be critically tested, and alternatives envisaged.

What we are suggesting is that a major reason for the dissatisfaction which many pupils find with schools is not so much a rejection of its purposes, but rather a reflection of the fact that they do not know what the purposes are. The school and its works and in particular the complex edifice of the curriculum are simply incomprehensible to many pupils.

PFL, by providing a common reference point for all pupils and teachers, may hold the key not only to a better understanding of what the curriculum actually is and what its purposes are, but may also provide a protected area within which a pedagogy more appropriate to the needs of adolescents might be worked out.

THE PROCESS OF CURRICULUM REVIEW

One notion which has emerged with increasing prominence over the last few years is that of curriculum review. Teachers have been exhorted to review their curricula and LEAs have been urged to support them in this task (DES, 1981a; 1981c). Somewhat surprisingly perhaps there has been little practical advice given on what such a process entails and how it might be carried out. The research model adopted in this project, and in particular that part described in chapters 2 to 6, both provides a way of conceptualising the process of curriculum review and a means of carrying it out.

236

We can think of the curriculum in terms of three distinct levels of analysis. First there is the way in which the curriculum is organised, i.e. the pattern of subjects taught, the methods of grouping pupils and teachers together to pursue specific learning activities under such headings as English, mathematics, careers education, etc. This most general level is illustrated in chapter 2 where the S4 and S5 curricula of the four project schools are analysed.

The second level provides a description of what is included under such subject titles as those mentioned above. This level then, is concerned with the content of the curriculum - however expressed, whether in terms of knowledge, skills, attitudes or values. Chapter 3 shows how the basic content of the PFL area of the curriculum may be revealed using a simple checklist instrument. Such a methodology can be applied to the curricula of several schools thus making possible a comparative analysis.

Finally at the third level the concern is with how the content of the curriculum is actually developed with pupils in the classroom. This includes the teaching and learning methods adopted, as well as the ways in which learning is supported both within and outside the classroom - something which may be called the learning milieu. An analysis at this level requires the observation of classroom activities.

In chapters 4, 5 and 6 particularly, a descent is made to this level by examining how some of the key themes of PFL, e.g. job choice, unemployment, etc. were actually developed in individual classrooms.

These three levels of analysis - which may be termed organisation, content and learning milieu - provide a description of the curriculum as it is. However description is only one side of the coin of curriculum review. The other side involves a comparison of that description against appropriate criteria. The completion of these two processes may then lead to an action stage in which some modification of the curriculum might take place. The criteria against which a curriculum description may be judged are likely to be broad educational or pedagogic ones. An example of this is provided by the critique of PFL courses outlined in the immediately preceding section of this chapter.

237

Project implications

NOTES

1   DES and EEC funding ceased on 31st August 1982.
    The LEA, however, decided to fund the
    appointment of a secretary, the secondment of
    teaching staff and certain resources for a
    further year so as to facilitate the production
    of curriculum materials and their dissemination.

APPENDIX: APPROACH ADOPTED IN THE   EVALUATION   OF
THE PROJECT

Our research approach involved us in talking
regularly with those involved in the project and
also took us frequently into the classrooms of
those teaching the project. This activity caused,
certainly in the early weeks of our work, some
anxiety amongst teachers. This was understandable,
and their concern that we were evaluating them was
perhaps natural. It was indeed difficult to
explain what we were doing, particularly as we did
not appear to be equipped with the highly
structured observational schedules favoured by some
classroom teachers (e.g. Galton et al, 1980).
Schedules of the latter kind were thought to be
inappropriate for the range of curricular
activities included within the project.
The aim of our visits was to provide an
account of what we termed the 'instructional
essence' of lessons. This was an attempt to strip
away the idiosyncratic details of routine
management and control of the classroom situation
to reveal the basic instructional core of concepts,
values or skills being developed. This meant in
practice concentrating on, and recording, the
details of the instructional content of teachers'
exposition and verbal exchanges with pupils as well
as noting, and collecting where possible, examples
of the teaching materials used. These classroom
accounts, and also those derived from informal
interviews with staff, represented a large body of
field notes. These, together with the mass of
papers derived from the committee and working party
activities of the project and from the schools
themselves, constituted a substantial research
archive.
We tried to take seriously the role of
facilitating a greater understanding of the project
by all involved by providing regular feedback
through short research papers. One of the
criticisms of educational research often made by
teachers and others is that feedback is not
provided or given so long after the event as to be
of limited value. One of our principal aims was to
reduce drastically the normally protracted time
scale of initiation, execution and dissemination of
research. The time scale of much academic research

is altogether too leisurely for the urgencies of
teachers. We therefore attempted throughout the
project to provide short studies focused upon
particular themes which, we hoped, would raise some
fundamental issues. In these studies data was
sometimes collected over several weeks and the
resulting paper written and circulated within a
very short time afterwards. This kind of approach
was similar to the notion of 'condensed field
work' suggested by Walker (1975).

Copies of the field notes were circulated
regularly amongst the research team. This provided
an opportunity for each researcher to know what was
happening in each of the schools and helped to
ensure a common approach to compiling field notes.
The circulation of field notes kept each researcher
in touch with what the others were doing and
provided the basis for a collective understanding
of the nature and progress of the project. The
field notes were also made available to the project
director to help him give leadership to the project
in the light of up to date intelligence from the
field.

The importance of collecting pupils' views of
the project was recognised from the very beginning.
The intention was to interview samples of target
group pupils in each of their last two years in
school and in their first year out of school. By
the end of the third year of the project (1980/81)
this had been achieved for a sample of the 1978/79
fourth year target group. By the same time a
similar sample from the 1979/80 cohort had been
interviewed twice, i.e. at the end of their fourth
year in 1980 and during their fifth year in 1981.

Teachers, the project careers officer, and the
education social worker were also interviewed
several times about their general reactions to the
project and their roles within it. Unfortunately,
limitations of time meant that it was not possible
to interview a wider range of adults concerned with
the target group, e.g. supervisors at work, as we
would have liked to do.

Data was also collected from time to time by
the use of questionnaire surveys, e.g. the account
presented in the chapter 'Teacher Views on the
Project after Three Years' is based on the results
of a questionnaire survey of teachers in the four
project schools.

All of the research reports and other
publications produced throughout the project were

forwarded to the national evaluator in London and to the European team (CAET) in Cologne.

Whilst we were able to maintain a regular and reasonably comprehensive cover of activities in the three project schools, time and resources did not allow us to treat those of the associate school in the same way. Although it was possible to involve the associate school in some of the research studies our knowledge of the detail of its programmes was very much less than that of the other schools. Such knowledge was also much more reliant on sources provided by the school itself. The greater research coverage given to the activities of the three main project schools was however consistent with the different role expected of them compared to that of the associate school. They were expected to be more heavily engaged in developing those areas of the curriculum concerned with preparation for adult life (e.g. careers education) than was the associate school. This was because the associate school was thought to have already developed considerably in this field and that one of its major roles in the project should therefore be to make its experience available to other schools.

Towards the end of the third year of the project the research team took the decision virtually to discontinue its field work during the final year of the project. This decision was prompted by two considerations. First the fact that the funding of the research programme was scheduled to cease with the project itself, i.e. there was to be no time allowed at the termination of the project to write the final report. Secondly it was increasingly apparent that the project was conforming to a '3 + 1' structure. In other words, the first three years represented a period of development and consolidation whereas the final year was expected to be essentially concerned with disseminating the materials, approaches and experiences arising from the earlier years. Thus in the fourth year (1981/82) the research team completed several studies which had been started in the previous year and began the formidable task of analysing the considerable body of research information which had been accumulated thus far in preparation for writing the final report.

THE PROJECT AS A CASE STUDY

The chapters which have gone before present an account of the development of the project over the three year period 1978/79 to 1980/81. In the main there is little reference to the 1981/82 programme. An account of something as complex as the project could not hope to be fully comprehensive - inevitably some aspects were omitted. We decided early on that the main emphasis of our research activity would be within the school context. Thus although information was collected on pupils after they had left school, obtained from careers office records and interview/questionnaire surveys, no attempt was made to observe or interview pupils in the context of their working and social environments. We saw the project as essentially a curriculum development one rooted in the school. Even the research carried out within the school context reflected prior decisions about selection, e.g. we did not observe all aspects of the project programmes in the schools, we did not interview all fourth and fifth year pupils but only a sample of the target group, etc. Finally, clearly not all of the vast amount of data collected over three or so years has actually been used in writing this account. What we have produced is a case study of certain aspects of a major curriculum development project in action.

There is a relatively well established tradition of case studies of schools represented by the work of Hargreaves (1967), Lacey (1970) and Ball (1981). Our study has some methodological similarity to these in that it was, in part at least, concerned with actors' interpretations of situations. It is different however in two significant ways. First, although observation was an important element of the research, we did not use a participant observer approach as did the other studies. Although we visited schools and classes and got to know some staff well (and pupils to a lesser extent) nevertheless we were there as detached observers (albeit fairly regular ones) rather than as engaged on-going presences. Secondly, our case study is based upon three, and to some extent four, schools rather than one. It is an example of a multiple site (three or four schools) multiple observer (three researchers) case study. [1]

242

The familiar methodological problems associated with single site case studies are compounded in the case of those involving multiple sites. Ebbutt (1981) has referred to this research area as a methodological minefield and has suggested that the actual processes of aggregating data across multiple sites have not yet been adequately worked out. Our approach to this problem was essentially one of 'progressive focusing' (Parlett and Hamilton, 1976). This involved us in reviewing regularly in meetings (both formal and informal) the growing body of research data generated by our observation, interview and other research activities. This was helped by a rapid turn-around in the conversion of field notes from longhand into typescript versions which were circulated amongst the research team. As the project developed our focus became increasingly sharper and we were able to identify a number of broad themes which seemed particularly fruitful to explore.

Some of these themes are summarised in the titles of several of the chapters of the book - others are to be found as sub sections of these chapters. Although the choice of some themes was not unexpected, e.g. careers education (chapter 4), some of the sub themes that emerged from a detailed analysis of the field notes were less predictable. Thus we show in the chapter on careers education that the ubiquitous rational choice model contains inherent contradictions which were more and more apparent as the juvenile employment market worsened. Looking back on our methodology we note some similarities to that adopted by the Cambridge Accountability Project (Elliott et al, 1981). Although the latter project focused on a different subject area to ours and involved more sites (six to our three or four) the methods adopted for generating themes across sites used a collegial mode not unlike our own.

In our case the field note archive played a key part in this process. By the end of the third year of the project the archive contained 230 field notes, some of which were several thousand words in length. Although in the first year approximately similar numbers of field notes were generated for each of the three project schools, thereafter the numbers varied somewhat from school to school. This reflected the differential complexity of programmes and our own commitment to progressive focusing. In order to prepare the vast amount of information in the archive for analysis one of the research team read through every field note and assigned each one to the main curriculum area or activity with which it was concerned. Many field notes were assigned to two or more groups since their content was relevant to more than one curriculum area. All the field notes relating to a particular curriculum group were then read again by one or more of the research team. After this one or more short papers were written on each of several curriculum areas. The purpose of these was to point up the issues considered important.

In preparing papers the researchers contributed to the building up of a cumulative cross reference index system. This meant that important points encountered in reading the field notes, which were not directly relevant to the title in hand, were recorded for possible use later on. The intention was that the draft paper would then be critically considered by the rest of the team, modified as necessary, before being circulated to relevant school staff for comment. Due to the pressures of time towards the end of the project however it was not always possible to realise this procedure fully.

Case Studies and the Problem of Generalisation

One of the perennial questions asked of case studies concerns the extent to which they can provide the basis for generalisation. For a multiple site case study there are at least two types of generalisation which may be made. First there are generalisations which relate to one particular site (school), e.g. the statement "in school A the amount of time devoted to careers education in the fourth and fifth year had increased over the period 1977/78 to 1980/81". Although this may seem to be nothing more than a descriptive statement it is also a generalisation albeit a low level one. It has been made as a result of looking at the arrangements for careers education for each of the years in the period concerned - it is a _general_ statement which summarises a situation of some greater complexity.

The second kind of generalisation is one which relates to more than one site, e.g. the statement "over the period 1977/78 to 1980/81 the amount of time devoted to the core curriculum in the fourth and fifth year had increased and that devoted to options had decreased" certainly describes the situation in three of the schools (A, C and D) during that period. These two kinds of generalisation can be termed <u>closed</u> <u>generalisations</u>. Bassey (1981) defines these as ones which are closed in space and time, which relate to a particular situation at a particular time and which cannot be extrapolated with confidence beyond that situation.

Closed generalisations are descriptive statements. In contrast <u>open generalisations</u> can be extrapolated beyond the observed results of the events studied to similar events. Open generalisations are both descriptive and predictive. In Bassey's view there are greater opportunities for making closed generalisations in education, e.g. about particular schools at particular times, than for making open generalisations. Clearly the two examples we have quoted are closed generalisations in Bassey's terms. We cannot use them to predict the situation in other schools over the same time period.

Much of the account of the project which has appeared in the previous chapters has been concerned with closed generalisations. They should not however be considered any the less for that. We agree with Bassey that the value of closed generalisations lies in helping teachers and others to <u>relate</u> what has happened in other situations to what is happening in theirs. Thus the merit of case studies lies not in their potential generalisability but in the extent to which practitioners can relate what they read in the case study to their own situations. This is close to Walker's view, i.e. that "generalising ceases to become a problem for the author (of a case study). It is the reader who has to ask, what is there in this study that I can apply to my own situation, and what clearly does not apply." (Walker, 1980, p. 34)

However, the formulation of closed generalisations in the context of multiple site case studies can be examined with a view to seeking evidence for the existence of underlying regularities and irregularities in the hope of formulating, at least tentatively, statements of wider generalisability. Such a process may also help in the creation of models or perhaps even theories of wider significance than the immediate situations to which the original case studies relate. This is what we attempt to do in our final chapter where we draw on our findings to establish a set of provisional guidelines for curriculum development within a local authority context. The realisation increasingly dawned on us as the project progressed and the data accumulated that what we were observing was really an exemplar of a particular model of curriculum development within an LEA context. If we strip away the details, e.g. the source of project funds (EEC and DES), the specific focus (transition from school to work) etc. we are left with a structural model for the organisation of curriculum development of considerable potential interest. Thus the overall purpose of our evaluation was two fold:

1. to illuminate for teachers, administrators, the national evaluator and others some of the significant issues involved in attempting to transform the curriculum of the last two years of compulsory education with a view to facilitating pupils' transition to working and adult life;

2. to clarify the general nature of the model which underpins the project and assess its feasibility for organising future curriculum development activities within LEAs.

The relationship between case studies and theory can also be approached in another way. Atkinson and Delamont argue that case studies can be analysed in terms of the analytic, abstract and formal categories of theory. Thus although "one cannot claim that one instance can be treated as representative and stand for all others in every particular ... (However) it is not only legitimate but imperative to draw upon and develop concepts which are of more general applicability than just the immediate setting under scrutiny. If that is done and done well, then to some extent the actual process of generalisation becomes one done by the readers of research reports, who can use the formal, comparative concepts as a resource for making sense of novel situations in which they are interested." (Atkinson and Delamont, 1980, p. 27).

The preceding chapters can be regarded as a series of connecting case studies which together

246

constitute the larger case study of the project as
a whole. It is hoped that they provide readers
with a sense of the project's reality and also an
opportunity to relate the particular instances
which are described to the general literature of
curriculum development and change.

NOTES

[1] Although each researcher concentrated mainly on
one school, each had some experience of
observing activities in at least one other.

ABBS, P. (1981)   Promoting new first principles', _Times Ed. Supp._, 28th August 1981, 10

ASHTON, D. N. and   'The function of academic and
MAGUIRE, M. J.   non-academic criteria in employers'
(1980)   "selection strategies"', _Brit. J. Guid. & Counsell._, 8, 2, 146-157

ASSESSMENT OF   _Personal and Social Development_, APU
PERFORMANCE UNIT   Exploratory Group, London: Department
(1981)   of Education and Science

ATKINSON, P. and   Strategies for Educational Evaluation.
DELAMONT, S.   University College, Cardiff,
(1980)   Sociological Research Unit

ATKINSON, P.   Social and Life Skills: The Latest Case
REES, T.   of Compensatory Education. University
SCHONE, D. and   College, Cardiff, Sociological Research
WILLIAMSON, H.   Unit
(1980)

AUSUBEL, D. P.   'Cognitive structure and the
(1963)   facilitation of meaningful verbal
                     learning'. Reprinted in: Clarizio, H.
                     F. et al (Eds), 1970, _Contemporary Issues in Educational Psychology_,
                     Boston: Allyn and Bacon

BALL, S. J. (1981)   _Beachside Comprehensive_, Cambridge:
                     Cambridge University Press

BALOGH, J. (1982)   _Profile Reports for School Leavers_,
                     London: Longmans/Schools Council

BASSEY, M. (1981)   'Pedagogic research: on the relative
                     merits of search for generalisation and
                     study of single events', _Oxford Rev. Educ._, 7, 1, 73-94

BATES, I. (1983)   'Participatory teaching methods in
                     theory and in practice: the Schools
                     Council 'Careers' Project in school',
                     Brit. J. Guid. and Counsell., 11, 2,
                     113-130.

References

BROWN, D (1983)   'Truants, families and schools: a critique of the literature on truancy', Educ. Rev., 35, 3, 225-235

BURGESS, T. and ADAMS, E (1980)   Outcomes of education, London: MacMillan

CLOSS, S. J. and BRODERICK, W. R. (1982)   'Choosing careers by computer', Education, 159, 17, 300

CAREERS AND OCCUPATIONAL INFORMATION CENTRE (1975)   The Sponge Mix, Southport: Careers and Occupational Information Centre

COPE, E. and GRAY, J (1978)   'Figures and perspectives on the national problem of truancy', Collaborative Research, Newsletter 3, Edinburgh: University of Edinburgh

CORBETT, C. PARKER, C. and SHANNON, M. (1981)   The Perceptions of members of the Advisory Committee of the EEC Funded Project on the Transition from School to Work. Unpublished M.Sc. Education Management Assignment, City of Sheffield Polytechnic

CORRIGAN, P. (1979)   Schooling the Smash Street Kids, London: MacMillan

DEPARTMENT OF EDUCATION AND SCIENCE (1973)   Careers Education in Secondary School, Education Survey 18, London: HMSO

DEPARTMENT OF EDUCATION AND SCIENCE (1979)   Aspects of Secondary Education in England: A Survey by HMI, London: HMSO

DEPARTMENT OF EDUCATION AND SCIENCE (1980)   Girls and Science, HMI Series: Matters for Discussion, London: HMSO

DEPARTMENT OF EDUCATION AND SCIENCE (1981a)   The School Curriculum, London: HMSO

DEPARTMENT OF EDUCATION AND SCIENCE (1981b)   Curriculum 11-16: A Review of Progress, London: HMSO

References

DEPARTMENT OF
EDUCATION AND
SCIENCE (1981c)

The School Curriculum, Circular 6/81,
London: DES

EAVIS, P. (1980)

'The development of a humanities
curriculum at Manor Park school', in:
EGGLESTON, J. (Ed), School-based
Curriculum Development in Britain,
London: Routledge & Kegan Paul

EBBUTT, D. (1981)

Three Approaches to Multi-Site Case
Study, Cambridge Institute of Education

EGGLESTON, J. R.
(Ed) (1980)

School-Based Curriculum Development in
Britain, London: Routledge & Kegan
Paul

ELLIOTT, J.
BRIDGES, D.
EBBUTT, D.
GIBSON, R. and
NIAS, J. (1981)

School Accountability, London: Grant
McIntyre

ENGEL, E. (1979)

'Health education in schools - a
philosophical dilemma', Health Educ.
J., 37, 4, 231-233

FINCH, J.
CLAYTON, S. and
CLEMENTS, J.
(1981)

'Health education and the school
curriculum: the case for infant
feeding', Health Educ. J., 40, 1,
19-23

FOGELMAN, K.
(1979)

'Educational aspirations of sixteen year
olds', Brit. J. Guid. & Counsell., 7,
1, 42-56

FREIRE, P. (1970)

'Pedagogy of the oppressed', in: BECK,
J., JENCKS, C., KEDDIE, N., YOUNG, M. F.
D. (Eds) (1976), Worlds Apart, London:
Collier Macmillan

GALLOWAY, D. M.
(1979)

A Study of Persistent Absence from
School in Sheffield: Prevalence and
Associated Educational Psychological and
Social Factors. Unpublished Ph.D.
dissertation, City of Sheffield
Polytechnic

References

GALLOWAY, D. M.
(1980)

'Problems in the assessment and management of persistent absenteeism from school', in: HERSOV, L. and BERG, I. (Eds), Out of School, London: Wiley

GALTON, M.
SIMON, B. and
CROLL, P. (1980)

Inside the Primary Classroom, London: Routledge & Kegan Paul

GRIMSHAW, R. and
PRATT, J. (1983)

Motivational Accounts and the Truancy Problem. School Attendance and Legal Action Project. Sheffield: City of Sheffield Education Department

HARGREAVES, D.
(1967)

Social Relations in a Secondary School, London: Routledge & Kegan Paul

HOPSON, B. and
SCALLY, M. (1981)

Lifeskills Teaching, London: McGraw Hill

IFAPLAN (1980)

European Community Action Programme: Transition from Education to Working Life, Project Information, IFAPLAN Gesellschaft fur angewandte Sozialforschung und Planung, Stadtwaldgurtel 33, D-5000 Koln 41

JENKINS, D.
(1974)

'Schools, teachers and curriculum change', in: SHIPMAN, M. D. Inside a Curriculum Project, London: Methuen

KEDDIE, N.
(1971)

'Classroom Knowledge', in: YOUNG, M. F. D. (Ed), Knowledge and Control, London: Collier MacMillan

KING, R. A.
(1981)

'Secondary schools: some changes of a decade', Educ. Res., 23, 3, 173-176

LACEY, C. (1970)

Hightown Grammar, Manchester: Manchester University Press

LAW, B. (1981)

'Community interaction: a 'mid-range' focus for theory of career development in young adults', Brit. J. Guid. & Counsell., 9, 2, 142-158

LAW, B. and
WATTS, A. G.
(1977)

School, Careers and Community, Westminster: Church Information Office

References

MANPOWER SERVICES COMMISSION (1983)
Technical and Vocational Education Initiative. Letter to Directors of Education in all LEAs in England and Wales. MSC Selkirk House, London

MARLAND, M. (1971)
Head of Department, London: Heinemann

MINISTRY OF EDUCATION (1963)
Half Our Future, a report of the Central Advisory Council for Education (England), London: HMSO

OXFORD CERTIFICATE OF EDUCATION ACHIEVEMENT (OCEA) 1983
The Oxford Certificate of Educational Achievement, Newsletter No. 2, Oxford: University of Oxford Delegacy of Local Examinations

PARLETT, M. and HAMILTON, D. (1976)
'Evaluation as illumination', in: TAWNEY, D. (Ed) Curriculum Evaluation Today: Trends and Implications, London: MacMillan

PRING, R. (1976)
'The integrated curriculum: curriculum organisation', in: Curriculum Design and Development: Educational Studies - A Second Level Course, OU E203, Units 11-13, Milton Keynes: Open University

REID, K. (1983)
'Retrospection and persistent school absenteeism', Educ. Res., 25, 2, 110-115

REYNOLDS, D. JONES, D. ST. LEGER, S. and MURGATROYD, S. (1980)
'School factors and truancy', in: HERSOV, L. and BERG, I. (Eds), Out of School, New York: Wiley

ROBERTS, R. J. (1980)
'An alternative justification for careers education: a radical response to Roberts and Daws', Brit. J. Guid. & Counsell., 8, 2, 158-174

RUDDOCK, J. (1976)
Dissemination of Innovation: The Humanities Curriculum Project, Schools Council Working Paper No. 56, London: Evans/Methuen

SAWDON, A. TUCKER, S. and PELICAN, J. (1979)
Study of the Transition from School to Working Life, London: Youth Aid

References

SCHOOLS COUNCIL (1972)
Integrated Studies Project, Exploration Man: An Introduction to Integrated Studies, London: Oxford University Press

SCOTTISH COUNCIL FOR RESEARCH IN EDUCATION (1977)
Profile Assessment System Manual, Edinburgh: SCRE

SHEFFIELD MDC (1977)
Transition from School to Working Life. Submission to the European Economic Commission for a Pilot Project. Sheffield Metropolitan District Council Education Department

SHEFFIELD MDC (1978)
Background, General Information and Current Activity. Sheffield EEC Project. Transition from School to Working Life. Bulletin 1, Sheffield Metropolitan District Council Education Department

SHIPMAN, M. D. (1974)
Inside a Curriculum Project, London: Methuen

STANSBURY, D. (1976)
Record of Personal Experience, Qualities and Qualifications, South Brent: RPE Publications

STANSBURY, D. (1980)
'The record of personal experience', in: BURGESS, T. and ADAMS, E. (Eds) Outcomes of Education, London: McMillan

STENHOUSE, L. (1978)
'Case study and case records: towards a contemporary history education', Brit. Educ. Res. J., 14, 2, pp. 27-39

STENHOUSE, L. (Ed) (1980)
Curriculum Research and Development, London: Heinemann

SWALES, T. (1979)
Record of Personal Achievement: An Independent Evaluation of the Swindon RPE Scheme, Pamphlet 16, London: Schools Council

WALKER, R. (1975)
'Case study research in education', in: CHANAN, G. and DELAMONT, S. (Eds) Frontiers of Classroom Research, Windsor: NFER

References

WALKER, R. (1980)   'The conduct of educational case
                     studies: ethics, theory and procedures',
                     in: DOCKRELL, W. B. and HAMILTON, D.
                     (Eds) Rethinking Educational Research,
                     London: Hodder and Stoughton

WATTS, A. G. and   'Career(s) education in Britain and the
HERR, E. L.   USA: contrasts and common problems',
(1976)   Brit. J. Guid. and Counsell., 4, 2,
                     129-142

WATTS, A. G.   'The implications of school leaver
(1978)   unemployment for careers education in
                     schools', J. Curric. Stud., 10, 3,
                     233-250

WHITTY, G. (1976)   'Studying society: for social change or
                     social control?', in: WHITTY, G. and
                     YOUNG, M. (Eds) Explorations in the
                     Politics of School Knowledge,
                     Driffield: Nafferton

WILCOX, B. and   Tooling up for Curriculum Review,
EUSTACE, P. J.   Windsor: NFER
(1980)

WILCOX, B. (1982)   'School self-evaluation: the benefits of
                     a more focused approach', Educ. Rev.,
                     34, 3, 185-193

WILCOX, B. and   'The coordination of secondary school
GILLIES, P. A.   health education', Educ. Res., 25, 2,
(1983)   98-104

WILLIAMS, G. and   'Attitudes of young people to school
GORDON, A.   work and the higher education system',
(1976)   T.E.S., 27th February

WILLIS, P. (1977)   Learning to Labour, London: Saxon
                     House

WINTER, R. (1976)   'Keeping files: aspects of bureaucracy
                     and education', in: WHITTY, G. and
                     YOUNG, M. (Eds) Explorations in the
                     Politics of School Knowledge,
                     Driffield: Nafferton

WOODS, P. (1976a)   'Pupils' Views of School', Educ. Rev.,
                     28, 2, 126-137

References

WOODS, P. (1976b)   'Having a laugh: an antidote to schooling', in: HAMMERSLEY, M. and WOODS, P. (Eds) <u>The Process of Schooling</u>, London: Routledge and Kegan Paul

WOODS, P. (1979)   <u>The Divided School</u>, London: Routledge and Kegan Paul

THE AUTHORS

BRIAN WILCOX

Brian Wilcox was formerly senior adviser in the City of Sheffield Education Department with specific responsibility for research and evaluation, and directed the evaluation programme associated with the Sheffield 'Transition from School to Working Life' project. His main research interests are in the areas of curriculum evaluation, learning methods and pupil assessment. He is currently chief adviser in the Sheffield Education Department.

JACQUELINE DUNN

Jacqueline Dunn has teaching experience in a variety of educational institutions and is currently working in adult education in Sheffield as a 'Return to Studies' co-ordinator and is running a Writers' Workshop. Her research interests lie in the areas of sexism in education and political education. She was senior research officer throughout the life of the Sheffield project.

SUE LAVERCOMBE

After graduating from the University of Leeds Sue Lavercombe did two years research in economics at the University of Manchester. From 1977-1980 she was research assistant on the Sheffield City Polytechnic project 'Young People's Attitudes to School, Work and Unemployment'. She was a researcher on the Sheffield 'Transition from School to Working Life' project from 1980-82. She is currently a full time mother.

LESLEY BURN

Lesley Burn was junior research officer on the project from 1978-80. Before that she studied developmental psychology at Sussex University and then completed a postgraduate teaching qualification at Homerton College, Cambridge. Since working on the project, and in need of a new direction, she has begun training in alternative medicine.

Printed in the United States
by Baker & Taylor Publisher Services